THE PLEDGE

LEONARD SLATER

SIMON AND SCHUSTER
NEW YORK

SBN 671-20465-3
LIBRARY OF CONGRESS CATALOG CARD NUMBER: 79-101883
DESIGNED BY EDITH FOWLER
MANUFACTURED IN THE UNITED STATES OF AMERICA
BY AMERICAN BOOK-STRATFORD PRESS, INC., NEW YORK, N.Y.

FOR LOU

CONTENTS

If I am not for myself, who is for me?
And if I am for myself alone, what then am I?
And if not now, then when?

—Hillel (c. 70 B.C.–A.D. 10)

PROLOGUE
January 3, 1948

The longshoremen, bundled into heavy jackets and thick gloves, their knitted caps pulled down over their ears, fastened the cables over each end of the big wooden case, and dashed back away from the ship into the open doorway in the side of the pier. They were grateful for the shelter of Pier F's corrugated iron walls and roof, grateful for the few minutes they now had to curse in peace. They cursed the fate that had brought them here to Jersey City on the New York waterfront on this miserable Saturday, January 3, 1948. They cursed Pier F and the ship, S.S. *Executor*, tied up alongside it in the oily slate-colored waters of the Hudson River.

Mostly they cursed the weather. They had stumbled and slid to work this morning over the sooty carcass of a storm that a week ago had dumped 26.4 inches of snow on the city and its vicinity—the biggest snowfall in sixty years, the newspapers said, bigger even than the blizzard of 1888. The storm had not been cleared, couldn't be, for as the new year began, there had been rain and sleet and more snow, day after day. All over New York and New Jersey, streets and highways were blocked, emergencies had been declared, traffic banned except for official vehicles and trucks carrying fuel, food, and medicine. Even their homes were cold; there was a fuel oil shortage. A black market had sprung up. Today the weather was clear but there was no relief in sight. The sun was a faint yellow blob behind the dark and jagged profile of Manhattan across the river.

Their foreman signaled the winch operator aboard the ship. The cables tightened and groaned, as if they too were cursing the weather, and the big case, about the size of a telephone booth, bumped and skidded on the asphalt floor of the pier.

One of the longshoremen walked over to the cargo checker and looked at his pad. He shouted to the others that the case, rising now from the pier, was number twelve. They had already seen eleven identical cases hoisted aboard the ship. Sixty-five more to go.

The cases lay in disorderly rows inside the shed, obviously from the same shipper. Each one bore the same stenciled black letters: "Used Industrial Machinery." Their destinations were the same: Palestine.

The longshoremen had read about Palestine in the newspapers lately: rioting, terrorism, a three-sided war. They cursed the Jews, the Arabs, and the British, but not equally. Since most of them were of Irish stock, they cursed the British with a special fury.

In the clamor of Pier F, a vast shed a city block long, from which three other ships besides the *Executor* were being loaded this day, the obscenities issued soundlessly from the men's mouths as short angry jets of vapor.

Seven hundred men worked on Pier F this morning. Trucks, cargo, cursing men made it a world of its own. In a matter of seconds, case twelve would join them with the larger world.

It hung now, rising slowly above the level of the doorway in which the longshoremen stood, perhaps twelve feet off the ground, swinging in the wind. Like the jaw of a rolling shark, one of its end boards was slowly opening, unaccountably jostled loose.

As the case swung, a black wooden box appeared through the widening hole. The men watched as more of it appeared. The black box plummeted to the floor of the pier with a sharp smack and tumbled over and over.

The longshoremen cursed and rushed forward, always curious to see what the cargo contained. Their foreman shouted, "Cooper! Cooper!"

Raymond Grimm, boss cooper of American Export Lines, was standing in a knot of truckmen, customs inspectors, and pier guards around a smoky fire burning in an oil drum near the customs shed on Pier F. A short chunky man, Grimm reached for his toolbox as soon as a longshoreman tapped his arm. He pushed his way through the circle of longshoremen around the black box. Grimm knelt and saw that one of the box's sides had been cracked by the fall. He reached for his hammer and began prying out the nails.

Grimm was adept at repairing anything, but he worked without gloves and his fingers were stiff from the cold. As he wiggled the

board free, he absent-mindedly read the labels on a row of tins
packed tightly inside the box. All said the same thing. In large black
letters: "TNT." In small letters: "Corps of Engineers, U.S. Army.
Trojan Powder Company, Allentown, Pennsylvania."

Grimm clambered to his feet and shouted, "TNT! Explosives!
Stand clear!" Then he ran for the port captain's office.

Grimm blurted out the news to Captain Sydney Blackledge, a
thin, dignified man in a business suit and red tie. Blackledge listened
calmly, as befitted a man who ran all of American Export Lines'
loading operations in the port of New York. As a ship's master, he
himself had carried explosives; during the war, as port captain, he had
supervised their loading many times in the special berths prescribed
by the Coast Guard. Explosives didn't panic him, but as contraband,
on Pier F, on this busy day, they were to be taken seriously. He stood
up, reached for his overcoat, and told his secretary, Eileen Ryan, to
call the Jersey City police and the Coast Guard. Then he followed
Grimm out onto the pier.

It took the police longer than usual to get to the Harborside
Terminal over streets slippery with ice. Detective Tom Hynes of the
Second Precinct picked up speed only as he entered the terminal's
interior roadway and turned into Pier F. He found Captain Blackledge giving orders to the longshoremen to get all the crates destined
for Palestine out of the *Executor*'s hold and back onto the pier. Hynes
heard the words "TNT" and "Palestine" and did what any smart
policeman would do under the circumstances. He went into Blackledge's office and phoned Chief James Wilson to come down and take
charge personally.

Work stopped along Pier F as Blackledge and the police took
over. They ordered everybody off the pier but thirty-two longshoremen needed to handle the *Executor*'s ominous cargo. A Coast
Guard cutter from the Battery in Manhattan chugged alongside the
pier and its officers climbed up, stiff with rank and weather. A
customs supervisor drove up and consulted with Blackledge, who
quietly passed an order to the foreman. The longshoremen began
prying open all of the seventy-seven cases marked "Used Industrial
Machinery." In twenty-six of them they found the same contents:
black wooden boxes containing tins of TNT. Some of the black
boxes didn't even have to be opened. The black paint had been
smeared on so thinly that the men could still read the legend on their
sides: "TNT. Corps of Engineers, U.S. Army."

The other fifty-one crates did contain industrial machinery. The customs supervisor, an old hand in the port, looked closely at one of them. It looked very much like a machine used in the making of ammunition. That too was contraband.

Blackledge, the police, and the customs and Coast Guard officials moved into Blackledge's office to make a number of phone calls. American Export Lines had to be notified; now the *Executor*'s sailing probably would be delayed, while all of its cargo was checked. A lighter had to be ordered up from the McAllister company to carry the seventy-seven crates to a safe anchorage in the harbor.

An investigation had to be started. Only a month ago Washington had put an embargo on the shipment of war materials to Palestine. It had caused controversy. The men looked at one another; they knew there was political dynamite in this shipment on Pier F. Someone suggested they call the FBI.

Newspaper reporters were waiting outside Blackledge's office. They gathered around a Jersey City police captain, Patrick W. Flanagan, and wrote down what his cursory glance had decided. "There's enough TNT here to blow Jersey City to bits," Flanagan said. He looked around. Jersey City was a tough town, like all waterfront and factory towns, but it was not often that its problems would make headlines around the world. "Five Jersey Cities," he added. The next day's newspapers carried Flanagan's remark authoritatively on their front pages.

Two neatly dressed young men made their way through the reporters and into Blackledge's office. They flashed black leather pass cases and listened intently to everything that was being said. The seventy-seven cases had been delivered to Pier F by the Hoffman Trucking Company of Belleville, New Jersey. It would be a routine matter to learn where they had come from, someone said. The FBI agents nodded, but they knew it wouldn't be routine.

In all the clamor on Pier F, no one noticed another well-dressed young man slip quietly from the sidelines, stroll back along the terminal's interior roadway, named Pennsylvania Avenue for the railroad that owned the building, and enter the Terminal Restaurant. There he waited for an empty phone booth and, carefully closing the door behind him, dialed a New York City number. All he said was, "Phil? I'm coming right back. The stuff is all over the pier."

Then he walked out of the terminal, crossed a parking lot, and descended into the Hudson Tubes station to take a train back to Manhattan, where it had all begun two and a half years ago.

PART ONE

I

THE MEETING

On that Sunday, July 1, 1945, New York lay somnolent in a heat wave. Even at 9 A.M. the city seemed a vast frying pan in which its millions of inhabitants were simmering. The radio said fifty thousand persons had slept out at the beaches the night before.

Rudolf G. Sonneborn had arisen early and instructed his houseman, Murray, to keep plenty of soft drinks on ice and to throw open the windows of his duplex penthouse on East 57th Street to catch the faint breeze coming off the East River. He himself arranged the chairs in his spacious high-ceilinged living room, with its dark green walls and white paneling. He wanted to make it as comfortable as possible for the guests he was expecting in half an hour.

He didn't know how many would come. In such heat, men thought of escaping the city, not coming into it. Nor did he know how interested his guests would be in the project at hand. The war in Europe had ended three months before. Hitler was dead. Japan was being bombed into submission.

Men's thoughts were on peace, on the good things peace would bring, on seeing their sons again and taking life more lightly. The news was all of impending victory and a return to normalcy. Not that there was much news, good or bad, that sizzling day. A strike of newspaper truckmen had crippled deliveries of the Sunday papers. In keeping with the mood of the city, Mayor Fiorello La Guardia would go on the radio later in the day and read the comic strips, so that people could keep up with the adventures of Dick Tracy.

Sonneborn was the secretary-treasurer of a multimillion-dollar corporation and scion of a wealthy German-Jewish family of Baltimore. In his youth he had played football at Johns Hopkins and been a naval aviator in World War I. With one simple voluntary step he could easily have passed into the assimilating arms of America's white

Anglo-Saxon Protestant aristocracy. Instead, he found himself taking more and more time from the affairs of his family's large oil and chemical business to concern himself with the fate and future of Jewish refugees who had been spewn across Europe in the aftermath of World War II.

Sonneborn was not even sure how many of his guests had received their invitations. They had been hurriedly invited by telephone and telegram from as far away as the Midwest and Canada at the behest of an old friend of Sonneborn's, a stubby white-haired Palestinian who was hardly known in the United States outside of Zionist circles: David Ben Gurion, chairman of the Jewish Agency Executive, a quasi-official organization which ran the affairs of the Jewish settlers in Palestine.

Ben Gurion had been in the United States for nearly a month and he had been talking all the time. He had been talking to Zionist organizations, to religious leaders, to pillars of Jewish society, to wealthy philanthropists. Everywhere he had run into a blank wall of incredulity, skepticism and distaste for the message he carried and what he had to propose.

Perhaps it was because he had to talk in parables and allusions, in hints and subtle probes. He was an alien and a guest in a foreign country; he could not openly propose measures which might violate the policies and, ultimately, the laws of that country. He could not frighten or offend his listeners upon whom he and his compatriots depended for so much. Yet he had to know how far he could count upon the rich and powerful Jewish community in America—the only group in the world, as he saw it, which could make the commitment he now sought.

The results had been discouraging.

Everything Ben Gurion saw confirmed the reports of earlier emissaries. The Jewish Establishment of the United States could be counted on for money to feed refugees, for sympathy for their plight, but not for the sort of undertaking Ben Gurion now had to propose. The stumpy Jewish leader, who had emigrated to Palestine from Czarist Russia when he was a boy and dedicated his life to establishing a Jewish nation there, was tired of talk. It was a time for action.

He turned to Henry Montor, who as director of the United Jewish Appeal was a walking encyclopedia of members of his faith. Were there, Ben Gurion wanted to know, ten, twenty, thirty men in the United States who were sufficiently interested in Palestine and sufficiently discreet to be told, frankly, with no holds barred, what he saw ahead? Could a meeting of such men be convened in a week or ten days, with a minimum of public notice? Montor drew up a list; the men were invited as individuals in the name of the impeccable Rudolf Sonneborn.

Six days later Ben Gurion, his white shirt open at the neck, a jacket slung over one arm, hurried through the lobby of the small residential hotel at 14 East 60th Street where he was staying and pushed his way through its revolving door. As he reached the street, the heat struck at him with a fistful of doubts. It was not a day to rally enthusiasm. He headed east, the sticky asphalt pulling at the soles of his shoes, and mopped his brow as he reached the haven of Sonneborn's penthouse.

They made an incongruous pair as they stood awaiting the arrival of their guests: Sonneborn, tall, suave, the elegant capitalist to his manicured fingertips; Ben Gurion, disheveled, emotional, with tufts of white hair framing his cherub's face, the intellectual torn loose from his library. The two men had met in 1919 when Sonneborn, at the behest of a family friend, U.S. Supreme Court Justice Louis D. Brandeis, had gone to the Versailles peace conference as secretary to an American Zionist delegation and afterwards had toured the Holy Land. Although they had arrived at their destinations by such different routes—Sonneborn the tourist in first-class; Ben Gurion the socialist in steerage—the two young men had become friends and had remained so through the years.

They exchanged a nod of satisfaction as they counted the arrivals. Seventeen men had been invited. Seventeen men were there.*

They were not the wealthiest nor the most influential Jews in America. Of the seventeen, only the host, Rudolf Sonneborn, would one day be mentioned in the 1967 best seller *Our Crowd*, an account of America's leading Jewish families.

None of the nineteen looked particularly Jewish—or particularly not. No distinction of dress, haircut, nose, or shape of head or body set them apart from any other random group of Americans. If they possessed one feature in common, it was a look of wariness that they carried with them wherever they went, even on this sweltering Sunday morning, even though they obviously were flattered by their

---

* Present also were the Americans Sonneborn and Montor—a total of nineteen. Besides Ben Gurion, there were two other Palestinians: Eliezer Kaplan, treasurer of the Jewish Agency, and Reuven Zaslani.

invitations to this meeting. One had come from Los Angeles, another from Toronto. The others came from Miami and Birmingham, from Philadelphia and Pittsburgh, from Cleveland and Columbus, Minneapolis and St. Louis, Newark and New Haven, the rest from New York. One was a rabbi; five were lawyers. The others were businessmen. One owned a chain of drug stores; one was in jewelry; another in the shoe business. Each one had his own success story, tucked away as carefully as his monogrammed handkerchief.

They listened silently as Ben Gurion told them that their destinies were linked with a desert strip 5,000 miles away and with ancestors who had been nomads on that desert 2,000 years ago. They had come to hear him speak because they were Jews, but, by that very fact, they would not accept easily everything he had to say.

Ben Gurion ran a finger around the inside of his collar, remembering wearily the many other men he had spoken to in the past month. Many simply had not been prepared to believe the grim evidence of genocide that was unfolding in the recently liberated Nazi concentration camps. Few could believe that the victorious Allied powers would not now set things right and see that justice was done, that old promises were kept, that the sufferers of persecution were redeemed. Above all, they had been upright American citizens, unwilling even to contemplate actions that might jeopardize their hard-won positions of acceptance and authority in American society.

The Palestinian wondered what effect his words would have today. He spoke quietly but quickly in strongly accented English. Five to six million Jews had been murdered by the Nazis, he began. The great centers of Jewish population in Eastern Europe—in Poland, the Ukraine, that crescent of the unwanted squeezed up against the Carpathian mountains—were no more. The Jewish communities of Western Europe were decimated. After years of hiding or living in concentration camps or, at best, in uncertain exile, those Jews who had survived the Nazi massacres were demoralized and displaced, not merely from their homes but from all recognition as self-sustaining human beings. The victorious nations would give their sympathy, he predicted, but they would not do more. Sympathy was a temporary thing; it easily soured into contempt. Already there were riots in the DP camps; the survivors not only wanted to get out of Germany, they wanted to get out of Europe.*

---

* On that same day—July 1, 1945—in Bavaria, forty-one representatives of Jewish DP camps met and drafted a petition to the Allied Big Three, who would meet in Potsdam later that month, asking them to support establishment of a Jewish state.

He looked around the room and asked a rhetorical question: Would America take these refugees? He didn't wait for an answer. Sonneborn had said there would be "open discussion" later on but no one, then or later, argued with Ben Gurion about the United States. They were sophisticated men; they knew all about cliques and quotas and what "New Yorker" meant in the South, and what "pushy" meant in business, and what "Hollywood" stood for in the West. They knew that while there might be a visa for a sister or a nephew, there was no room in the United States, or, for that matter, in any other American or European country, for more than a handful of the human wreckage that had escaped the Final Solution. As practical men, they knew all about unsteady applecarts. They were Jews and every Jew's image of himself is conditioned by the least anti-Semite's view.

Ben Gurion said there was one country that wanted the European Jews and to which the Jews, especially the young Jews, wanted to go. That country was Palestine. It not only wanted them, it needed them, for it was not yet a country but only the promise of one. There were 600,000 Jews and 1,000,000 Arabs and it could only be a homeland if the Jews reached a majority. The Jews had made history in the Land. They had survived because they believed in that Land; the promise of that Land held them together. He said he would not argue the merits of Zionism, and there were smiles all around.

Everyone present knew, at least sketchily, the modern history of Palestine. After World War I, the League of Nations had given Britain a mandate over Palestine with a view to fulfilling the Balfour Declaration of 1917, which had promised the "establishment in Palestine of a national home for the Jewish people." Acting on that promise, thousands of European Jews had emigrated to Palestine. In 1920 the then Colonial Secretary Winston Churchill had reaffirmed the pledge, but one year later, to provide a kingdom for the Emir Abdullah of Syria, Churchill had agreed that all of Palestine east of the Jordan River be split off to form the Arab state of Transjordan. The League of Nations had concurred. More than half the loaf was gone, but there was still the promise. In 1939, on the eve of the Nazi holocaust, Britain had issued the infamous White Paper limiting Jewish immigration "unless the Arabs of Palestine are prepared to acquiesce in it." That had killed even the promise.

Ben Gurion glanced at his audience and gulped down a glass of water. The temperature outside had reached a sizzling ninety-seven degrees, and even in the airy vastness of Sonneborn's living room it was close.

He had just come from London, Ben Gurion continued, and he was convinced that the British Labour Party would win the forthcoming election against the wartime Churchill government. His listeners murmured their approval; the Labour Party had always supported the idea of a Jewish national home in Palestine.

But Ben Gurion was not smiling. He said he had become convinced in London that the Labour Party, once in power, would do nothing to support its promises. In fact, it would go back on them.

Not only would the White Paper stand, but "in two or three years" the British would give up the mandate. The Foreign Office bureaucracy was convinced that stability in the Middle East meant a Palestine dominated by Arabs. It would persuade the Labour government to see things its way.

Nor did Ben Gurion expect the U.S. State Department to view the situation any differently from the British Foreign Office. They spoke the same language—status quo.

Again Ben Gurion tried to appraise his audience. Were they with him? Even among his own people he stood almost alone in his analysis of how events were likely to develop. Other Palestinian leaders, old line socialists, pacifist by tradition and policy, still put their faith in political solutions, in negotiations, treaties and the good will of the great powers, especially a Labour government in England. Only a handful of members of Haganah, the secret Jewish defense force in Palestine, shared his apocalyptic view of the future. Ben Gurion had made this trip to the United States with the knowledge but by no means with the unanimous support of the Jewish Agency. Many of its members considered him alarmist and foolish. Did these well-tailored, well-fed Americans think the same? He pushed on with his argument.

Once the British gave up the mandate, Ben Gurion predicted, there would be a vacuum in Palestine, a vacuum of power, not of pronouncements and promises. The Arabs in Palestine made no secret of their plans to fill that vacuum. Their fellow Arabs in the countries around Palestine, although divided in their objectives and often squabbling among themselves, would, in Ben Gurion's view, invade, including the 10,000 well-equipped British-trained men of Transjordan's Arab Legion.

It would no longer, he said, be a question of what the British would say or what the United States might want or what the new United Nations Organization might someday recommend. There would be no time for any of that. It would be a bare-knuckled fight for survival. There was only one course open to the Jews of Palestine.

They would get the Jewish survivors out of the DP camps by themselves, by whatever means they could devise, on their own ships. Despite prohibitions, blockades and White Papers, they would bring them to the homeland and establish them there. They would heal the sick, whether of body or spirit. They would train the able-bodied with the help of the thousands of Palestinian Jews who had served in the Allied military forces and were now coming home.

And when the British left, and the Arabs struck, there would be no marching into the slaughter pens, no filing aboard the refugee boats, no surrender. There would be a battle.

This time the Jews would fight.

The meeting lasted throughout the day; afterward some of the men wondered where the time and the heat had flown.

They had smoked and they had drunk quantities of Coke and ginger-ale—this was not an alcohol-drinking crowd—and shortly after noon Sonneborn's servant had laid out a spread of cold meats and cheeses, salad and iced tea.

Late in the afternoon, as the first breeze rose off the East River, the assembled men got the promised chance to "put their oars in." They made suggestions and Ben Gurion nodded. They asked questions and he answered. Some of them had to leave to catch planes and trains. Ben Gurion stayed on with the others, elucidating, affirming and asking nothing specific, as if he found in their presence and their interest commitment enough to do whatever might be necessary.

No notes of the meeting were taken; no specific promises were asked for or made. What was remembered best by each of the participants was the uncertainty he felt at the end about what was expected of him.

Writing a confidential aide-memoire several years later, with at least a touch of hindsight, Rudolf Sonneborn noted, "On that memorable day, we were asked to form ourselves into an . . . American arm of the underground Haganah. We were given no clue as to what we might be called upon to accomplish, when the call might come, or who would call us. We were simply asked to be prepared and to mobilize like-minded Americans. We were asked to keep the meeting confidential."

By fall the war in Asia had ended; the atomic age had dawned. And, one by one, as if history were following some inexorable outline written by Ben Gurion, each of the predictions he had made to the men at Sonneborn's apartment regarding Britain and Palestine came to pass.

A Labour government had replaced the Conservative wartime administration of Winston Churchill. Its new Foreign Minister, Ernest Bevin, a tough trades-union man with a background of Zionist sympathy, had acquiesced to the Foreign Office professionals and upheld the White Paper. Legal Jewish immigration into Palestine ended in September with the arrival in Haifa of 340 refugees from Barcelona, where Franco had sheltered them from the Nazis. The DP camps of Europe were bulging with the restive survivors of the Final Solution. And no one in Europe and America wanted them.

II

THE JOB

Philip Alper had stayed on in Berkeley after graduation, putting things off, taking a couple of courses in American history and Russian, holding down "a flunky job" with the university's mechanical engineering department. He was a slender handsome youth of twenty-one, high-spirited and romantic, and he dreaded the kind of routine job a brand-new mechanical engineer from the University of California would be offered immediately after V-J Day.

He had missed out on the war because of a heart murmur, while his two older brothers had been in service, and it bothered him. "Not just the duty and the patriotism," he readily admitted, "but the glamour, the excitement." His father, who owned a clothing store in Alhambra, a small town near Los Angeles, urged him to come home and go to work for one of the big Southern California aircraft companies. Instead, Phil thought of Alaska, but he never got there. In September 1945 he decided to hitchhike to New York.

He passed air bases clogged with grounded planes, Army camps whose barracks suddenly seemed shabby and uninhabitable, Army trucks that no longer looked warlike but more like ungainly junk, war plants plastered with posters announcing their reconversion. And everywhere there were men on the road, ex-GIs going home. Soldiers were being released from the Army at the rate of 500,000 a month. President Truman had announced that 5½ million would be discharged in the next eighteen months. War contracts were being canceled, assembly lines halted. Shipyard workers laid off in California were heading back to Oklahoma, Massachusetts, North Dakota. Washington economists predicted that 5 million war workers would be out of work by October. The stock market was nervous.

In New York Alper moved in with an uncle, Louis Ross, a widower who kept house with his three grown children. Alper began reading the classifieds. There were openings for engineers in the exciting new postwar world the ads talked about. But not in exciting Manhattan. There were jobs in Connecticut and upstate New York and New Jersey; with General Electric in Schenectady and Caterpillar Tractor in Peoria.

Now that he had made his way to New York, Phil was determined to stay there, close to the action. The only solid offer he got in Manhattan was with Babcock and Wilcox as a draftsman. Excellent engineering firm, good prospects and about as glamorous as the drafting tables in California which he had fled. He was talking with his uncle about it one evening in the apartment in Forest Hills when the telephone rang. It was a friend whom Phil had looked up shortly after arriving in New York. Phil and the friend had once belonged to a Zionist youth group. Phil's parents had been interested in Palestine and he had studied Hebrew, sang the songs and gone camping—but he had long since left that behind. His friend, however, had maintained his interest in Zionism.

"Phil," the friend greeted him buoyantly, "I have a job for you."

"I'm not interested in any Zionist missionary work," Alper said warily. "I'm an engineer."

"It's engineering," the friend assured him.

"I have to know more than that."

"It has something to do with Palestine," he conceded. Then, after a long pause, "That's all I can tell you."

Alper pressed for details but the other remained mysterious and cryptic. Alper could coax no more information out of him.

"Do you want it or don't you want it?" the friend finally demanded impatiently.

Phil thought of Peoria and Schenectady. He thought of the war he had missed and the drafting boards waiting at Babcock and Wilcox. "What the hell," he decided, "I'll take a chance."

The next day he met his friend at the Hotel Commodore near Grand Central Station. Phil still looked the Berkeley senior: open-collared blue shirt, gray slacks, sports coat, scuffed loafers. The friend was more soberly dressed and Phil was sorry he hadn't worn a tie. The elevator stopped at the twelfth floor. The two young men got off and walked down what seemed like an endless labyrinth to a room in a back corridor. At their knock, a door was opened by a stocky Slavic-featured man. His face was unsmiling as he admitted them to the room.

Phil looked around. All he could think of was that it had been silly to worry about a necktie. This was the smallest room he had ever been in. There was a narrow bed, a tiny desk, a wooden chair, a window and the walls closing in. Its single occupant wasn't wearing a necktie either.

Still unsmiling, the man bowed slightly, extended his hand to Phil and said, "Slavin."

Haim Slavin had arrived in New York that same month wearing a sports shirt and slacks beneath a borrowed topcoat that was two sizes too large. To improve his English, which was negligible, he carried a 1924 edition of Sherlock Holmes, which he laboriously read with the aid of a dictionary.

He was a stocky man of forty-four with a ruddy face, sandy-colored hair, and piercing blue eyes. His eyes were the first thing people noticed about him—second was the fact that he rarely smiled. He was an engineer, a specialist in irrigation and hydroelectric projects, and he was also the Haganah's specialist in the secret production of arms.

He had been sent to the United States by Ben Gurion* with a short list of names of "important men" and instructions to steer clear of the usual Zionist channels. He had never been in the United States before. His first night in New York he spent in a hotel on West 49th Street that had been recommended by a friend in Tel Aviv who had stayed there thirty years ago. Times had changed and so had the hotel. Haggling whores kept Slavin up most of the night.

Tossing sleeplessly, after his ninety-hour flight from Tel Aviv, uneasy about what lay ahead, he thought, Here I am, Haim Slavin, in America, with big plans and no way to know how to do it.

The next morning he telephoned a couple of the men whose names had been given to him by Ben Gurion. They were cordial. Henry Montor, as soon as he heard where Slavin was staying, arranged for him to move to the Hotel Commodore, no easy feat in crowded postwar New York. Rudolf Sonneborn took him to a plush restaurant for lunch. Slavin was so impatient he could hardly sit through the meal.

"I was a man from work," he recalls. "I didn't know if twice before I went to America I tried out a necktie. I was all out of table

* Ben Gurion would say years later: "I considered that with the end of the war the United States would begin to find some of her arms factories surplus to her needs, and would wish to dispose of expensive machinery fairly cheaply. This was just what we needed. . . . To equip an army, we now had to manufacture not only ammunition and explosives of a type and on a scale hitherto unknown in the country, but also actual weapons, even though limited to small arms."

manners and all these things. There were all kinds of forks and knives and I had not the slightest idea what to do with all this stuff. So I told this fine man, 'I don't know how to use all these tools. You just go ahead and I will follow.' "

Slavin would say little about what he wanted. "I have a plan but I haven't the people. I need some engineers, some technical people—not politicians, not good Jews—but people that I can speak technical questions to them."

He was given the name of a man in Chicago who might help.

Again, the well-dressed businessman. Again, the cordiality. Slavin, desperate about his inability to communicate, tried to tell a little more about what he had in mind.

When he had finished, the man smiled at him as though he were a child. "For what you want to do," he told Slavin, "you need tools, you need machines, you need export licenses."

Slavin exploded. "For this advice I didn't have to fly six thousand miles and then come to Chicago."

Discouraged, Slavin returned to New York. He was shivering—he had caught a cold on the train—and his right foot hurt from an ingrown toenail. Nevertheless, he couldn't stay in his hotel room. He limped over to Times Square and stood in a doorway. "I just had a vision of myself in the frame of this big Broadway with all the lights and the thousands of people all free, all going to have some fun, and I thought, My God, Slavin, your people put their hopes in this man who cannot walk because of a nail in his toe. I was shaking from grief. I was thinking over my days in America, spending money, nine dollars a day, going from appointment to appointment and just making nothing. So I just forced the lights out of my mind and I was in the stillness of a farm in the Galilee in the pure of the night, with the fear all around. And the comparison of this fearful dark night and the Broadway lights just shook me. I decided, with toenails, without toenails, I have to do something."

The next morning Slavin disobeyed Ben Gurion's order. He telephoned a man he knew from Palestine, a man who knew Slavin's Haganah specialty. The man sent him to see another man at a youth organization. Slavin said only that he needed "someone with a technical background for a little job—a simple little job." His listener nodded. He had recently met an old friend from California who was now an engineer.

Alper sat down on the only chair in the tiny room and waited expectantly to find out why he was there. His friend had left. Slavin had perched himself on the edge of the bed and was regarding him intently. Finally, speaking slowly, in hesitant English, Slavin asked Alper about himself. "Good, good," the older man said when Alper volunteered that he knew a little Hebrew and a little Russian. After that, conversation went more easily in a halting combination of the three languages. Learning that Alper was a graduate engineer, Slavin nodded his approval. That was what he needed, he said, a technical man. Alper paused, hoping to hear what sort of technical work would be expected of him, but instead Slavin began to talk about himself. He had emigrated to Palestine from Russia in 1924, he said, and gone to work for the Palestine Electric Corporation. He had been working on an isolated hydroelectric station when the Arab riots of 1929 broke out. "We were surrounded there," he recalled, "maybe seven hundred people, and all our protection was six hand grenades." Quickly taking over, Slavin had sent a few men to Haifa to get pipe fittings and explosives. Then he had put the men to work stuffing each two-inch pipe section with dynamite and a four-second fuse. Several hundred of these homemade hand grenades were made and distributed to the scattered farm settlements in the area. "Of course, it was a very simple thing," Slavin explained, "but still, to give the people courage, it was good. If you are holding something in your hands, it can do for your courage more than anything. With nothing in your hands, morale goes down fast."

After the riots, Slavin recounted, he and others decided "we should start to do something more serious to protect ourselves." But it was difficult. None of them knew anything about the manufacture of arms; very few had even Slavin's technical training. He divided his time, "making my days for the Palestine Electric Corporation and my nights for the Haganah." He helped set up small secret workshops to manufacture crude grenades and mortars. With the outbreak of World War II Haganah asked him to give up his job and devote full time to this underground work.

Even the simplest materials were hard to come by and there was always the threat of discovery and arrest by the British, who had forbidden the Jews to arm themselves. Slavin's ingenuity took endless forms. He wanted to make mortars. "We had not the pipes, the simple pipes that you buy on the market for so many pennies. So we took a false order to the Royal Navy and brought out sheet iron three inches thick and from this we made pipes. Now that was very good and all very nice but to make it shoot, you have to have gunpowder. How to do it? The only thing you can get is a license for a half pound for a man who is going to hunt, a hunter, so you can't exist."

Some of Slavin's "boys" had noticed that the British were dumping outdated cordite—which disintegrates after five years—into the Mediterranean. Slavin sent down divers to bring it up, then put a roomful of young women to work with improvised machines made of razor blades to chop up the congealed chunks and dry out the explosive. "It was a great victory," Slavin assured Alper.

"All during World War II," he continued, "we were struggling to prepare ourselves for everything: for the Arabs, for the Germans who maybe would be coming in. We wanted to sell our lives as high as possible."

When the war ended, Slavin, like Alper in Berkeley, had taken stock. But his was not a personal stock-taking; he was measuring the situation of his people: The worst had not happened; the Germans had not reached Palestine.

Haganah had grown and now had a mobilized elite shock force, known as Palmach, of about two thousand young men and women as well as a small cadre of full-time officers and several thousand reservists with varying amounts of military training. Hidden away in secret caches around the country was Haganah's motley arsenal of home-made weapons and a few thousand rifles, Sten guns and light machine guns bought clandestinely, in neighboring Arab countries and from British and Arab Legion soldiers. That was all to the good, Slavin explained to Alper, but not enough. "I clearly saw that when the time would be coming that serious Arab groups will come with arms, we will be shot down. I knew how much we had, how much ammunition, how many rifles and I saw that we will not hold up." Slavin's mission in the United States, he gravely told Alper, was to somehow acquire and ship to Palestine the machinery necessary to set up a small-arms industry. Then the Jews there would manufacture the weapons to protect themselves right inside the country. Slavin wanted Alper to help him get the information, the know-how—to do the legwork that he could not handle with his poor English and unfamiliarity with the country.

Alper had listened quietly to the older man's recital and he hardly knew what to say.

"I thought it was crazy," Alper recalls. "The British were in Palestine and I could not imagine how the Jews could make arms and ammunition while the British were in the country. But it was not my business to say how they were going to do it."

He did have a personal reservation: "Will this be against American law?"

Slavin had been expecting the question. In his own mind there was no doubt about the morality of his cause—the right of his people to arm and defend themselves. He was equally convinced that America, of all nations, would see the justice of this. But at the moment there were complications. All the great nations were preoccupied with their own postwar problems; the international situation was confused; the political outlook for Palestine uncertain. American law on buying and exporting armaments and the machinery to make them was complex, contradictory, and constantly changing, subject to the vicissitudes of a shifting foreign policy.

He wanted to say these things to the young American, but language kept them apart, so he spoke, again, in "baby talk," as simply as he could. "A law has to have a frame," he said. "You cannot live without a spirit in the law. That is why you go to a judge, and not to a machine that says yes or no, automatically. Every man in America, when he has the picture of the night that is coming to Palestine and the dark forces coming around us, will understand."

Alper wanted to ask for a few days to think it over, but Slavin was watching him with such anxious intensity, he said, instead, "All right, I'll start Monday."

"What's the matter with tomorrow?" demanded Slavin.

III

THE GUN

<hr/>

Slavin took getting used to. When Alper got to work the next
morning, a Friday, at 8 A.M., he found Slavin pacing as best he
could in the tiny hotel room. Phil realized that 8 A.M. was late for
Slavin. Alper was resolved, after a long talk over breakfast with his
uncle, to bring up salary. Again Slavin was waiting for him: "You are
just graduated from university, yes?" Alper had composed his arguments on the subway, but he never had time to use them.

"Yes," he said. He could not argue so early in the morning with
a man who looked so exasperated.

"How much are getting salary, the graduating engineers?"

"The big companies, like General Electric, pay beginners fifty
dollars a week," Alper replied.

Slavin pointed a stubby thumb at his chest. "I am not General
Electric," he said, with what seemed to Alper to be a smile. "Thirty-
five dollars a week is okay?" Alper nodded.

He had signed on for an adventure, but all Slavin had him do at
first was go to the New York Public Library and look in the engineering index for the titles of articles on arms and ammunition
manufacturing that had been published in technical magazines since
1939. As Alper scanned each article, he found references to earlier
articles and these too he wrote down: the names of the magazines, the
dates of the issues, and the numbers of the pages on which the articles
had appeared. But not the titles. "I didn't want to walk around
carrying a list of titles like 'Bullets by the Billions' or 'Turning Out
Garand Rifles in a Tractor Plant.' " Taking this little precaution
made him feel more like a secret agent, and less like an underpaid
librarian. From time to time, as he sat quietly in the library, he would
slowly turn around to see if someone was looking over his shoulder.

No one was interested in what he was doing, except Slavin. After the library, armed with a list of magazines and dates, Alper visited the back-issue magazine shops along Sixth Avenue near 42nd Street or he took the subway up to H. W. Wilson Company, in the Bronx, where he found the best selection of all. Slavin gave him ten dollars a day for his carfare and purchases and insisted he sign a receipt for it each time.

He brought the magazines and journals back to Slavin's tiny room and together they spent hours going through them, Alper reading the articles and explaining them in a mixture of English, Russian and Hebrew that only served to make Slavin more impatient and more frustrated. But the system worked. They were learning together. Slavin, Alper discovered, was "very competent technically, a brilliant man, a good engineer, but he knew nothing about manufacturing arms and ammunition. He had been sent to the United States because he had had some experience, on a very small scale, in making weapons surreptitiously. He was a wonderful organizer, but he was starting from scratch."

Slavin would take notes and he would talk about the kinds of weapons his people needed—pistols, rifles, light machine guns, ammunition—the level of technology of which they were capable. And Alper would clip out the articles that seemed pertinent. He also collected advertisements. The great wartime arms industries were closing down or reconverting to peacetime production; recent issues of the magazines bulged with ads offering machinery for sale. Slavin began a card file of machines that would do specific jobs.

"One article would be very sketchy," recalls Alper, "on, say, the manufacture of thirty-caliber cartridges. It might have certain details and highlights on the equipment but not a comprehensive study of the whole process. Another article would hit other highlights and by taking all of these articles that had appeared over a number of years, we were able to piece together a fairly complete description of the manufacture of the equipment we were interested in. Making ammunition is a very complicated process with many operations, quite a lot of machinery and many, many techniques connected with metallurgy that can be very tricky. What we put together from these articles was a sequence of operations, and the kind of machine used for each operation—either with a picture or its specifications. It was like doing a big jigsaw puzzle."

They pasted excerpts from the articles and the illustrations or specifications on loose-leaf pages and then organized the pages into a book that, for all its similarity to a child's scrapbook, grew into an impressive production manual on the manufacture of small arms.

Slavin's card index listed all the machines that could do the jobs by manufacturer, number, and even an approximate price.

On the days they worked together in the hotel room Alper and Slavin lunched at an Automat and Slavin immediately wrote down to the penny the meager amount he had spent.

It was then, over an extravagant second cup of coffee, that Slavin would talk in guarded terms about his most urgent project: The Gun. The scrapbook, the machines, the plans for an arms industry in Palestine were for the future. What he wanted, right away, was a gun—a versatile, powerful automatic weapon with which the settlers in Palestine could defend their homes, their women and their children from the terrorist bands which already were harassing them; a gun which a member of Haganah could hide easily, learn to use effectively, and take with him when he got a sudden call, like a volunteer fireman, to fight. Slavin wanted to acquire the machinery for making that gun and smuggle it, piece by piece, into Palestine, as quickly as possible.

Carl Ekdahl, a hard-working Swedish-American, had never planned to retire at the age of fifty, so when the job offer came he didn't ask many questions.

Ekdahl had emigrated to the United States from Sweden in 1910 when he was eighteen years old, settled in Connecticut, and learned cabinetmaking. But during World War I, he had found himself working as a gunsmith. New England was the center of the United States small-arms industry and for twenty-six years he had worked at that specialty, for Marlin, for Winchester, for Harrington & Richardson, and then, until 1942, for Johnson Automatics, Inc., in Providence, Rhode Island, where he had helped design the Johnson light machine gun that had won high praise in the ordnance field for its simplicity and versatility.* A heart attack in 1942 forced him to quit work. He had been an active, loquacious man who enjoyed work, hunting and fishing, good food and drink, and convivial evenings

* The Johnson light machine gun, which had been used by Marine parachute and raider units in the Pacific, and Army Rangers in Europe and the Aleutians, weighed only 12.5 pounds empty and could be quickly dismantled into three parts, none measuring more than two feet long, so that it could be packed handily into a canvas bag. Assembled in ten seconds, it fired 60 shots per minute on semi-automatic, 150 per minute on automatic, operated by one man, and 250 per minute operated by two. An overheated barrel could be changed in ten seconds.

harmonizing old Swedish songs. He was still slowly and impatiently recuperating from his heart attack, working part time at his former trade of cabinetmaker to make ends meet, hoping one day to get back to gunsmithing but doubting there would be much chance of it, with the war over, when he received a call one day in October 1945 from a Harry Levine, who identified himself as the friend of a friend. They met and Ekdahl came away exhilarated. Levine, a precise, urbane man, was a millionaire, the owner of a large plastics manufacturing firm in Leominster, Massachusetts, and he had been in the arms business during the war as one of the owners of the New York Safe and Lock Company, which had made parts for the Swiss Oerlikon gun under license.

Would Ekdahl be interested—Levine wanted to know, after they had talked awhile about other things—in designing another machine gun, similar to the Johnson, for a small research and development project Levine had in mind?

Ekdahl agreed to meet Levine the next day at the Hotel Commodore in New York to talk over the details with Levine's "brilliant associate."

Slavin was waiting impatiently at the door as Ekdahl and Levine walked down the hotel corridor toward his room. He had sent Alper out on errands for the afternoon and piled the magazines in the closet. Slavin's eyes went quickly from Ekdahl's thin sensitive face to the package he was carrying, a canvas case which, by its unmistakeable profile, held a machine gun. Slavin's jaw dropped. He grabbed Ekdahl's arm and rushed the visitor into his room. In Palestine it was worth several years of a man's freedom if the British authorities so much as found a pistol in his house and here was this American carrying a machine gun in broad daylight through the lobby and corridors of a busy hotel.

Slavin's technical vocabulary in English had improved from his work with Alper. He also found that he could understand Ekdahl's slow Swedish accent more readily than the hurried slur of words that most of the Americans he had met threw at him. "Anyway," Levine recalls, "they communicated beautifully by drawing lines on blueprints."

The conversation concentrated on technical details. If Ekdahl was curious about the setting, the unimpressive room, Levine's obviously foreign "associate," so unlike what he would expect from a man as important as Levine, he gave no sign. He broke down the machine gun, explained the various parts and discussed the sort of modifications he had in mind for a simpler, improved version.

Levine recalls that "Slavin was smiling for the first time since we'd met."

As Ekdahl put the gun back together and slipped it into the canvas pouch, he agreed to meet Slavin again in Providence in a few days.

As he boarded the train for Providence, Slavin was feeling ill. He was coughing and running a fever as he got to Ekdahl's modest home. Mrs. Ekdahl, a sweet-faced, retiring woman, took one look at him and put him to bed with tea and aspirin. "There I was," Slavin recalls, "a stranger and a Jew—in New England they are not so much liking Jews—and it was as though it was my family."

He didn't have to ask Ekdahl what decision he had reached about designing the gun. The answer was obvious. The two men, Slavin propped up in bed, Ekdahl hunched on a chair beside him, pored over drawings and lists. There were many details to discuss. Ekdahl would not only design the gun but all of the tooling—the machinery—that would be needed to manufacture each part of it. To do the entire job properly, Slavin realized, Ekdahl would have to know more.

So Slavin took a chance on another American. His fever might have relaxed his normal guard. He told Ekdahl that he was a Palestinian, that there would soon be a Jewish state in Palestine, and that the gun was needed to arm his people against their enemies. He stopped as Ekdahl broke in.

He hadn't known many Jews, the Swedish-American was saying, but he was sympathetic. He felt all people had a right to a homeland. He had always wondered why Jews never defended themselves against persecution, and now he would be glad to help.

They settled the business details that evening: Ekdahl would receive $17,000 for the job. He estimated that he could do it in six months. The next morning, as they drove to the railroad station, Ekdahl asked Slavin some questions about other aspects of Slavin's work. "Look, Carl," Slavin replied, "there is very little I can tell you in truth. So let's make an agreement. You will not ask and I will not lie."

Slavin went to bed to recuperate after his trip to Providence. When he first told Phil about the successful negotiations with Ekdahl, he appeared happy and confident, but inactivity inevitably brought out his worst fears. Alper came back one day and found him brooding that the hotel was not safe, that the chambermaids were spying on him; too many people had access to the room.

The next day when Phil came in, Slavin was hanging up the phone.

"Phil," he said, "no more work today. We are moving to a safe place."

They set about packing the magazines, the clippings and loose-leaf books wrapped in manila paper and tied with twine that Slavin, in spite of his illness, had gone out to buy. Slavin packed his few belongings, including the dogeared copy of Sherlock Holmes, in his battered suitcase.

Phil suggested a bellhop. Slavin merely grunted.

They carried the suitcase and bundles through the lobby and into a taxicab.

"We are going to a good place," Slavin said, as the cab started uptown. "Safe. Much more room. This is going to be a big business."

IV

THE APARTMENT

The five-room apartment at 512 West 112th Street was in the neighborhood where Columbia University, Harlem, Chinese restaurants and kosher delicatessens huddle together, as if to avoid the icy blasts off the Hudson River. There Slavin's "operation" quickly settled down to a routine of work that he considered normal—eighteen hours a day, seven days a week.

Slavin believed in a man living close to his work, so he talked Alper into taking a room in the St. Mark Arms, a residential hotel two doors away. He would have preferred having Alper in the apartment itself but he already was sharing it with a Palestinian family, headed by a journalist named Pines which in Hebrew is pronounced "penis." Pines, stubbornly refusing to adopt the American pronunciation, once startled Alper by walking into a room and belligerently introducing himself to two young American women: "Ladies, my name is Penis, and don't laugh!" Pines, his wife and young daughter occupied the kitchen, the living room, and two of the apartment's three bedrooms.

Slavin's office was in the front bedroom and he slept there—when he slept—on a cot. The room's other furnishings consisted of a desk for himself, a table for Alper—"I worked most of the time standing up"—and an increasing number of makeshift shelves on which Slavin "filed" the papers they were accumulating, European-style, flat, in layers.

Slavin worked until he was completely exhausted. Then he would fall asleep, get up in a few hours, start work again "and look around for me" recalls Alper. Alper, more involved in this strange occupation than he liked to admit, had decided "It was all crazy, but fortunately for Slavin, I was very young, very naïve, very energetic and very enthusiastic. I didn't think about money or time or a career any more." His boyhood interest in Palestine was reviving. "I figured that in a few years I would go to Palestine and live on a collective settlement where everyone lives in one room anyway and you don't need money."

Money was very much on Slavin's mind. He was making plans to spend tens of thousands of dollars on equipment for Palestine. But he shuddered, his face whitened and his blue eyes glared when Alper submitted an expense account listing three taxi rides. Alper was still ferreting out magazines and reference books; his prime source, the H. W. Wilson Company, the largest dealer in back-issue magazines, was in the Bronx. Slavin, who had bought a map of the subways, would suggest to Phil the fastest (and cheapest) way of getting to Wilson's and back from the apartment. They also had arranged with Harry Levine to use his New York office at 256 West 38th Street as a mail drop. Every morning Alper picked up the mail at Levine's office by a route that Slavin insisted he take. Alper hoped it had something to do with eluding the British secret service, but nobody followed him— unless it was Slavin with his little brown expense book. Alper, the former California lifeguard, grew pale from so many hours spent indoors in libraries and underground in subways.

Once a week Slavin sent him to the Western Union office on Broadway and 107th Street to send off a cable to Palestine reporting on their progress. Slavin's code name was "Auerbach"; Alper never knew why. He often wondered what the Western Union clerk thought about his regular visits and cryptic messages, but if the sleepy young clerk felt any curiosity, he didn't show it.

On a rare evening off, Alper would retire to his room in the St. Mark Arms, "a room so small that if you opened the door, you couldn't open the closet." He would shower off the dust of the old magazines, change into his good suit, tiptoe down the stairs, and sidle out the door, half expecting that Slavin would be waiting outside to summon him back to work.

He had met a girl, but had no serious plans yet. How serious could a man be when he was earning, as he once calculated, twenty cents an hour?

For days on end, their monastic isolation on Morningside Heights was interrupted only by the shuffling sounds of the Pines family as they tiptoed along the corridor, or by the smell of Mrs. Pines's cooking. But, as the magazines were culled of their pertinent articles, and the articles were correlated into the thickening loose-leaf books, Alper managed to convince Slavin of a logical next step.

American manufacturers would be only too pleased to send them, to send to anyone, catalogues, price lists, and additional specifications, if they wrote for them. For this phase they would need a secretary.

Slavin refused to entertain the notion, so at first Alper himself pecked out the letters on a battered typewriter, the cheapest machine Slavin had been able to buy, but as the first replies came back, Slavin grew convinced. Through one of his "contacts," he obtained a secretary, a young woman who could be trusted to work for minimum salary and with maximum discretion. She was a tall buxom young woman whom nature had equipped only to work in large offices. Her breasts were so large that Alper had no peace; they seemed to be everywhere in the narrow office in which the three of them now worked. Slavin, noticing his assistant's flushed face, replaced her with another young woman, who asked a larger salary but was suitably slim.

Jerry Schweitzer turned out to be a bargain that Slavin could appreciate. Her twin sister, Diane, was a secretary at the American Economic Committee for Palestine and when Jerry was working late at West 112th Street, Diane would come uptown to wait for her so they could go home together.

In such a situation Slavin could be charming and gallant. He began asking Diane to help out so that Jerry's work would be finished sooner, and when the two sisters worked late into the night, he would treat them to a taxicab ride to their parents' apartment in the Bronx. They didn't mind. Both were ardent Zionists and Jerry found the work much more to her liking than the civil service job she had left. Slavin never told her exactly what he was doing, and Jerry was too discreet to ask. "After a while, it began to dawn on me," she recalls, "but I never discussed it with anyone except my sister. To this day, I don't know what a lot of it was about."

A nook had been found for Jerry in the crowded apartment, a small room just to the left of the narrow entry hall. In it Slavin jammed her desk (a secondhand wooden table), some makeshift shelves to hold her papers (filing cabinets were another luxury he considered unnecessary) and a battered studio couch. It now was Jerry's job to take care of the requests for catalogues and handle Slavin's correspondence. "He always answered every letter immediately," she recalls. He left it to her to compose the letters, which he outlined in halting English.

None of Slavin's "contacts" ever visited the 112th Street apartment. There were few callers of any kind. Mail was still routed through the 38th Street office of Harry Levine; Jerry now picked it up each morning. It was as though the apartment did not exist to anyone but its little band of regular occupants.

Alper's work gradually entered a new phase. He was getting around more, and not only to the Bronx to buy old magazines. The United States government had formed the War Assets Administration to sell its surplus war plants and military supplies. The arsenal of democracy was to be auctioned off for a fraction of its cost—everything from olive-drab brassieres to aircraft carriers. The WAA and the big surplus dealers flooded prospective buyers with advertising, and with invitations to come to the depots, factories, navy yards, and surplus warehouses to see and finger the bargains for themselves.

Alper and Slavin got on every mailing list they could; they studied the offers and when they saw something that fitted the plans in their scrapbooks and card file, Alper went out to take a look at it.

The twenty-two-year-old youth from California, who only a few months before had been hitchhiking across the country, aimlessly eying the vacant military bases and arms plants, suddenly found himself inside them.

At the Remington Arms plant in Bridgeport, Alper made his first big buy—six tons of machinery to produce .303 ammunition for the gun which Ekdahl was designing.

The machinery was highly specialized; nothing could be substituted for it. Yet, since it was usable for no other purpose, the WAA sold it as scrap for seventy dollars a ton. It was not new, Alper explained to Slavin, but it was the most modern type of ammunition-making equipment available in the world.

Under terms of the sale the machinery had to be removed from the Remington plant immediately. Alper had stored it in a Bridgeport warehouse, but this was a temporary—and risky—expedient. It was imperative that it be moved to secure quarters in New York and Alper had made arrangements with a trucker to bring it down; the first truck loads already had arrived at the warehouse of a shipping firm on the Lower East Side of Manhattan which had agreed to crate it for shipment to Palestine. Although it was an unseasonably warm day at the end of a Manhattan winter, Slavin felt chilled by a premonition. He hurried downtown, walked out of the pale sunshine into the firm's garage and, as his eyes grew accustomed to the darkness, he shivered.

A knot of men was gathered around a truck which appeared curiously upended. He went closer. One of the truck's wheels had

cracked the wooden flooring of the garage and the men were prop-
ping up a crate on the truck so it would not slide off. Enraged, Slavin
sought the head of the firm upstairs.

"What kind of sloppy work is this you are doing?" he demanded.

"Look, Slavin," the warehouse owner said, "I'm doing this only
for expenses. I can't worry about your crates. I have my own business
to worry about."

Slavin's suspicions exploded. He asked, "How much are these
expenses?"

The boss leaned back in his chair. "A thousand a week for me,
seven hundred a week for my two partners."

Slavin's fist crashed down on the desk. "Look, who gets a
thousand a week for a business like this? My salary is one hundred
dollars a week."

The warehouseman grinned. "Slavin, don't try to make a comparison between you people coming from the Middle East and we
Americans with our high standard of living. I have three kids. My
wife has her own car."

"How much? How much?" Slavin was pounding the desk. "I
won't pay."

"Mr. Slavin," the truckman said, "maybe you know there is an
organization with the name of FBI. They would be interested in
you."

"Nothing I'm doing in this country is against the law. This
machinery can be bought by anyone."

Slavin raced down the flight of stairs and out of the building. On
the sidewalk, he heard the office window on the second floor being
thrown open. The trucker stood there, wagging a finger at him.
"You'll pay, Slavin, you'll pay."

Slavin ran through the streets of New York, "like a crazy man,"
to the office of the textile jobber who had recommended the trucking
firm. There was nothing he could do, the man said after phoning the
truckman. Slavin met with some of his American friends that night.
He shouted, he pleaded, he threatened to shoot the truckman on
sight. But he told Phil afterward, "There were people there more
wise than I. If we don't pay, the whole thing could end. We cannot
frighten people in the United States. The British cannot learn what
we are doing."

Now there was no time to lose. Another sanctuary had to be
found for the machinery at once.

With some leads from Harry Levine, Slavin went looking for a warehouse to buy, one where he could control the costs and the security of the operation. But finding a suitable site was difficult. Precious days were lost while Slavin tramped the streets of New York, looking at buildings which proved to be either too expensive or poorly situated for secrecy and easy shipping. His last hope was a building that someone had told him about at 4366 Park Avenue—the same Park Avenue that stood for elegance all over the world, but not its Bronx extension. The building, unfortunately, had been sold recently but perhaps the new owner would consider reselling.

Negro children were playing in the oily slush of a snowstorm when Slavin saw the building for the first time. It was a derelict, unoccupied for years, without heat, with smashed windowpanes and holes in the roof through which snow had fallen to melt in sooty pools on its third floor. However, it did have concrete floors that could hold heavy machinery and a loading dock that opened directly onto the street. What's more, the price was right. Slavin had been told that $3,000 cash, and a friendly bank's mortgage, should swing the deal if the owner was willing to sell. Slavin turned to the young man whom the building's owner had sent to unlock the door for him.

"Take me to Zysman," he told the young man.

Zysman dealt in secondhand refrigerators. His shop smelled of rancid food and machine oil. He busied himself among refrigerators while Slavin shouted that he was interested in buying the building.

"Who says I am ready to sell?" Zysman's head popped out from behind a refrigerator door. "I just bought it."

"I will give you a profit in addition to your three thousand dollars and take over the mortgage," Slavin coaxed.

Zysman's head disappeared into another refrigerator. The youth hissed at Slavin. "His wife. See his wife."

"Mr. Zysman," Slavin shouted at a refrigerator that seemed inhabited. "This is the first and last time in my life I ask a man to invite me for dinner. I want to meet your wife and we can talk about this matter."

Zysman stood up in the midst of his refrigerators like a walrus rising among icebergs. "Why not?" he shrugged.

The Zysmans lived in a small apartment and dinner was served in an alcove between the living room and kitchen. After each course Mrs. Zysman disappeared into the kitchen, summoning Mr. Zysman to follow her. Slavin sat there trying to look relaxed. He had repeated his offer of the day before.

Zysman emerged from the kitchen carrying a golden brown loaf of bread, its crust braided into an ornate design and sprinkled with poppyseed. "Seven thousand," he said.

"Four thousand," said Slavin, reaching for a slice.

Zysman disappeared and came back with chicken soup afloat with homemade noodles. "We're not selling," he announced.

They haggled through the roast chicken, the carrots and peas and the compote. Slavin went up to five thousand as Mrs. Zysman brought in the pastries and disappeared back into the kitchen. Zysman, bearing lemon for the tea, brought back the answer: "We're not selling."

Late that night, Slavin told Alper, "Nine times they decided to sell and ten times not to sell." Slavin didn't sleep that night. Skipping breakfast the next morning, he rushed uptown to Zysman's shop. Zysman was tinkering inside a refrigerator; Slavin addressed his remarks to his bottom.

"I want to borrow the keys," he said. "I want to look over the building again."

"What do you have to look at?" Zysman's voice was muffled among the ice trays. "We're not selling."

"Zysman," Slavin said, taking a familiar tone—after all, they had broken bread together—"twenty times you changed your mind so maybe you will change it twenty-one times and sell."

Zysman handed over the keys.

That afternoon, as the trucks from Bridgeport were rolling down the Post Road toward New York, Slavin led a group of young men—sent over hurriedly by his friend at the youth organization—into the warehouse. They nailed boards over the gaping windows, swept out the first floor, hacked away at the debris in the loading dock so that trucks could discharge cargo. Slavin telephoned one of his contacts: "If they catch me, what?"

"If they catch you, you will go to jail."

"And the machines?"

"That depends on what Zysman says."

"I'll take care of Zysman," Slavin said. By nightfall the trucks were unloaded and the machines were safe.

The next day Slavin returned the keys to Zysman's shop and confessed what he had done. "I will put you in jail. You will be thrown out of the country," Zysman threatened. Slavin let him blow off steam. Then he began talking and suggested Zysman make a few phone calls. Slavin would furnish the names and numbers.

Zysman threw up his hands in a sign of surrender. Slavin again came to dinner at his house. Before the main course—stuffed breast of veal—he handed over a check for $5,000.

"We have a warehouse," he reported jubilantly to Alper. "Open to the sky, full of snow, but still a warehouse."

V

GOLD, PURE GOLD

Alper could now step up his buying. He was looking primarily for machinery that could be used to make Ekdahl's gun and other small armaments of immediate interest to Haganah. But making the rounds of WAA sales, he couldn't help casting a covetous eye on some of the other machinery, designed for making bigger guns, which, he reported to Slavin, was being snapped up by buyers from all over the world in the biggest closeout sale in history. Someday the Palestinians would need these large machines too. Perhaps their enemies were buying them right now.

On one trip to a government depot at New Bedford, Massachusetts, Alper found "lines and lines of beautiful machines, practically new, for making gun barrels, 20 mm., 40 mm., all the way up to 75 mm." He described them to Slavin over the telephone. "Put in a scrap bid," Slavin advised—this was the price the machinery would be worth as scrap, about seventy dollars a ton. It was almost inconceivable that Alper would get them for that, but then they weren't on his list anyway. To his amazement, when the bids were opened, his was the highest. "We got mountains of the stuff, six trailer loads." When Slavin first saw the machines in the Bronx warehouse, he gasped, "Gold, pure gold." For slightly over $10,000 Alper had bought machinery worth perhaps a quarter of a million dollars and capable of manufacturing the most modern weapons.

Together Alper and Slavin took a train trip through the Midwest, stopping off at Buffalo, Detroit, Chicago, Rockford, Cincinnati. "Slavin couldn't go into the official government depots because he wasn't a citizen," recalls Alper. "I'd often run into obvious foreigners, Asians and Latin-Americans, but they must have been there under better auspices, maybe official government buying missions. Slavin would stay in the hotel and then pump me for every detail of what I'd seen."

When they went to visit private dealers, Slavin would take over. "He had a very keen sense of values and he had learned a lot about machines in a very short time." Alper marveled at his technique. "We'd look up some man whose name had been given to him. He might be a dealer or he'd take us to a dealer. Slavin would act mysterious, just say he was an engineer from Palestine and then he'd carry on in that broken English that somehow, by will power alone, got the points across. We scoured their warehouses and yards and Slavin was always able to get what he wanted for half what the dealers asked. Some of them simply handed the stuff over to us when they guessed what it was all about." The WAA was so anxious to get rid of surplus war machinery that it paid dealers a commission for acting as brokers in sales to their registered customers. Slavin often talked the dealers into rebating that commission to him too.

Sometimes he used bombast, sometimes his fractured eloquence. Sometimes he'd be humorous.

In one city a dealer took Slavin into a room full of old machinery and offered it for sale. Slavin looked around, nodding his head seriously. Then he looked the dealer up and down. Finally, his blue eyes bright with anticipation, he said, "Before I came here, there was a big meeting in Tel Aviv and a man stood up and said, 'Make sure we don't send a fool to America. They have their own.'" The dealer burst into delighted laughter and took him next door where he had "the real stuff."

On another visit to a machinery company in Worcester, Massachusetts, Slavin proudly invited one of the executives of the prosperous firm to take a ride in the automobile he had just purchased. It was a wheezy old 1936 Chevrolet which Alper had talked him into buying on the grounds that they would save money on train and bus fares. The executive chuckled as Alper tried again and again to start the jalopy. At last the aged ignition caught and, with a gnashing of gears, the car lurched down the street. The executive was white-faced and smiling wanly by the time they got back. Slavin was delighted. "This car is going to save us five thousand dollars," he whispered to Phil. "Now that they've seen how poor we are, they'll knock that much off their price."

Roaming the country, Alper and Slavin found more and more to buy. There was one wild day at the Colt Arms plant in Hartford, Connecticut. All of the machinery in the building was up for sale. The WAA had classified it, priced it, and announced it would be sold on a first-come, first-served basis starting at 9 A.M. of a given date.

Slavin and Alper spent hours studying the WAA lists, marking the things that interested them.

Several hundred eager buyers were waiting at the door the day of the sale. Among them were Alper, Slavin and a sympathetic executive of a large machinery firm, Botwinik Brothers, who had volunteered to help them, William Horowitz (now a banker and a fellow of the Yale Corporation, the governing body of Yale University). When the door opened, the three sprinted in, each in a different direction. Working from the lists they had prepared, they darted from one machine to another, putting their tags on the things they wanted. At the end of an hour the three men met. Triumphantly they surveyed their lists: they had managed to outdash the other buyers to most of the equipment they needed.

In a technical magazine Alper showed Slavin an article on a new safer and simpler method, the Olsen process, for the manufacture of smokeless powder, the explosive used in all small arms ammunition.

"Write a letter," said Slavin, a convert to the amazing American facility for obtaining the most advanced technical information by mail.

Alper sent fifty cents to the United States Patent Office and got back a copy of the Olsen process. "Not very complicated," he declared, after reading it. "But it must take a lot of know-how to do it right."

Slavin came up a few days later with the name of a chemical engineer, Abraham Brothman. The firm of A. Brothman Associates, consulting chemists and engineers, was headquartered in Queens, the bedroom borough across the East River from Manhattan. Slavin consulted his subway guide and decided it would save time if Brothman met him in Manhattan. The chemist suggested on the phone that they meet at the Russian Tea Room.

Slavin's irritation rose the moment he entered the restaurant on West 57th Street, near Carnegie Hall; it was not a tea room. Brothman led Slavin to a table laid for dinner, introduced him to his "partner," a hard-faced sullen woman named Miriam Moskowitz, and called for three menus. Business negotiations that stretched through a long and expensive meal always irked Slavin, and this first and later meetings with Brothman over plateful of borscht, blinis, and chicken Kiev were not made more digestible by the presence of Miss Moskowitz, whose appetite seemed insatiable. Her mutterings between mouthfuls carried decisive weight with the equally hungry chemical engineer, but she spoke seldom. At first Brothman was reluctant to "do anything that might get me into trouble." Slavin assured him, "I want nothing from you except some expert information." Brothman waited for Miss Moskowitz to finish dessert, then held a whispered conference with her. Only then, patting his mouth with a napkin, did he reply to Slavin: "In this specific field, I am the expert."

Brothman asked for a down payment of $2,000 to finance the project on a pay-as-you-go basis, and then returned to the Russian Tea Room to demand additional $2,000 payments. As the months went by, as Slavin's investment reached $20,000, all Brothman would do was reassure him, over dinner, that his "report was almost ready except for a few details." Slavin had had enough. He rode out to Queens and demanded to see some of the work, in whatever state it was in. Brothman handed over a sheaf of blueprints. Slavin scanned them furiously. "I recognized everything right away. It was nonsense, the same stuff I had been reading in the simple textbooks." Slowly and deliberately rolling them up, Slavin put them into Brothman's wastebasket and walked out of the office.

He had nothing to show for his grandiose dream of a smokeless powder plant; the money he had diverted for its design was gone.

He went to Harry Levine and "cried on his shoulder": "I can't spend public money this way."

Levine, through his plastics business, knew a laboratory owner, William Grosvenor, and he asked him for advice. Grosvenor recalled that eight years previously he had sponsored for membership in the Chemists' Club of New York one Ignace Grageroff, a Russian-born explosives specialist. The Chemists' Club's files showed that Grageroff, now sixty-seven, was working in New York.

There was no way to ascertain Grageroff's sympathies. He was an extremely quiet, dignified man about whom little was known. All Slavin could learn was that Grageroff had been born in Odessa, had fled Russia in 1904, had studied chemistry at the University of Berne, and then had come to the United States. In World War I he had worked in Canada. In World War II he had been employed in the Keystone Ordnance Works in Geneva, Pennsylvania. In 1946 he was working for Fraser-Bruce Engineering Company in midtown Manhattan and living on West End Avenue. There was nothing about his background to suggest anyone other than a man who practiced a rather arcane specialty and wanted to be left alone.

Slavin insisted Levine call him for an appointment. Grageroff said he could spare only fifteen minutes at 4 P.M. Levine went along to make sure "Slavin didn't lose his temper because not everybody felt the way he felt." They found Grageroff to be a stocky man with a broad forehead and a stoic Russian manner. Levine began slowly, but Slavin soon interrupted in Russian. When Levine tiptoed out an hour later, Grageroff was inviting Slavin home to meet his wife.

Slavin exulted later, "Our meeting for fifteen minutes was the longest fifteen minutes of my life. At two o'clock the next morning I took the subway home from Grageroff's apartment."

In those ten hours he had told Grageroff "the story of the Jewish people for the last forty years." Grageroff had been born a Jew but—an important difference in Tsarist Russia—he had been raised as a Russian. His wife, Slavin discovered as they entered Grageroff's apartment, was "a big woman, a sick woman, sitting in a big chair like a queen, very Russian and very nice. And there was a collection of people there, old people from Russia who spoke only Russian and thought only about Russia. They had led hard lives since leaving the old country; they always dreamed of going back. They talked about Russia as if the Bolsheviks had never happened. I now had to lecture on Palestine. I spoke the best Russian I ever spoke."

Alone with Slavin later, Grageroff said he would help. "I will do all that my conscience allows me. I am not prepared to give you drawings or specific data." Slavin assured him he was not interested in military secrets, only basic technical know-how.

"I will give you no details," Grageroff agreed. "I will tell you the story of how plants of this kind are built, what is important, what is not important. And another condition: I don't want you to take any notes."

And so began a strange series of lectures, ten of them, each lasting two hours, delivered in a quiet corner of the Chemists' Club library at 52 East 41st Street, Grageroff speaking quietly, carefully, Slavin sitting there, brow furrowed, staring at the speaker's face as if it were a blackboard on which formulas were written. "I have a special memory," Slavin told Alper one evening, "but this is overtaking me, not making a noise for two hours, not moving even my foot. I am trying to hold my head quiet not to shake anything out." After each lecture, he rushed to the office to write down all that he could remember.

At the end of the tenth lesson Grageroff permitted Slavin to ask some questions. "Some he answered; some not. He gave me a course in chemistry, that was all, and he never told me if I got a passing grade."

The smokeless powder plant turned out to be too ambitious a project for Palestine in 1946. It was not until 1949 that Slavin acquired all the equipment for his homeland's first smokeless powder plant.

In 1950 Slavin, at his home in Tel Aviv, and Alper, in his New York apartment, each read in their morning newspapers that Abraham Brothman and Miriam Moskowitz had been arrested by the FBI as members of the same Soviet "atom spy" ring that included Klaus Fuchs, Ethel and Julius Rosenberg, and the government's chief witness in the trials that followed, Harry Gold, a chemist who had worked for Brothman from 1946 into 1948. Another important government witness, Elizabeth Bentley, a self-confessed former Communist and courier for Russian agents, testified that in her meetings with Brothman "usually we first had something to eat. By this time it was fairly late and then during the meal I would explain the latest . . . policy and theories to Mr. Brothman and he would talk a bit about himself and then afterwards he would hand me the blueprints and sometimes he would dictate a very involved technical explanation of what the blueprints were all about."

Gold testified that Miss Moskowitz was present during dinners he had had with Brothman and that (like Slavin) he found Brothman dilatory in delivering materials he had promised.

In his 1950 Federal trial Brothman said in his defense that the material he had delivered to Miss Bentley and Gold consisted largely of "commonly known processes . . . well known and easily available." Brothman and Miss Moskowitz each served prison sentences of two years and paid fines of $10,000 for attempting to impede a Federal grand jury investigation. As he followed the trial in the newspapers, Slavin says, "sweat broke out all over me." Alper says that the Brothman case "brought back to me all over again the whole crazy, funny, dangerous atmosphere on West 112th Street."

Ekdahl had estimated it would take six months to design The Gun and make the tooling needed to produce it in Palestine. Half that time had elapsed and the designs were not finished; the manufacture of a prototype and tooling had not even begun.

Slavin was about to telephone Ekdahl in Providence when the lanky Swede showed up at the office on West 112th Street. He was oddly hang-dog and silent. Perhaps the plans were not working out, Slavin worried; perhaps Ekdahl had been out of designing for too long and no longer had the touch. He was a drinking man, Slavin had discovered. But he could nip all day "for my heart" without any noticeable ill effect. Slavin drew him aside and asked what was wrong.

"Hai-yum," Ekdahl began—he never could pronounce the guttural *ch*. "Something very funny has happened. I've been approached by a group of Egyptians. They want exactly what you want, tooling, and they are willing to give me a hundred thousand dollars for the job."

It was the kind of nightmare Slavin kept locked in one corner of his mind—there were so many other things to worry about. But there it was, out. He looked at Ekdahl. "He was very upset. I knew the man. I knew he was not rich; he had a small pension, maybe four hundred dollars a month, and a large family. I had eaten with them, stayed with them. They were like my own people."

"Take my advice, Carl," Slavin said, his heart sinking lower with each word. "You owe nothing to the Jewish people. You are very fair up to now and you have done everything you said you would. I free you from the contract."

Ekdahl looked even sadder than when he had entered. He stammered, "Hai-yum, it's not as simple as that. It's not just the money." Slavin thought, He wants me to argue with him, with his conscience, but in my heart I can't do it. Many Jews are doing nothing; why should I expect something extra special from Carl Ekdahl?

Ekdahl persisted. "Come with me. Let's go talk it over with my old lady."

Slavin put his worn jacket over the shabby sweater he habitually wore in the office and the two of them rode silently down in the elevator and walked out into the icy wind whirling off the Hudson River. For once, they took a cab. They spoke little on the train to Providence. Slavin remembers saying only, "Look, Carl, your wife is safe. Your children are safe. You are not worrying about your nights. No enemy will come in the night, only dreams good or bad. I don't know about dreams. Our wives are waiting for the killers but you don't have to worry about that. Your nights are safe, your days are safe, and you are a man who must worry about your own security. Take my advice and break the contract. Take the one hundred thousand dollars." Ekdahl said nothing and Slavin lapsed into silence, sorry that he had spoken so bitterly.

At the house in Providence Mrs. Ekdahl came in from the kitchen and sat down in the living room. "She was not smiling,"

Slavin noted, and the fear that these were not his people and would never understand swept over him as he saw her there, in her spotlessly clean living room with its well-used overstuffed furniture and the photographs of the Ekdahl children on the mantelpiece. Carl was saying, "Momma, I have something to tell you," and Slavin listened as Ekdahl told her about Slavin's mission, Palestine, Jewish independence and then about the Egyptian offer.

Mrs. Ekdahl looked at Slavin carefully, as if she was seeing him for the first time, and then she looked over at her husband.

"Carl, you have a contract with this man?"

"Yes, Momma," he said.

"Is this man fulfilling his obligations?"

"Of course. Oh, yes, of course." Ekdahl seemed relieved.

"Well, then," she said—and Slavin would never forget the musical lilt of her Swedish accent—"there's nothing to talk about. Just to get on with the job."

VI

THE PORT

Jerry Schweitzer arrived for work at the West 112th Street apartment one morning to find that another table had been jammed into her cubbyhole of an office. She would, Slavin announced matter-of-factly, be sharing it with "a real expert."

Two hours later Elie Schalit breezed in, a handsome husky blond man of the world, aged twenty-two. He was courtly and expansive, and he had the gift of tongues. He spoke English with a British accent to Alper, seemed to take on a Southern accent when he addressed Jerry, and rattled off Hebrew that was obviously more fluent than Slavin's. His wide-eyed associates would soon learn that he also spoke German, Arabic, and smatterings of Portuguese, Spanish and French.

The grandson of a celebrated Jerusalem physician and the nephew of the administrator of the Baron Rothschild's pioneering colony, Schalit was a *sabra*—with the native-born Jewish Palestinian's bravado but with talents that went far beyond reclaiming the land. Even while in high school, he had joined Haganah in a student unit that participated in some of the operations of the colonists' secret paramilitary force. He had worked on farms in his homeland, but he also had lived in Highland Park, Illinois, and Houston, Texas, and attended Texas A.&M. as a student of military science and tactics. He also had studied at the University of Reading in England, spent some months in Brazil, served in the Royal Canadian Air Force, and graduated from Louisiana State University with a degree in agricultural economics (and a research project in shipping). Then he had come to New York to work for the American Economic Committee for Palestine. He had been there only a few months when someone in Palestine realized that, with his special background, he was a natural candidate for Slavin's operation and, as soon as Schalit was told about it, he knew that was where he really wanted to work.

His insouciance with Slavin astounded Jerry and Phil Alper.

They watched him sail in and out of the office, arriving later than they ever dared, leaving when he wished, even taking taxis (he was always late), and wondered when Slavin's temper would erupt and demolish the newcomer. It never did. Slavin might complain, "Elie, if you are an hour late to see me, I'll wait an hour and three minutes more. Just don't rush into my office so fast that you blow the papers off my desk." But he would say later to Alper, "That Elie is an artist with the telephone. He sits and holds that telephone in his arms, making love to it, hour after hour. I never saw a man working with the telephone like that. In ten minutes he is speaking with twenty people and he is in the picture."

Slavin's patience had its reasons. Schalit's job was to be a dangerous one, and every bit of bravado he possessed would be needed.

There was nothing illegal about Alper's purchases of machinery. The War Assets Administration was selling it to all comers as fast as it could. Most of the machines had peaceable applications—even if only as scrap. But getting it to Palestine was to be Schalit's responsibility, and that could give the whole game away. If the American authorities found out that the machines were being shipped abroad and reassembled for their original purpose of arms manufacture it would not be long before they cracked down. It was against United States policy to allow the export of arms machinery without specific permission from the State Department. At the receiving end, it would mean jail sentences for the Palestinians if the British learned that crates arriving in the port of Haifa contained machinery for making armaments.

It would be Schalit's job to devise a means of packing and shipping the machinery, to shepherd it through the bureaucratic maze of shipping documents, export licenses and port authorities, to satisfy prying customs inspectors at both ends.

As Slavin's and Alper's purchases piled up in the Bronx warehouse on Park Avenue, Schalit worked out his system.

Some of the machinery was standard: lathes and milling machines which were used in many sorts of manufacturing. Proper export licenses could be obtained for them through friendly American companies, like Botwinik Brothers; proper import licenses could be obtained by legitimate factories in Palestine. They could be crated and shipped like any other merchandise. But the equipment specifically designed for making arms, the cartridge-making machinery, the tools and dies for gun manufacture, these had to be carefully camouflaged.

"We knew," Schalit would recall, "that a customs inspector in

New York or Haifa wouldn't know whether a lathe was to be used to make shovels or guns, but some of the sophisticated equipment we were sending had only one use, and that stuck out all over, that had to be disguised."

A painstaking system was evolved. First the machines were completely dismantled and each part was labeled with a number. The number and a description of the part then went onto a card and into a file—which eventually would list 70,000 separate parts. A schematic drawing of each machine was made showing how to reassemble the numbered parts. The disassembled parts were then separated, scrambled and packed at random among other machinery or as loose parts in misleading containers.

Schalit used crates labeled "agricultural implements" or "textile machinery," but this didn't satisfy him. He wanted something more secure for the really risky—and precious—items.

On one of his buying forays Alper noticed that several war surplus plants were selling huge transformers that consisted of steel cases with heavy lids. He described them eagerly to Schalit: "The insides are full of copper wiring but once you take that out, what you have is a steel chamber that can hold all kinds of things." Schalit sent a few of them in his next shipments. He found that their mere size and appearance discouraged customs inspectors. "They were monsters," he recalls. "It took heavy cranes to lift them and it was difficult and expensive for us to transport them. But their size made it discouraging for someone to say, 'Just carry that over here and let me look inside.' Furthermore, they were psychologically awesome and repulsive. We left all the wires and rods sticking out so that subconsciously even a customs inspector would be frightened." Alper went ahead and bought more of the transformers, "enough to light up the Jordan Valley like Times Square."

He also bought large boilers, which were cut apart, emptied of their tubing, stuffed with assorted parts and then welded together again. Any sort of large equipment which could be gutted, and which had a conceivable use in Palestine that would justify shipping it there, took on another dimension to Alper and Schalit; whatever it looked like to someone else, their eyes appraised it in terms of how much it would hold and how well it would fool a customs inspector. It all went out as "used industrial machines."

As the pace of activity at the Bronx warehouse became more frenetic the volunteer services of a Zionist boys' club were used to help crate some of the equipment. The ideological purpose for the

Zionists was to teach these youngsters from the sidewalks of New York some of the manual arts they would one day be called upon to use in Palestine. What interested Slavin was the chance to save money.

Ten youths and a professional carpenter who would serve as their instructor were admitted to the warehouse one blustery winter day. The most gaping holes in the building had been repaired but it still felt like a wind tunnel in midwinter and the inside temperature had dropped so low that Slavin, who had come up to witness the event, was bent with cold and couldn't stand up straight.

The youngsters bounded in, shouting Hebrew imperatives, humming snatches of Palestinian songs, and listening with round-eyed solemnity as the carpenter explained the elementary principles of hammer, saw, boards and nails. They tackled the job as if it was a desert that had to be reforested by nightfall. By midafternoon their Zionist zeal had been numbed by fingers stiff with cold and raw with bruises. The warehouse looked like an emergency ward. The warehouse's first-aid kit was running low on bandages and adhesive tape. Ominous questions were being asked about insurance claims. "I had another good lesson in America," Slavin reported, "how you can be a good Zionist and still not know from what side to hold a hammer."

Retreating to his office, he decided the warehouse would never again be used as a training school. Packing would be left in the hands of the warehouse's regular "professional" staff.

Schalit, following the usual recruiting methods of the underground, had talked his next-door neighbor on Central Park West into giving up his job with a machine tool firm to supervise the drafty activities on Park Avenue. Jules Chender, a young Frenchman who had come to the United States in 1941, took in stride the arrival at the warehouse of arms-making machinery and giant transformers to ship it in, Slavin's tempers and Schalit's brainstorms. It didn't even surprise him when he was made the nominal lessee of the warehouse (Levine was its nominal owner). What Chender couldn't get used to was the hours he was expected to work. To help him in the handling and packing of the machinery, Schalit had brought in a group of young Zionists who were living together in a beach cottage in Brooklyn while awaiting an opportunity to embark for the Promised Land. Their zeal was matched by their strength. One of them, Chender recalls, stood only five foot three, but he could lift "anything." Chender came from a less rigorous milieu. Moreover, he was engaged to be married.

"We started work at seven in the morning," he still remembers wryly. "The boys would come by in a car to pick me up to make sure I got there on time. I'd call my fiancée at the lunch break to say I'd meet her at seven in the evening. At seven I'd call to say I would be there at nine. At nine I'd say eleven. We'd finally meet at midnight." After six or eight months of this, Chender was exhausted.

Chender began talking nostalgically of returning to France, which he knew was war-weary, poor, short on food and creature comforts but where a man was not expected to neglect his fiancée for seventeen hours of work a day. Schalit and Alper would talk Chender into staying and would keep him away from Slavin, who could never understand a man who didn't enjoy working a ninety-hour week.

As the warehouse filled with desperately needed arms machinery, Schalit and Alper urged Slavin to streamline their operation by adopting more open and direct procedures. They wanted to form a company, a legally registered aboveboard company for purchasing and exporting machinery. Slavin, Alper recalls, "after so many years in Palestine under the British, was accustomed to doing things secretly, through other people and other firms. It was almost inconceivable to him that we could make an appointment, walk into a factory and buy machinery ourselves."

Talking it over late one night in the apartment, the two younger men pointed out that anyone could start a business in the United States, print a letterhead, write letters, make phone calls, get information, buy merchandise and dispose of it. Schalit argued that even for the sort of underground work in which they were engaged, "the best way to operate in the United States is as much in the open as you can." The experience with the blackmailing warehouseman had demonstrated the dangers of being at the mercy of others.

Schalit even came up with a name for their company: Machinery Processing and Converting Company, a name sufficiently broad to give it scope for manifold activities. Levine's downtown mail drop would serve as an impressive address. An attorney, in answer to a theoretical question, had advised them on how to set it up. On paper the company would be owned by two Palestinians, temporarily living in the United States, who could quickly leave the country should anything go wrong. The apartment at 112th Street and the people working there would remain behind the scenes. But Machinery Processing and Converting would be an active legally incorporated firm, able to negotiate, bid, buy, sell, store and export machinery.

Slavin, still skeptical, agreed.

Now the problem was to keep the mounting pile of machinery moving across the Atlantic.

Schalit learned that nothing moves in the port of New York unless there is muscle behind it pushing, or muscle ahead of it clearing the way. It can be union muscle, company muscle, Mafia muscle, or political muscle. It can take the form of a quiet word or the vicious slice of a longshoreman's baling hook. In its simplest form, muscle begins to operate when currency changes hands, as any first-class passenger off a luxury liner quickly learns when, helpless, suddenly grimy, he stands amid the maelstrom of the pier with his monogrammed leather luggage and finds all the taxis "taken," all the porters blind, all the policemen vanished. Only then, or when there is a longshoremen's strike or a Marlon Brando movie, do most people think of the port of New York as anything that affects them personally.

To twenty-two-year-old Schalit, scheming to get tons of forbidden machinery to Palestine, the port of New York became a second home. Not just the passenger-ship piers of Manhattan, but the cargo docks and warehouses in Brooklyn, Queens and New Jersey that the public never sees. The port of New York runs for 771 miles of water frontage and of its 200 piers (in Schalit's day) only eight handled most of the passenger ships. The cargo that moved through the port each day required 815 railroad cars, nearly 2,000 lighters, and 25,000 individual trips by motor trucks. These carried, floated, lifted and lowered about 26.5 million long tons of merchandise a year, about a third of United States foreign trade and most of its luxury cargoes—furs, jewels, watches, household appliances, cars, and electronic gear. West Coast and Gulf ports might achieve volume through the oil that is piped, cleanly and efficiently, aboard tankers; but in the port of New York everything had to be manhandled—by back-straining labor more often than by modern machinery—through overlapping jurisdictions, jealously held official fiefs—up the sides of ships and down into the holds.

Schalit got to know it all, the longshoremen waiting around for the morning shape-up—two men for every job; the loansharks collecting their "vigorage"—10 per cent was minimum interest on a loan; the crap games, and the foremen, the cargo checkers, company cops and union representatives who ran rackets of their own. The bigger rackets were run by bigger gangsters.

Anyone who had any muscle used it—not just the longshoremen and the loansharks but also the neat soft-speaking executives in their carpeted offices at the tip of Manhattan who bemoaned the "jungle" which their glass-plated offices overlooked but made deals with union bosses, politicians and the underworld to keep the men working and the cargoes moving.

Schalit, coolly, systematically studying the port, as was his way, noted the muscle and the men who wielded it and decided to make as few alliances as possible. In his view, "You could make alliances with professionals, like the mobs, and pay whatever they asked. Or you could make alliances with legitimate interests that were sympathetic and didn't want money. But there you ran the risk of embarrassing them if something went wrong, or of being inhibited by them if they got wind of something you were planning that they didn't like." Instead, Schalit decided to go it alone. He became his own "shipping company," with a pocketful of calling cards, a half-dozen company names, a downtown address and a thorough knowledge of the requirements and procedures for the export of machinery from the United States.

He already knew the other end, the British requirements for import licenses to Palestine and how to handle the letters of credit and allocations of foreign exchange.

Schalit scrambled for space on the overloaded postwar shipping lines, worked his way through the piles of official papers required for each shipment and checked out the ruses for getting his cargo past inquiring officials. He worked closely with Alper and with Jules Chender at the warehouse to make sure that the crates being shipped out conformed—or at least would appear, under close scrutiny, to conform—with the documents he secured. It was a trio of inexperienced twenty-year-olds against the system, and so far they were ahead.

Schalit had "one Golden Rule" about shipments: someone had to be on the pier whenever material was being loaded. Usually it was Schalit himself. On freezing nights or on days so hot his shoes stuck to the asphalt, he went down to the docks to watch his shipments being loaded, grinning, nodding amiably to the foremen and the cargo checkers, his hands casually tucked into his pockets, comforted by the folded twenties he always carried just in case. He knew that crates sometimes dropped and disclosed their contents; that there were dock workers who even took advance orders for the contents of those broken crates.

One day an accident befell one of his transformers on a Brooklyn dock. "The ship's hook had lifted it off the low-bed trailer when something went wrong with the crane and it dropped. Normally, it would not have meant anything, because a transformer is a very solid thing and the top is bolted shut like a bank safe." But this time something was jarred loose. As Schalit watched, horrified, a tinkling trickle of bullets fell out and rolled crazily around on the ground. Schalit's eyes darted about to see if anyone else had noticed. Everyone was standing back, clear of the transformer, engrossed in the efforts of the crane operator to get another grip. When the transformer slowly rose again, Schalit was the first to walk beneath it. As casually as he could, he leaned down, scooped up the handful of bullets and dropped them in his pocket. When the transformer was safely on board, he handed the foreman one of his folded twenties; he was never sure how much the men on the dock had seen or how much they knew, and a little extra muscle always helped in the port of New York.

VII

CANADA

The idea of going to Canada with The Gun had come up in a setting that was for Slavin as much of a celebration as he allowed himself. New Year's Eve 1945; Times Square—the same Times Square through which he had limped so dismally not so many months before. Now he, of all people, was showing a visitor the town.

They watched the lighted ball descend at midnight from the top of the Times Tower; they watched the roistering crowds, and Slavin kept asking about the wages paid to tool and die makers in Canada. The visitor was Norman Grant, a friend of a friend, and he was in New York with his wife on his first holiday in years. Throughout the war he had been chief engineer of the York Arsenal in Toronto.

Grant, a dapper, smooth-talking man, answered Slavin's questions as patiently as he could as they pushed their way through the throng. Wages were lower in Canada, he said, and gave examples, but as he tired and Slavin's questions went on, he tried to close the subject with "Let me know what you want, and I will try to help" or "Come up to Toronto and we'll talk it over."

On their way back to Toronto Grant told his wife, "Apparently he wants me to design a small-scale version of York Arsenal in secret and then run it. He has some kind of operation going in New York but he never let me see it."

Canada popped up in Slavin's mind again when Ekdahl delivered some of the blueprints and the first estimates for manufacture of the tools, jigs, and fixtures. To Slavin the estimates seemed excessive; Grant had said Canada would be cheaper.

He went to Toronto and looked up Grant. Together they went to see Samuel J. Zacks, a onetime financial writer who had made a fortune in gold mining and was president of the Canadian Zionist organization. Zacks had been the sole Canadian among the nineteen men who had attended the meeting with Ben Gurion at Rudolf Sonneborn's penthouse several months before. He had been waiting "to help in any way I can." With Zacks's endorsement, as with Sonneborn's in New York, doors would open and friends would appear.

Grant agreed to take on the job. Harry Levine rented the second floor of an automobile dealer's garage on Bay Street, signing the lease as president of the Industrial Research Laboratories which, Levine told the landlord, was going to do some scientific research for Palestine, adding that "it would be best if not too many people know about it." Fortunately, there was only one stairway to the second floor; nobody could enter without being observed. The ramp from the ground floor was sealed off.

Alper and Ekdahl came up to lend a hand. The first jobs were farmed out to several machine tool shops in the Toronto area; the work was divided up and so spread out that no one shop could guess precisely what was being made. War veterans who were members of Zionist organizations took on odd jobs. Ben Ocopnick, who had been a wireless operator and gunner in the RCAF, remembers driving Ekdahl's old Mercury from one machine shop to another distributing blueprints and picking up parts.

Working in such piecemeal fashion, there were delays and snags. But the most punishing delay occurred when Grant took on another secret job for Palestine.

Through friends in the surplus business he had heard that some 150 tons of Bren gun parts were about to be put on sale by the Canadian Department of Munitions and Supply and he had quickly raised the money to buy them.

Ocopnick, the courier, was one of the young men asked by Grant to sort out the parts and truck them away. One evening an Ontario provincial policeman stopped one of the trucks for a traffic violation, searched it, and discovered the gun parts. The surplus had been legitimately bought; no one was arrested. But a local newspaper reported the discovery and Toronto's Zionist leaders became alarmed.

They notified Grant that they wanted the Industrial Research Laboratories, whatever it was doing in the way of industrial research, to shut down.

Slavin, Ekdahl and Levine rushed to Toronto and into a stormy meeting in a suite of the Royal York Hotel. What happened next is not too clear. Grant thinks Slavin drew a pistol and threatened to kill anyone who opposed him. Levine recalls that Slavin only talked about a pistol. Zacks remembers that Slavin had said on another occasion that he was prepared to kill if necessary. Slavin says that "Zacks and Grant were white-faced, looking at me as if they expected me to shoot them." Ekdahl broke the tension by suggesting that he and Slavin dine in their hotel room, while the others talked things over in the suite. There, Levine, calm and persuasive, told the Canadians that the work of the Laboratories was almost finished and urged them to let it finish its job. They agreed, providing he would keep Slavin out of Canada.

However, the Canadian operation never regained its momentum. Caution overruled every other consideration. What should have been finished in a few months took several more. Slavin fretted and fumed; Alper and Ekdahl spent as much time in Toronto as they could, but they were behind schedule in their own work.

Ocopnick, the courier for the Laboratories, got so bored that he quit to go to Europe and serve aboard one of the illegal immigrant ships. With his departure, Grant looked for another loyal young man. He made a lucky find. Max Brown, a university student and former pilot in the RCAF, had been a machinist. Dedicated, intelligent, and extremely hard-working, he became Grant's foreman and much more, the man who kept the Laboratories going.

Phil Alper could report to Slavin after a trip to Toronto, "The first six guns, the prototypes, will be perfect."

Brown was a paragon, but there was, mused Alper, something discomfiting about him as an underground operative. With his nervous gestures, slouched walk, sallow narrow face, and long slick black hair, he looked "like a Hollywood mobster; it was like seeing a young George Raft. You would always take him for the bad guy."

VIII

NIAGARA FALLS

A cable to "Auerbach" from Tel Aviv in the fall of 1946 ordered him, when he had decoded it, to make preparations to leave the United States. Alper, Schalit and Jerry Schweitzer couldn't believe their ears when Slavin summoned them into his office one morning and told them he would be going home before the end of the year.

Yet, as the three of them talked it over in the West 112th Street apartment while he was out seeing "a friend," they realized that the events in Palestine over the preceding twelve months—the twelve months that Slavin had been in the United States—had made the prospect of a secret arms-manufacturing operation in Palestine increasingly precarious. The British response to terrorism from both Jews and Arabs, to illegal immigration, and to Haganah's "demonstrations of strength" had been to turn the Holy Land into a garrison state. There were now 100,000 British troops in Palestine whose search-and-seizure methods against Haganah's secret bases were increasingly effective.

The danger was now at the receiving end. Alper and Schalit could carry on the work of purchasing and shipping in New York, but the next phase would require the personal fanatic supervision that only Slavin could give: quietly, efficiently assembling the machinery in Palestine, organizing it into production lines, accumulating the new materials and training the labor, planning the production schedules for the showdown struggle that Ben Gurion and a few others were convinced was coming—and doing it under the noses of the British and the Arabs.

Subsequent cables from Tel Aviv to Auerbach laid out Slavin's itinerary. He would go to Switzerland, where a World Zionist Congress had been called for December, a crucial conference to consider the entire political situation in Palestine, the precarious position of the Jewish settlements and the continuing misery of the Jewish refugees in Europe. Britain had rejected appeals from both President Truman and an Anglo-American Commission to admit 100,000 Jewish refugees into Palestine immediately. In saying no to the refugees, the British government was in effect saying no to the Jewish national home it had proposed thirty years before and which it had been mandated by the League of Nations to bring into being. At Ben Gurion's insistence, the Jewish Agency in August had approved the first sizable appropriation it ever had made for buying arms, $3 million, a mere trifle in the world arms market. In Switzerland he hoped to win support for large-scale acquisition of heavy armaments. He wanted Slavin there to report secretly on his work in America, to show what had been done.

Slavin would then go on to Palestine. As soon as the Canadian machine tools reached him, The Gun would go into production.

Slavin summoned Grant and Ekdahl to New York. How much longer would it take for Industrial Research Laboratories to finish the six prototype guns? "About two months," Grant said. Slavin's face fell; he had hoped to be on hand when the guns were tested.

In a sentimental mood, Grant and Ekdahl went to a toyshop and bought an electric train for Slavin's son. They gave the package to Slavin, who opened it gingerly, as if he were being handed an expense account. He didn't say anything, didn't even look up at them as he examined the parts of the toy—the pieces of track, the shiny locomotive and cars. "We thought he didn't know what it was," Grant recalls, "so we told him. He was crying. Slavin crying! It was the first time I had ever thought of him as an ordinary man, like the rest of us."

Slavin flew off carrying in his old suitcase microfilms of Ekdahl's blueprints, the schematic drawings of the machinery Alper had bought and Schalit had shipped, and the card file listing the thousands of disassembled parts.* He left Sherlock Holmes behind.

For Alper, at first, it was as if Slavin had never left. He reported directly to Slavin by coded cable. Whenever he made so bold as to raise his arm to hail a taxi, Slavin's spirit seemed to appear, tugging at his sleeve.

Phil moved out of the St. Mark Arms and into the office-

---

* Another copy of the microfilm was smuggled into Palestine by an American woman tourist, purportedly in her brassiere. It is a measure of the effectiveness of Slavin's system that when he returned to Palestine to supervise reassembly of the machines, not one important part was missing, not one machine failed to work.

bedroom Slavin had vacated. In her alcove down the hall Jerry continued to take care of the correspondence, bills and bank account of the Machinery Processing and Converting Company.

Elie Schalit moved out to office space in the shipping district at the foot of Manhattan, closer to his scene of operations. Slavin had left instructions that if something arose that neither they nor Levine nor an exchange of cables could solve, they should take it to another Palestinian, Jacob Dostrovsky, who lived in a small hotel on East 60th Street. Alper had met Dostrovsky a couple of times. He was a pleasant, self-assured man who had been in the country for several months and had something to do with money.

From Toronto Grant and Ekdahl informed Alper that they were ready to transport two prototypes of The Gun to Ekdahl's farm in Vermont for testing. They would have preferred some remote place in northern Ontario, but Slavin had instructed Alper to invite Dostrovsky to the test and Dostrovsky said he did not want to risk crossing a border.

Taking the guns across would be simple, Grant and Ekdahl said—a commonplace ride across the border by the same route that tens of thousands of tourists took every year. A drive across the Whirlpool Bridge to get a close-up awe-inspiring look at Niagara Falls, brief stops at the Canadian and American border posts at the foot of the bridge, and then a shuffle off to Buffalo. It was said of the American and Canadian customs and immigration inspectors that they could spot a smuggler at a glance, probably by the shifty look in his eye. But shifty looks were not uncommon at Niagara Falls, for many of the "honeymooners" crossing the border had not yet seen a minister or gotten a license. Professional smugglers—the gangs that smuggled silver fox pelts, or cattle to relieve the American meat shortage, or gold—usually crossed in less accessible areas of the 3,000-mile-long border, patrolled by only 210 U.S. Border Patrolmen scattered in groups of twos and threes. At Whirlpool Bridge the smuggling was petty—a bottle or two of Canadian whiskey, a fur parka, a couple of toy totem poles.

On the morning of February 24, 1947—a wintry Monday—Grant, Ekdahl and Max Brown left Toronto in Ekdahl's 1942 Mercury. In the trunk, clanking ominously, were two of the six prototype machine guns, each disassembled into three main components—stock, barrel and firing mechanism—and a hundred rounds of .303 British Army ammunition, much easier to obtain in Canada than in the United States.

At Hamilton they stopped to pick up a second car, loaned to

them by business friends who were also supplying a driver, a young employee named Andrew Noseworthy, who would drive Max Brown to Buffalo and bring the car back. It would be safer, they had decided, to split up for the trip. Noseworthy knew nothing of the purpose of the trip but had been instructed to answer any questions at the border by saying he was going to Buffalo to pick up a friend of his employer's and had invited Brown, who was going to Buffalo anyway, to come along for the ride.

Out of sight of Noseworthy, Ekdahl hurriedly divided the gun parts and ammunition between the two cars. He stuffed the firing mechanisms and ammunition into paper sacks. It took time and he became rattled. He shoved an armful of the parts beneath the front seat of Noseworthy's car. "We drove off very fast, about fifty-five miles an hour," Brown recalls, "and this stuff kept coming out from under the seat. I kept kicking it back."

In New York Phil Alper sat by a telephone waiting to hear that the men had reached their designated rendezvous, a roadside cafe on the American side of the border. He wished that Slavin were there; the call from the border was overdue. Alper had spoken twice with Dostrovsky, Slavin's friend in the midtown hotel. Just wait, he advised the young American.

It was midafternoon when Alper's telephone finally rang; he heard Grant's voice at the other end.

"Carl and I crossed over," Grant began. "We had no difficulty. We went to the cafe and waited for Maxie to come. There was only a distance of three or four cars between us. We waited an hour. He didn't come to the cafe so I said, 'Let's go back to the bridge and see.' We got to the bridge and found that the police had Maxie and the chauffeur in tow." Grant's voice was thin with anxiety. "We got right out of there," he concluded flatly. He was calling, he said, from the Statler Hotel in Buffalo.

Alper, summoning up all the *sang-froid* he had acquired in the past year, told Grant to wait where he was. He and Dostrovsky would come to Buffalo immediately.

Grant reported to Ekdahl that help was on the way. Then the two men sat down and took stiff drinks from the bottle Ekdahl always carried.

Afterward Brown would recount what had happened to him at the border.

"We come to the American border guard and he comes around to my side and he asks me how long am I going for?

" 'Three days,' I said. What for? To visit a girl friend. Those were reasonable answers.

"Then he goes to the driver's side of the car and asks him what he is going across for?

"And the driver says, 'Oh, I am just taking this fellow across for my boss. I am going right back.' Completely different from what Grant told me the answers would be. With those answers I knew we were in trouble.

"The guard says to me, 'You must have a very special friend to send you a car to take you down to Buffalo.' Then he says, 'Do you mind stepping out?'

"I get out and he looks inside the car, you know how they do it, and he puts his hands under the seat and starts taking the stuff out . . ."

In New York Alper and Dostrovsky, hurrying to catch a train to Buffalo, tried to figure out what had gone wrong. What could Brown have done at the border to arouse suspicion? As they attempted to reconstruct the scene, the answer suddenly came to Alper: "Maxie didn't have to do anything. He's the nicest guy in the world, but he *looks* suspicious whatever he's doing. Probably the border guards just took one look at him and started searching."

In Florida Harry Levine and his wife were unpacking resort clothes, looking forward to two weeks in the sun. The telephone rang; it was Dostrovsky. Levine hung up and turned to his wife who was standing with a linen dress over her arm and a bemused look on her face. "I have to get to New York," he said. "Something has come up."

"I know," she said. "I'll go with you." She put the linen dress back in the suitcase.

For three days Brown stood firm under questioning in the Erie County jail in Buffalo. He was questioned at different times by different men. They came in pairs—two men from the FBI and two men from the Royal Canadian Mounted Police. He answered their questions as naïvely as he dared: He had been a university student, he now worked in a small machine shop. His father was a tailor. Yes, he had been a member of a Zionist organization, but what did that have to do with it? Brown was not adept at small talk, but he did his best. He felt that all he was going through—from the fingerprinting and mugging, to a turnkey's threat to "put me in the end cell with Daisy," a rugged homosexual—was worth it because as long as he didn't talk, there would be time for the others to cover their tracks and warn their colleagues in Canada. "I just kept on and on, repeating, 'I don't know what you're talking about. I never saw this stuff before.' I figured that if I kept my mouth shut, Grant and Ekdahl would have time to warn Toronto to get the shop on Bay Street cleared out."

Brown refused to telephone anybody, but nonetheless a lawyer turned up, and three days after the debacle at the border he was freed on $4,000 bail, as was Noseworthy. Brown went to a house where Dostrovsky, Alper and Levine were waiting.

There he learned that for all his stubbornness, nothing in Toronto had escaped the Mounties. They had quickly traced him to Industrial Research Laboratories. They had impounded the Laboratories and its machinery before anybody there thought of evacuating it. Only one precaution had been taken on time—and as Brown heard this detail he became more upset than at any time in the past three harrowing days. Someone had telephoned Brown's father, a quiet little tailor who thought his son was still a university student, informed him that Max was in serious trouble and instructed him to burn all his private papers. The bewildered elder Brown had just finished incinerating Brown's school certificates, diplomas, service records—everything—when the RCMP arrived. A couple of questions convinced the Mounties that the father knew nothing and they left without even asking to see Max's room.

The important thing now, everyone agreed, was to keep the border incident from escalating into an international affair. That would be up to the lawyers. Meanwhile, they would disperse quietly. Brown and Grant went to New York to separate hotels; Ekdahl and Levine to their respective New England homes; Dostrovsky to the hotel on East 60th Street; Alper to West 112th Street to confer with Schalit and call a temporary halt to shipments.

So far the affair looked like a small independent venture by a few Canadians. An unnamed American customs official was quoted in the newspapers as suspecting "gangsters . . . We have every reason to believe that such a smuggling ring is operating over the border." But the Mounties might still get their man. Brown's arrest had led to Industrial Research Laboratories and thus to Grant, who was arrested as soon as he returned to Canada. But the greatest danger was that the name of Harry Levine would be uncovered; he had signed the lease for the Laboratories. It was known that the RCMP exchanged information with the FBI, and if the FBI investigated Levine, they might uncover more than a trail—a broad highway leading to West 112th Street, to the Machinery Processing and Converting Company, to the Bronx warehouse, to Alper's machinery purchases and Schalit's shipments. It would then be merely a matter of days before the British were informed and cracked down in Palestine on Slavin and his hidden arms plants.

The lawyers decided on a strategy. They acted as if Toronto were the headquarters and the ruse worked. Grant pleaded guilty and was fined; the Mounties suspected he was operating for Palestine but they could not prove it. At most they assumed he was making a few guns; they never guessed that the tools, dies and jigs were to be sent too. After Grant had paid his fine, all of the machinery was returned to him.

Max Brown's case did not come up before the Federal court in Rochester, New York, until May. His lawyer kept postponing it. He was, he explained to Brown, "waiting for an Irish judge." What sort of argument would he make before an Irish judge? Brown wanted to know. "I'm going to ask the judge just one question," the lawyer assured him. "I will ask him, 'Have you seen *The Informer?*'" Brown shook his head. These things were beyond him.

It wasn't until late that night that he realized the lawyer was referring to the celebrated movie about Irish resistance to the British.

When his case was heard, the trial was brief. There was a whispered consultation between Brown's attorney, former State Supreme Court Justice David Diamond, and Judge Harold Burke. Brown never knew for sure what they said but the sentence was light. He was fined $100 and told to stay out of the United States for a year.

Home in Leominster, Levine was still worried. He mulled over a conversation he had had with Dostrovsky in Buffalo. Levine hadn't known Dostrovsky; but observing him in Buffalo under such tense circumstances, he sized him up as a man who was extraordinarily knowledgeable, resourceful and decisive. During the excited consultations Dostrovsky had suggested that they mend the damage caused by Brown's arrest by dealing with the American authorities on a high level.

Levine went to New York and talked it over with some men he trusted. One of them picked up a telephone and called Washington. The next day Levine, Dostrovsky and a representative of the Jewish Agency went to Washington. They conferred there with Robert

Nathan, the economist, who knew J. Edgar Hoover, the director of the FBI. Nathan arranged an appointment with Hoover. The meeting was more relaxed than Levine and Dostrovsky, pacing the floor at their hotel, could have imagined. "I talked very frankly," Nathan recalls. "The RCMP had asked the FBI to cooperate in tracking down the sources and personnel involved and maybe prosecuting. I told Hoover, 'This is not anything damaging to the United States. But it is not straight up and aboveboard. Some prominent people and some important organizations could be hurt.'"

Hoover wanted to know whether any of the weapons were to be used *in* the United States? "No," Nathan assured him. Were any of them to be used *against* the United States? "Absolutely not," Nathan replied.

"Hoover made no promise," Nathan recalls, "but the indication was that he would cooperate. He was sympathetic."

The Gun had been reprieved once more. After three near disasters—Ekdahl's encounter with the Egyptians, the discovery of the Bren gun parts near Toronto and the arrest of Max Brown at the border—the long laborious project was drawing to an end. Instead of six months it had taken more than a year. But Slavin's dream of mass producing in small secret workshops an automatic weapon with which the men and women of Palestine's settlements could defend themselves was in sight.

There was just one sizable hitch: the prototypes and the tooling still had to be gotten out of Canada, across the ocean and into Palestine. Slavin cabled anxiously—his code name now was "Millman"— asking when he could expect their arrival.

It would be a simple matter to ship most of the machinery of Industrial Research Laboratories from Canada to Palestine; it was the normal equipment of any machine shop. But the special dies designed by Ekdahl were something else. They might be recognized as impressions for parts of a gun and the border incident repeated all over again.

The ticklish job of getting these specialized parts to Palestine was turned over to shipping expert Elie Schalit. He decided to bring them to New York and send them out scattered among his regular shipments of machinery. Schalit was reasonably sure the gun dies would slip through, in the bowels of a boiler or transformer, along with everything else. But first, of course, he must get them to New York.

In his usual methodical manner he scanned maps of the north-eastern United States and Canada, made three trips to Toronto, and studied the terrain. He refused to be rushed by the urgent cables from Millman. "I wouldn't move until I had figured it out," he recalls. "With the right concept, it is as easy as pie. But you must have the concept." He came back from his third trip to Canada with a scheme.

As soon as the weather was warm, he returned to Toronto with his twin sister, who was now living with him in the United States. They were well dressed, carrying smart new luggage. They checked into the Prince Edward Hotel, where several friends called on them and a young man delivered some packages—the product, perhaps, of a shopping trip.

Another visitor was a Toronto clothing manufacturer, who invited them to take a cruise on Lake Ontario in his thirty-foot yacht. A few friends would be going too. He gave a cocktail party at the dock before their departure. Schalit recalls, "When the whole crowd went down to the boat, our bags looked like the normal luggage for the jet set going on a cruise." The boat was loaded with fishing and bathing gear, with picnic baskets and bottles of wine. It was a pleasant sunny day. Within a few hours the boat had crossed Lake Ontario and reached Rochester, New York. At the harbor breakwater it passed a customs inspector. Everyone hailed him, glasses in hand. He waved back and motioned them into the harbor. After another round of cocktails at the yacht club there, Schalit and his sister waved goodbye to the gay party, piled their luggage into a car that was waiting for them and sped off to New York.

With all of the delays, the dies reached Palestine a year behind Slavin's original time schedule, a fact which would have important repercussions for both him and his cause.

PART
TWO

IX

HOTEL FOURTEEN

From his alcove beneath the gilt stairway Ruby Barnett screwed a sharp eye on all the comings and goings in his hotel and tried his hardest, his very hardest, to be philosophical about it.

Opposite his desk, on the other side of the lobby, were the grilled cashier's cage and the narrow registration desk, utilitarian departments joined by a proscenium of plywood stained mahogany—a rather makeshift note amid the lobby's high-ceilinged solidity of marble walls and fluted pillars. To his left Ruby could see the revolving door that led to the other, larger world of East 60th Street, New York. The Hotel Fourteen—its name came from its address, 14 East 60th Street—stood roughly halfway between Madison Avenue, with its smart shops and office buildings, and Fifth Avenue, lined by larger hotels and apartment houses and, across the avenue, the green relief of Central Park. To Ruby's right he could see, marching down the length of the lobby, a lounge with overstuffed chairs, entrances to the bar and to the Burgundy Room featuring "French American cuisine," and the two banks of elevators which carried Ruby's guests to the three hundred rooms above.

Barnett, a nervous little man, given to peering over the tops of his spectacles, was relatively new to the hotel business. He and his wife, Fannie, had bought the Hotel Fourteen in a Federal bankruptcy sale in 1944 for some cash and an $800,000 mortgage. Ruby, who had been a lawyer and an accountant, had found in the hotel the kind of vocation he enjoyed. "I never was able to maintain a dialogue with certain businessmen," he liked to tell Fannie, a placid, handsome blonde. "A hotel, you know, is a world in microcosm." Ruby had an office on the second floor of the Fourteen, where he kept the books. But whenever he could spare the time, he came down to the lobby and sat behind his desk in the alcove to "watch the ebb and flow of

human affairs." Ruby fancied himself a philosopher, able to view the
world with detachment. With a competent manager to worry about
reservations and a housekeeper to fuss over the inventory of sheets
and pillowcases, Ruby was able to concern himself with "the big
picture," "the human element," and "the historical context." His
hotel, although small, provided plenty of scope for his ruminations. It
was, Ruby liked to confide to Fannie, a hotel with a "split personality."

Its daytime personality, aboveground and entirely aboveboard,
was that which its architect, in 1902, had planned it to be: a stately
residential hotel, as befitted its location, genteel and sheltering, attractive to elderly widows of means and breeding and to couples down
from New England for the long winter season. Many of its accom-
modations were small suites with high ceilings, marble fireplaces and
even modest cooking facilities. In taking over the hotel, Ruby, who
prided himself on his taste, had resisted the practical temptation to
convert the suites into single rooms and, instead, had refurbished
them with deep sofas and armchairs covered in pastel stripes, tables
and chairs with curved carved legs, and lacquered lampshades, in a
style that he vaguely described as "Florentine."

He also had installed in the Burgundy Room a French chef who
was paid $10,000 a year and insisted upon a saucier who got $150 a
week.

That Ruby had succeeded in keeping the Hotel Fourteen's
dignity intact was evidenced by the fact that it still was a home away
from home for nearly half its guests, most of them little old ladies
who tiptoed into the lobby to ask if perchance their mail—long envelopes with return addresses of banks and attorneys—had arrived.

There was among them even a Mrs. Morgan who, while she was
not of the banking family, had a daughter who was, by marriage, a
genuine Vanderbilt: Gloria Vanderbilt, whose daughter also was a
Gloria Vanderbilt. Mrs. Morgan's other daughter—the girls were
twins, celebrated in New York and London society in their day—was
Thelma Lady Furness and she, Ruby knew, for a philosopher must
understand the endless ramifications of the human element, had once
been linked with Edward VIII of England, now the Duke of Wind-
sor. The Duke and his Duchess might stay at the Waldorf-Astoria,
but there was a kinship there that Ruby recognized.

All of the Fourteen's guests, permanent and transient, eccentric
and not-so, valued the hotel's quiet withdrawal from the bustling
city, the security they found within its thick walls. Their privacy was

further guaranteed by the Irish housekeeper who sometimes sat behind the registration desk, out of sight to passersby, but able to watch the elevators. When a young man went upstairs, she would quiz the operator about him—did he look suspicious? Where was he going? Perched there in the shadow like some omnipresent guardian, Miss Houlihan represented the daytime personality of the Hotel Fourteen.

Its other personality popped out only at night, from the big basement. Long before the Barnetts took over, the basement had become a night club—the Copacabana, sexy, bold and as raffish as the hotel was sedate. Earlier nightclubs on the same site having failed—a butter-and-egg man's version of Versailles and a shrine dedicated to the crooner Rudy Vallee—someone had hit upon the name Copacabana which provided an excuse for a lush flagrantly artificial tropical decor and a chorus line of young ladies who wore only a few pieces of imitation fruit over strategic points of their tall, lithe anatomies. Thanks to the Copa Girls and to performers like Martin and Lewis, Lena Horne, and Joe E. Lewis, the Copacabana had survived in that most transitory of industries, and, when the Barnetts took over the hotel, was paying $2,500 a month rent, a considerable contribution toward Ruby's mortgage payments. It was not the first time that a respectable little old lady had been supported in secret by a scarlet sister. In this case few people realized they occupied the same building.

The Copacabana was visible at night from outside the hotel as a lighted canopy that cut a slash in the darkness down the street from the hotel's larger and dimmer entrance. Inside the hotel only an unmarked and locked door, down a corridor behind the elevators, led from the lobby to the night club. Occasionally, Ruby and Fannie used it to drop in for a visit as guests of the Copacabana management; more often, the management took an early and quiet dinner in the Burgundy Room. Martin and Lewis once stayed at the hotel and Ruby noticed that on Sunday, like other young New Yorkers, the two comedians went out to Central Park with a softball and bat to hit a few. Jimmy Durante too had been a guest upstairs, tirelessly playing the piano until the early hours to amuse his entourage. But the hotel's quiet atmosphere had absorbed these entertainers, just as the walls absorbed Durante's music.

The schizophrenia was well under control; the personality of the hotel's basement seldom revealed itself to the upper stories and vice versa. But this happy equilibrium seemed threatened. Amoebalike, the

hotel's psyche seemed to be splitting again; a *third* personality had
appeared. Actually, Ruby fretted, his wife, Fannie, had brought it
home, the way some women bring home orphaned kittens.

It had begun almost as innocently in the late spring of 1945.
Fannie had asked—it was a usual sort of question for a hotel-keeper's
wife—if there was a room free for a Palestinian friend?

Fannie had been interested in Palestine since childhood and after
high school had taken a temporary job with a Zionist group that
seemed to have a name longer than its membership rolls and a future
slimmer than its payroll. It eventually became the Jewish Agency for
Palestine, but in those days it was some provisional-committee-or-
other. "I was supposed to be there for two weeks, but after the two
weeks I wasn't fired, so I went to ask why," Fannie recalls. "They
said, 'If you leave us alone, we'll leave you alone.'" And so, efficient,
good-natured Fannie had stayed.

She had married Ruby, a year older than she. They had had two
sons and while Ruby prospered, Fannie, whenever she could and
whenever she was needed, worked for the Agency. When its president, the renowned British scientist Dr. Chaim Weizmann came to
the United States during the war, she served as his secretary. In 1945
the Agency had asked her to come back to take over a new job with a
Palestinian named Reuven Zaslani, who explained cryptically, in his
clipped British accent, "We will try to help Haganah."

Zaslani was the Palestinian friend whom Fannie had brought to
the Hotel Fourteen. Ruby observed him from his alcove: medium
height, sallow complexion, dark hair. He came and went quietly.
Occasionally he sat for a few moments in the lobby, chain-smoking,
eyes hooded, silent as an Arab feigning sleep in the shadow of a
wall.

"Who is this Zaslani?" Ruby had asked Fannie.

She replied as well as she could: "From what I gather he was one
of the great spies for Palestine in the Arab countries. But I don't
know what he is doing here."

Her only work for him so far had been writing letters to Zionist
groups asking if Zaslani could meet with them to discuss the needs of
Haganah. Most had declined, alarmed by the mere hint of armaments
or armies, and Zaslani had sent a confidential memo to David Ben
Gurion, the Agency's head, back in Tel Aviv, reporting that official
Zionist organizations could not be counted on to help with this particular mission. Another approach would have to be found.

Soon after that, Ben Gurion himself had arrived and held the momentous meeting at Rudolf Sonneborn's apartment. Ruby had watched the two men, the excitable stumpy Ben Gurion trailed by the silent Zaslani, in the early summer of 1945. Ben Gurion had left. Then Zaslani had disappeared, as mysteriously as he had come.

"Fannie's friends," Ruby had sighed in his alcove, balefully regarding the Hotel Fourteen's lobby. He was almost afraid to look toward the revolving doors. There was no telling who would walk through next. Fannie had told him to expect another guest, her new boss at the Jewish Agency who would be coming soon from Palestine.

X

DOSTROVSKY

Jacob Dostrovsky had arrived in January, a brisk man with a tanned and freckled face, fringed with a final corona of what had been a head of sandy hair. Ruby breathed a sigh of relief as soon as he saw him. Dostrovsky had a rugged, open, outgoing manner which impressed Ruby, as it would other Americans. His horn-rimmed glasses gave him a gentle and scholarly air, yet he obviously was a man of action, relaxed yet purposeful, proud and determined.

In short, the New Palestinian.

He had much the same effect on Americans as his earlier American counterpart Benjamin Franklin had had on the French 170 years before. Franklin, welcomed in Paris as the New American, a symbol of the ebullient democracy emerging in the rebellious Thirteen Colonies, had persuaded the French to send military supplies to the American insurgents. Dostrovsky, the New Palestinian, had been sent by Ben Gurion to perform the same mission in the United States.

Haim Slavin had arrived three months before and already had recruited his young American assistant Phil Alper. In the months ahead, while Slavin worked to develop The Gun and Alper haunted WAA surplus sales, while Jules Chender and his crew labored in the warehouse and Elie Schalit maneuvered to get their crated merchandise on board Palestine-bound ships, Dostrovsky would work quietly at the Hotel Fourteen, organizing other projects, enlisting the help of other experts, prodding, advising, listening, mediating, explaining.

Few of the people involved would know one another. In the interests of security, each undertaking would operate separately. But Dostrovsky would know everyone. He was the coordinator, the grand strategist, the master planner.

The survivor, at age six, of a pogrom in his native Odessa, Dostrovsky had grown up in Palestine. He had fought with the

Jewish Legion of the British Army during World War I. During the Arab riots of the early 1920s he had developed a new kind of frontier settlement, composed of young men and women who were trained to use both plowshares and swords. It had become the backbone of Jewish self-defense in Palestine and would be the prototype of similar soldier-farmer settlements in developing countries as far apart as the Congo and Vietnam.

By World War II, Dostrovsky had risen to high rank in Haganah, the secret volunteer militia organized on a local, part-time basis. As soon as the war had begun, Haganah—although officially banned—had offered the British a first draft of 13,000 volunteers. The Imperial General Staff, critically short of Middle East man-power, nonetheless turned down the offer. However, British intelligence agencies, like thirsty travelers, had been unable to pass by this oasis of skilled and zealous manpower without drawing from its pool. Haganah intelligence units operated for the British behind enemy lines in the Balkans and the Middle East.

The offer of Jewish volunteers to fight in organized groups like the Free Poles or the Free Greeks was renewed again and again, and repeatedly rejected. The alternative was for Palestinians to volunteer individually, and this they did: they served in all the Imperial services, including the Indian Air Force, and some even made the long and expensive journey to recruiting stations overseas to serve in the American and Canadian armed forces. It was not until 1944 that the Churchill coalition government and the Imperial Staff agreed to the formation of a Jewish Brigade Group, which fought briefly but with distinction during the last forty days of the war.

Dostrovsky now set up headquarters in the United States like the military man that he was. At his office at the Agency which he main-tained for the public side of his activities—speech-making and fund-raising—he put up a huge map of the United States. It covered almost an entire wall and, like the battle maps which it resembled, it was studded with pins of different colors: one color for meetings, another for personalities; one size for plans, another for results.

His room at the Hotel Fourteen was kept "like a West Point cadet's," Sam the valet reported to a curious Ruby, "everything in its place." Sam also passed on the information that Dostrovsky was able to look meticulously neat, his trousers in a knife-edge crease despite the fact that he always wore the same suit, because he actually owned two identical suits, like a civilian uniform; when one was being pressed, Dostrovsky wore the other.

At the Agency office Dostrovsky dictated letters to Fannie and watched the slow progress of his "battle plan" on the map. It was dreary work for a man of action, mostly begging letters and parlor meetings and straining to understand rapid American voices asking clarification on some point that he felt was as clear as panic on a child's face.

Fannie typed the letters.

To a department store owner: "You will recall no doubt my conversation with you. At that time you were kind enough to show an interest in our vital undertaking. Because of the urgency of the work may we call upon you to assist us in our efforts. . . . Very sincerely yours, Jacob Dostrovsky."

In five days the answer came: "Dear Mr. Dostrovsky: Your letter of May 8th arrived in the absence of . . . When he returns to his desk, which will be the latter part of this month, please be assured that your letter will be brought to his attention." It was signed by the great man's secretary, but the initials showed it had been typed by still another secretary on an even lower echelon.

Outgoing: "On April 25th you were kind enough to pledge $1,950.00 for our special work. To date we have not heard from you. I wish to take this opportunity to thank you for attending the meeting and to call your attention to the urgency of our cause . . ."

Incoming: "Dear Mr. Dostrovsky: As soon as the elections are over, I hope to be able to give more time and energy to this work which I feel is most important at this time . . ."

Dostrovsky would wearily turn from the letters to projects more attuned to his active nature. One of the most urgent was the acquisition of ships to carry illegal immigrants from the DP camps in Europe to Palestine.

The British had turned down a recommendation of the Anglo-American Commission to admit 100,000 refugees. The Jews of Palestine were now determined to run the British blockade and bring in the immigrants by whatever means they could. Palestinians already were in the DP camps organizing the exodus. Ben Gurion wanted ships to transport a minimum of 10,000 illegal immigrants a month.

He had sent over a young red-headed Palestinian named Danny Shind to work under Dostrovsky on this project. Shind set up the first of a dozen dummy companies which he and Dostrovsky would use during the next year to assemble a motley fleet of small vessels. To avoid suspicion, each company—the names ranged from Caribbean Atlantic Steamship Company to Pine Tree Industries and their offices were scattered through the downtown shipping district of Manhattan—

would buy only a few ships. Sailing under various flags, most often Panamanian, the ships would cross the Atlantic, pick up an overload of refugees in French or Italian Mediterranean ports, then attempt to run the British blockade with their human cargo. Some would get through to Palestine, landing at night on lonely beaches. Many would be intercepted and confiscated by the British; their despairing passengers were interned in yet another camp, in Palestine or, as these filled up, on the island of Cyprus.

The ships that got through would make repeated trips until they were either captured or wrecked on the Palestine coast. In years to come the epic story of illegal immigration would be told again and again. Yet it was just one of Dostrovsky's activities in the United States.

Dostrovsky and Slavin met often at the Hotel Fourteen. The two men, both Haganah veterans and specialists in the defense of settlements, conferred earnestly about The Gun and the small-arms industry which Slavin one day would assemble in Palestine from the surplus machinery which he and Alper were buying.

There were other specialized needs of the Palestinian settlements which Dostrovsky also sought to fill. One of his key discoveries in the United States was a young American electronics engineer from the New York suburb of Yonkers named Dan Fliderblum. A baby-faced boy who always looked sleepy, Fliderblum had been too young for the draft and was later deferred; during the war he had taught Army Signal Corps trainees at New York University.

At Dostrovsky's request, Fliderblum had assembled a group of electronics whiz kids, most of them veterans of the Signal Corps who were up on the latest gadgetry. They had sat, grinning like a roomful of radio dials, as the short balding man from Palestine told them what he wanted: a secret radio network to link the isolated settlements and forewarn them of British search parties seeking illegal arms (whose visits, all too often, were followed by Arab raiding parties).

The youngsters had gone to work in a loft under the twenty-one-year-old Fliderblum. During their free hours, after jobs or classes, they had manufactured a handsome radio set in a mahogany veneer case which even bore its own trade name: Musica. Actually, it was a transmitter disguised as a receiver; the only difference was in the crystal.

Fliderblum next began scanning surplus stocks of radio equipment for items that might be useful to Dostrovsky. He turned up a dozen National MC57 receivers and two dozen Hallicrafter S-38s, which were purchased and sent to Palestine. One day he came across a bonanza: nearly one hundred excellent sets, good as new. He triumphantly reported his find to Dostrovsky, who told him to meet him in front of a Broad Street building. Fliderblum struggled to suppress his excitement as Dostrovsky shepherded him upstairs into a brokerage office.

His excitement turned to amazement as he watched Dostrovsky speak with great familiarity to the occupant of the office, an impressive-looking businessman who nonchalantly twiddled open a vault, lifted out a large stack of bills and handed them over to Dostrovsky. Dostrovsky turned to give the money to Fliderblum but paused, as though to take a fresh look at the pink-cheeked youth who tinkered with wires and tubes and said he had found valuables among the debris of a complicated war. "Are you sure it is good stuff?" he asked. Fliderblum, tongue-tied, nodded. Dostrovsky shrugged and handed over the cash.

The man who so obligingly had produced the money was Louis Rocker, a highly regarded stockbroker whose personal vault had become the underground's bank. Dostrovsky, often accompanied by Fannie, made frequent trips to Broad Street. Looking very much like a middle-class couple on their way to visit the Aquarium, they would board the IRT Lexington Avenue subway, Fannie tightly gripping her purse, which bulged with thousands of dollars. Later Fannie often made the trip alone, sometimes to deposit money, sometimes to withdraw it for disbursal. So involved did she become in the financial affairs of the underground that years later, when a friend in business was going over the books of the Machinery Processing and Converting Company to make sure they were in order for an income tax review, he shouted, "Who's Fannie? On every page I see the name Fannie. You can't run a business with a ledger that says, 'Money from Fannie.' "

At the Hotel Fourteen Dostrovsky received an increasing number of visitors: dark-suited American businessmen, Palestinian youngsters who breezed excitedly through the lobby in old Army jackets, men with strange accents, women with strange authoritative manners —some of these latter Fanny would identify to Ruby as female members of Haganah. If they did not always look to Ruby Barnett like "the sort of person which ordinarily we are getting in the hotel," still, they bothered no one. Dostrovsky spoke with them quietly in the hotel bar, ordering a brandy, neat, for himself, or, more often, in his own orderly room. Ruby had no complaints, maybe only a speculation or two.

"What is Dostrovsky doing," he would slyly ask Fannie, "writing a sequel to *Crime and Punishment*?" For all their years of happy marriage, Ruby, who had served with the Canadian Army during the First World War and remained a confirmed Anglophile, had never quite shared Fannie's enthusiasm for Palestine. But it was no use, he had learned long ago, trying to argue with Fannie. Instead, he took his doubts one day directly to Dostrovsky.

"What right do you have," Ruby began, "to change the face of the world by creating another ghetto, which instead of two by four, it's two hundred by four hundred?"

Dostrovsky, patient as always, had smiled his winning smile and explained that it was precisely to be free of ghettos, of the confinement and fears and frustrations of ghettos, that the Jewish settlers had gone to Palestine to found a nation of their own. He spoke of their historic association with the Land, of the struggle to wrest it back from arid disuse and of their determination to raise up there a redeemed people, a phoenix rising out of the smokestacks of Auschwitz. Ruby nodded. He liked Dostrovsky's "philosophical viewpoint that there was something new being born on this earth" and accepted his invitation to talk some more over lunch the following Thursday.

Ruby Barnett trotted behind Dostrovsky as they entered the lobby of the Hotel McAlpin, across Herald Square from Macy's and Gimbels. The Palestinian headed familiarly for the hotel directory of the day's events and pointed to one of the announcements: "Luncheon in honor of Rudolf G. Sonneborn."

THE INSTITUTE

E ver since the portentous meeting with Ben Gurion on July 1, 1945, in his penthouse, Sonneborn had been meeting irregularly with small groups of men, friends and their friends. The conversation inevitably got around to Palestine, but it might warm up with other subjects—a man's business, the names of some of his friends who also were interested in Palestine, their businesses. Sometimes Sonneborn took short trips out of town to see some of the eighteen other men who had been in his apartment that day and to suggest they hold similar meetings.

Often Palestinians, arriving in the United States to raise funds, would start their tour at one of Sonneborn's meetings and be passed on by him to friends in other cities.

Soon after Slavin's arrival Sonneborn had lunched with him. He had not asked Slavin to speak at one of his informal gatherings; Slavin's English was not good enough and he was in the United States on a different kind of a mission. Sonneborn referred him to men he hoped could help. He had his doubts; a lot of missionary work remained to be done. He had spoken about Slavin later to Montor, to Levine, to others and had got back encouraging, but generalized, reports. He knew only vaguely of the existence of the apartment on West 112th Street and of the drafty warehouse on upper Park Avenue in the Bronx. He had met Elie Schalit as a young man who occasionally spoke at fund-raising meetings. He had never heard of Phil Alper; he would never meet Carl Ekdahl. He preferred not to know too much about such matters.

A few months after Dostrovsky's arrival Sonneborn had received the specific instructions he had been waiting for ever since Ben Gurion had asked him and the eighteen other men at his apartment to hold themselves "in readiness." Ben Gurion, Dostrovsky informed him, would pay another visit to the United States. Again invitations went out for a "private and confidential" meeting at Sonneborn's penthouse. This time, Sonneborn would recall, "it was decided to form ourselves into a working committee and to assume definite responsibilities." For the moment these would be mainly financial: raising money to buy ships for illegal immigration and to finance other projects at which Ben Gurion only hinted.

"The Sonneborn Institute," as the group wryly dubbed itself, held its first meeting in late July 1946 at the Hotel Astor. Only six men were present, an inauspicious beginning but some prescient current may have passed among the half-dozen men as they sat around the luncheon table and listened to Dostrovsky interpret the latest news from Palestine.

The British, in their most successful arms seizure to date, had found and confiscated some six hundred rifles, pistols, mortars, and light machine guns which had been hidden by Haganah in underground storerooms at a settlement near Haifa. On Black Saturday the British had rounded up the entire leadership of the Jewish Agency in Palestine. Ben Gurion had escaped arrest only because he was in Paris. The Palestinians would continue their struggle for statehood, Dostrovsky emphasized, but—like Irish, Czech, Polish and Arab nationalists before them—they could do only so much in the face of severe repression. Every fight for national independence, he concluded, depended in some measure on sympathizers abroad. He paused and smiled, looking around the table.

As the number of men around the table grew, it became a horseshoe. The luncheons were fixed for every Thursday noon and moved on to the more convenient Hotel McAlpin, where they were usually held in the El Patio Room on the second mezzanine.

Sonneborn had suggested the weekly luncheons. He knew from long experience how much businessmen could accomplish over lunch, without the distraction of their wives, relaxing among men they could feel were their equals, in the midst of a trying day when they might feel equal to nothing else.

Luncheon was light, often a buffet, so that the busy men could get away promptly at 2 P.M. "Part of our work can be done while we are eating," Sonneborn would explain, for the benefit of newcomers. "Discussion of confidential matters will take place after we are all served and the waiters leave the room."

Sonneborn's opening remarks were always the same.

"I want to stress, as we always do at these meetings, that all of you here are either close collaborators or friends of our colleagues who have vouched for you. In the course of our discussions we expose certain of our activities. I know you will understand the necessity for extreme discretion in disclosing what you hear. Much of what we say will be useful to you in your task of helping us reach the public, but you must be guarded in how you disclose any information obtained here."

In July he said, "Our plan of campaign is very simple. In each of thirty-five or forty industry groups we want one man to act as our representative." This man, he said, would hold meetings and solicit support; those who attended the meetings and volunteered to do more would in turn be asked to hold meetings of their own.

On August 28, 1946, Sonneborn gave some idea of the variety of the Institute's "membership": "We have been able to get additional key men in industries previously untapped—dairy products, radio, sewing machines, advertising, marine supplies, and blouses."

The October 17, 1946, meeting decided to try to raise $100,000 a week for the remainder of the year—a cool one million. The goal was reached, but it wasn't enough. Sonneborn told the December 31 meeting, "Within the next three weeks we must have a rather considerable sum of money. I would like to suggest that everyone here arrange a small parlor meeting in the next two or three weeks. Let's see if we can have two or three a night."

More ships, including two surplus Canadian Navy corvettes, had to be bought for the illegal immigrants. And Slavin's secret purchases, which were mounting in volume, had to be paid for.

On February 13, 1947, Sonneborn reported that in the preceding week meetings had been held in Hamilton, Ohio, and Memphis, Tennessee, and that "forty more were scheduled for February as far west as Albuquerque, New Mexico." Palestine was on the front pages with stories of rioting, terrorism, repression. In the same February week that the British announced they would turn over the Palestine problem to the United Nations, Sonneborn told his luncheon that twelve more meetings had been held in Camden, New Jersey; Cedar Rapids and Iowa City, Iowa; Baton Rouge and Alexandria, Louisiana; Dallas and Tyler, Texas; and Washington, D.C. (The speaker there was Elie Schalit, who said little about himself.)

By April 17, contributions for 1947 had reached $505,177 and the twenty-seven men at the weekly luncheon were given heartening eyewitness accounts of the landing of two of "their" ships in Palestine.

All through the spring the news was ominous. The British

hanged three members of IZL, one of the Jewish extremist groups, and Irgun hanged two British sergeants in reprisal. The Arab extremist groups, Young Chivalry and The Helpers, took a toll of Jew and Briton alike. On May 13 a United Nations Special Commission on Palestine was established and began one more study of the problem. The Institute discussed that, but they also talked, more quietly, about an old Chesapeake Bay excursion steamer, the *President War-field*, which they had bought and refitted in Baltimore. It would become the immortal immigrant ship *Exodus*.

On July 5, 1947, Sonneborn scheduled a cocktail party at the Hotel New Yorker. The holiday weekend, he felt, would be a good time to remind his "collaborators" that they would have to stay on the job all summer. He asked the hotel to list the party as "the first anniversary of the Sonneborn Institute." John F. McDonnell, the hotel's banquet manager, wrote him, acknowledging the reservation and suggesting that an orchestra be hired: "I personally feel it would be a good idea and I know music would add to the merriment of the occasion."

Whenever a member of the Institute made it plain that he was prepared to contribute more than money, Sonneborn and Dostrovsky would decide just what influence, skills and resources he could bring to the cause. There were many men who did small favors, once, twice or several times, guessing the purpose, but never knowing the end result. They arranged bank credit, office and warehouse space, meetings with ship brokers, machinery dealers and truckmen, or they transferred funds through their own accounts. But there was one man in particular upon whom the Institute would call again and again.

He was Adolf Robison, whose father had visited Palestine with Sonneborn immediately after World War I. A mild-mannered, genial man, he was a successful textile converter in New Jersey. His hobby was musicology. He also possessed a phenomenal memory for figures, names, and shipping routes, and he was able to devote a few days each week to the cause. He became Sonneborn's deputy at Institute meetings and, eventually, its direct liaison with the Hotel Fourteen.

The Institute spawned a public subsidiary when it became obvious that nothing was confusing American sympathy for the Jewish settlers of Palestine so much as the issue of "terrorism." The two principal extremist organizations, Irgun Zvai Leumi (IZL) and the Stern group (LHI), were ideological rivals of Haganah. Thousands of well-meaning Americans who would have disagreed with their beliefs were contributing to the extremist groups in the belief that only they were "doing something."

The Institute was especially concerned about the flamboyant advertising of a razzle-dazzle organization calling itself the American League for a Free Palestine which supported IZL. Ben Hecht, the author, wrote its advertisements, which often likened the British to the Nazis and the news from Palestine to another holocaust. Such unbridled emotionalism—and Hecht's energy—attracted supporters from the world of show business and, playing upon the American fascination with massed pageantry, they were drawing huge crowds to spectacles which included musicians, chorus girls, singers, celebrities, and even a chorus of fifty rabbis, praying in unison. A pageant, *We Will Never Die*, written by Hecht and produced by Billy Rose, had drawn 40,000 people to one performance in New York and was purported to have raised more than $1,000,000 around the country. An audience watching a line of shapely chorus girls waving papier-mâché tommy guns might not realize that most of the settlers in Palestine abhorred Irgun and supported Haganah. The Institute decided to form Americans for Haganah, which then published a newspaper, distributed publicity releases, rounded up its own celebrities, and held its own mass meetings. While it never made as much of a splash as the American League for a Free Palestine, it switched some of the money that might have gone to Irgun to where it would do more permanent good.

The Institute reached the point where it needed an office and a full-time staff. The Institute's first paid employee was Harold Jaffer, a bright, nervous public relations man who had begun as a volunteer and impressed Sonneborn with his ideas. Jaffer brought in Isaac Imber, who had been in the machinery business, and Imber in turn recruited Julius "Rusty" Jarcho, a red-haired former editor of trade newspapers in the garment industry. All three had done organizational work before and they knew the pressure points between a pledge and final payment.

It was hard to get office space in crowded New York, but one of the Institute's members was part owner of the 26-story Fisk Building at 250 West 57th Street, at the corner of Eighth Avenue, just below Columbus Circle. He wangled space for the Institute's staff. The only name that appeared on the door of Room 1905 and on the directory in the lobby was that of Harold Jaffer.

Although Sonneborn continued to insist that his weekly luncheons had "no formal organization, no committees, no letterheads," the "Institute" had become an institution.

Thousands of American Jews who had never been interested in Zionism before had been so shocked by the Nazi atrocities that they were taking a new—or a first—look at the idea of a Jewish national home in Palestine. A dormant Jewish consciousness had been aroused. Motivated by humanitarian concern for their co-religionists in the DP camps, by fear for their own fates, by moral indignation and by a hard-headed appraisal of the world political situation, they were receptive to the message of the Sonneborn Institute's emissaries. Speakers at the weekly McAlpin meetings brought the latest news from Palestine. "Key men" passed on the message, like a bucket brigade or a human chain letter, to other men who held meetings in living rooms, rumpus rooms and country clubs, at Sunday brunches and cocktail parties across the country.

The meetings were always private, informal and confidential. They were held outside the framework of organized Jewish philanthropy and Zionism. Their instigators took care not to conflict with the fund drives of established charities which were engaged in the herculean task of raising millions of dollars for the relief of refugees. Money given to the Institute, it was made clear, must be in addition and apart from other contributions; it was destined for other purposes.

About these purposes they said what they could. Sometimes the veil slipped a little.

In the spring of 1947 Sonneborn announced at a Thursday luncheon that Dostrovsky was returning to Palestine. In paying tribute to the spruce little military man who had been his "close collaborator for more than a year," Sonneborn said, "He was the inspiration for the organization of the work in this section." And then, even though he had prepared his remarks in advance, Sonneborn went on to explain what he meant by "this section." Dostrovsky, he said, "has had the responsibility for handling the security problem here and did so with the utmost care and confidence."

That much candor from Sonneborn was surprising, but he was masking an even greater secret—one that it must have pained him not to be able to disclose. Only he and a very few others in the Institute knew that Dostrovsky was returning to his homeland to resume the job he had held before coming to the United States. He was chief of staff of Haganah.

XII

RABINOVICH

Things weren't the same at the Hotel Fourteen. Ruby Barnett brooded, balefully regarding from his alcove under the stairs the man who had replaced Dostrovsky. A chunky former British Army major named Shlomo Rabinovich, he was ostensibly in the United States to work for Palestine Exhibits, a firm which more or less, and increasingly less, set up exhibits to show the material progress made in Palestine. That was his cover. But there was something about Rabinovich that negated the suggestion that he would ever exhibit anything. He was a wary, secretive man whose suspicious nature had not been softened by years of underground work for Haganah. Ruby Barnett could discern in Rabinovich nothing of the philosopher, nothing of the inquiring mind, no desire to enjoy a relationship of patient prophet to brilliant disciple. Rabinovich responded to Ruby's opening parries with a harsh thrust of his chin and silence except for a few cryptic questions about the hotel: Who had the room next to his? Who answered the telephones?

Short and stocky, Rabinovich had joined Haganah as a runner at fifteen and worked his way up through the ranks; he had fought mosquitoes and Syrian snipers as a member of a settlement in the Huleh marshes; he had reached the rank of major in the British Army, serving during World War II in the Middle East and Italy. By the time he came to the United States to replace Dostrovsky, he calculated he had been fired at forty-two times from a distance of less than twenty-five yards.

No wonder Rabinovich treated even Ruby Barnett's overtures like an ambush. He was a man who looked every gift horse in the mouth to see if its teeth had been wired for sound by the British secret service. He was no less gentle with Dan Fliderblum, the young electronics genius who had been discovered by Dostrovsky.

A request had come from Tel Aviv for Mark 19 tank radio sets, sophisticated communications equipment which had been used by the British, Canadian and Russian armies. Fliderblum found some on sale in Canada and was instructed to buy two hundred sets. The price for each set, brand new with all accessories, was only nineteen dollars. "My own judgment," he recalls, "was that at that price it didn't pay to repair the sets or even to stock spare parts; it would be cheaper to replace them, so I went ahead and bought four hundred." When he returned to New York and reported the purchase to Rabinovich, the Palestinian muttered, "Do you think we are going to give radio sets to every shoeshine boy in Palestine?"

Rabinovich cast the same jaundiced eye on all of the proliferating American operations. Unlike Haim Slavin, who a year and a half earlier had had difficulty finding one person to help him, Rabinovich was flooded with offers, passed on to him through the Sonneborn Institute, Americans for Haganah, and other interested organizations and individuals.

He would have preferred to keep tabs on everyone and everything himself, to turn over every application, to draw up orderly lists of the help he needed, to choose the candidates worth cultivating and ignore the others. Easily, he could have had two of every kind. He was no Noah; his ark was in danger of being swamped by a flood of demobilized American know-how. One day he was introduced to Paul Shulman, a former U.S. naval officer, an Annapolis graduate, scion of a prominent American Zionist family, who asked what plans were being made for a navy. Soon after, at one of the Sonneborn luncheons, Hal Gershenow, another former U.S. naval officer, graduate of MIT and a specialist in ship repair, came up to offer his services. Rabinovich sent both young men to a downtown office which handled ships for illegal immigrants. A navy? "With all due respect to ourselves," he would later observe, "at that time we were not thinking so big."

Nevertheless, he made a note of their names.

Another young man found his way to Rabinovich's office at the Agency with an even more fantastic proposal. He was an athletic-looking fellow with a Germanic name—Adolph Schwimmer. He was, he explained, a flight engineer for TWA on the Cairo to Washington run.

"I just wonder whether I can help," he said in a dry New England drawl.

Rabinovich, trying to drown his suspicions in a lukewarm smile, asked a few tentative questions about what had brought him in. No ideological basis, Schwimmer replied. He had simply been moved by events in Palestine.

"I've been reading the newspapers. Airplanes might make a difference."

Airplanes? Another big idea, Rabinovich thought. Where would the Palestinians get airplanes? They had almost no pilots, no place to train them under the eyes of the British, and even less prospect of assembling the complex supporting system of airstrips, weather stations, repair shops and armament that back up an air force.

With a heavenward glance of resignation, Rabinovich took down the visitor's name and gave him an invitation that had become routine for testing the depths of a volunteer's enthusiasm: "Come in again sometime."

"In our situation," he would explain later, "you always had to calculate the costs, the political risks. You had to be careful of stool pigeons. You had to go slowly. When a man comes to help, he wants to give you his life—quickly. But you can't move so quickly. How to hold him in abeyance for a time until you can really make use of his good will and his contribution? It becomes a pure human problem of contact and trust."

There *were* people that Rabinovich wanted. Ben Gurion had asked him to look for some top military men who could help develop a new concept of national defense, one that went beyond guarding buses and patrolling farms.

The situation in Palestine was as ominous and uncertain as ever despite Great Britain's decision in February to refer the whole problem to the United Nations. Whether the UN's recommendations would be followed was unclear. Colonial Secretary Creech Jones said Britain was asking only for advice and many of Bevin's advisers were known to feel that the net result of the maneuver would be a strengthened British mandate when either the Arabs, the Jews or both asked Britain to stay to save the country from chaos. The Arab nations in private meetings quarreled among themselves about what stand to take; each had a slightly different stake in Palestine and its own dreams of aggrandizement.

The ambiguity of the British position left everybody guessing. In

Palestine Jewish leaders debated what course to follow. Their primary efforts now were concentrated on the political fight at the United Nations, where a Special Commission on Palestine (UNSCOP) was formulating recommendations. Few believed that either the British or the Arab states would defy a UN decision favorable to a Jewish state. Their military planning, accordingly, was aimed primarily at obtaining additional small armaments to enable Haganah to handle dissident bands of Palestinian Arabs and protect the Jewish settlements during an era of relatively orderly transition. Ben Gurion, however, continued to predict that the British might not leave Palestine unless forced to by Jewish intransigence and that the Arab states might invade, UN decision or no.

He was trying to plan ahead accordingly. He had even written to Mrs. Blanche Dugdale, an English friend and a niece of Lord Balfour, and asked her to send him some books on military strategy. Haganah had experienced military men, skilled in the arts of commando warfare, but none who had served in positions of senior command or on a general staff. These were the sort of men Ben Gurion now asked Rabinovich to find.

Colonel David "Mickey" Marcus, a West Point graduate who had been a civil affairs officer on the staff of General Eisenhower's SHAEF headquarters during World War II, was restive in his civilian job as Commissioner of Correction for the city of New York. Pugnacious—he was a former prize fighter—politically ambitious and bored, he was quick to accept Shlomo Rabinovich's invitation to make a trip to Palestine.

Under the nom-de-guerre of Mickey Stone he toured the country and quickly became a symbol to the Palestinians of an American commitment to do more than contribute money to their cause. He returned to the United States a convert, ready to do whatever was asked of him. Rabinovich saw Marcus not so much as a commander— he had not had much actual field experience—but as a magnet for recruiting other combat-trained American staff officers and as, perhaps, future adjutant to a senior American officer, yet to be found. Together they mounted a search for such a man.

The most likely possibility was retired Major General Ralph Corbett Smith, a former Army division commander whom Marcus had known in the Pacific.

Rabinovich and Marcus flew to San Francisco to see him. Smith

took them to lunch at Fisherman's Wharf, where Rabinovich ate his
first lobster. As the men removed their paper bibs, the general, who
had been listening intently, began plying them with questions.
Rabinovich was elated by his obvious enthusiasm, but Smith's decision, he soon made it clear, hung fire on one question: Would service
as an adviser to this national army-in-the-making endanger his U.S.
Army pension? Like most professional military men with years of
underpaid service behind him, he was dependent upon that pension
for his old age. The answer that Marcus got from the Pentagon was
disheartening: It might. General Smith regretfully declined and
Marcus and Rabinovich had to settle for lower-ranking specialists,
two American officers who quietly slipped into inactive duty and
flew off to Palestine with Marcus: a Marine Corps captain who
advised Haganah on field communications, and an Army intelligence
officer who helped to plan strategy in the headquarters of Chief of
Staff Yaacov Dori, formerly Jacob Dostrovsky of the Hotel Fourteen. They worked anonymously in secret jobs, their presence known
only to their superiors in Tel Aviv.

Rabinovich and Marcus next turned their attention to Canada.
Harold Jaffer, director of the Sonneborn Institute's secret offices at
250 West 57th Street, had come back from a fund-raising trip to
Canada with a Blue Book, published by the Jewish community of
Canada to record the accomplishments of its co-religionists in the
Canadian armed forces. One of the names that stood out was that of
Benjamin Dunkelman, who had been a major in the Queens Own
Rifles, a regiment of the Third Canadian Infantry Division; he had
landed in Normandy on D-Day and commanded the first troops to
reach and take up a permanent position on the Rhine.

The Dunkelman family, wealthy clothing manufacturers and
retailers, were longtime Zionist sympathizers; Ben had ridden with
settlement watchmen during childhood visits to Palestine. He was
now a tall, dark, saturnine man, surprisingly shy for a combat officer.
Rabinovich and Marcus flew to Toronto to talk to him. He was
hesitant; he had so recently returned from five years of war; he had
considerable responsibilities in the family business. He agreed to think
it over and, meanwhile, scout for others who might help.

Eventually, in March 1948, Dunkelman did go to Palestine,
where he became commander of the Seventh Brigade, which spear-
headed the fighting in central Galilee and occupied the northern
part of the country to the Lebanese border. While there, he again met
Colonel Marcus, now a military adviser to the new Jewish armed

forces. Touring the Jerusalem front in early June, Marcus was accidentally shot and killed by a nervous sentry while visiting the headquarters of his old friend and colleague Brigadier Shlomo Shamir —formerly Shlomo Rabinovich of the Hotel Fourteen.*

* Marcus's body was brought home for burial at West Point, escorted by two officers, Yosef Hamburger and Moshe Dayan. Hamburger used the opportunity to ask the Institute to send over naval vessels, while Dayan, on leave from his commando unit, requested more reconnaissance airplanes.

XIII

THE SCHOOL

Nahum Bernstein, a prominent Manhattan attorney, was not surprised when Rabinovich approached him at an Institute meeting in the early summer of 1947 and, in a guarded elliptical way, asked if Bernstein would be willing to take on a special job.

A handsome man with an engaging personality and seemingly boundless energy, Bernstein agreed immediately to help "in any area in which I am particularly qualified."

His background was diverse. He had made a name for himself as a young lawyer by exposing an insurance claims racket that had been costing insurance companies millions of dollars. His reputation as a lawyer-investigator had gotten him into the OSS during the war. After considerable service in the field, he had been assigned as an instructor to a secret OSS school in a secluded cove on Catalina Island, off the coast of California. Since the war he had re-established himself as one of the city's most energetic and promising young attorneys. A friend had brought him to one of the McAlpin luncheons and Bernstein had introduced himself to Sonneborn, casually mentioning his OSS experience. "We clicked immediately," Sonneborn would recall. "From that time on, he was one of the boys."

Bernstein assumed that Rabinovich wanted legal advice or an appointment with a local politician. But instead, the Palestinian explained: "We now want to find in the United States more than money, but also Americans with special skills to train our people in areas they know absolutely nothing about." As their conversation continued, Bernstein realized that it was his OSS background which interested Rabinovich; he was being asked to organize and run an extraordinary educational venture—a secret school, right in the heart of New York City, which would train young Palestinians for intelligence work.

It was impossible, the Palestinian explained, to give such training in Palestine, where the British had decreed a death penalty for the mere possession of a gun. Nor were there instructors available in Palestine with Bernstein's up-to-date expertise in the advanced techniques developed during World War II, nor the equipment needed to demonstrate the increasingly sophisticated and electronic methods now used. Bernstein nodded; it was a job he would relish.

While a group of young Palestinians were quietly summoned to New York, some from abroad, others already studying in the United States, Bernstein got to work on campus and faculty.

Finding suitable facilities momentarily stumped him; his was definitely not the kind of school that could use an ivy-covered campus and stadium, even had they been available. Bernstein finally and covertly borrowed classroom space at an Orthodox religious institution, the National Council of Young Israel, on West 16th Street, where his school's classes could be inconspicuously intermingled with Young Israel's regular evening courses for young adults.

Bernstein's faculty consisted of carefully chosen volunteers. He had difficulty at first recruiting a teacher for the subject he considered most important: the use of codes and ciphers in transmitting secret messages. He went to one of America's top cryptologists, a Jew, and was "turned down cold." He then approached another expert whom he had met in the OSS, Geoffrey Mott-Smith, a forty-five-year-old Episcopalian from Schenectady, New York. A dark-haired man with heavy eyebrows and a mustache, Mott-Smith claimed some American Indian blood and an ancestor who had been the first governor of New York. Both of his parents had been artists; he had attended Union College and, in addition to being a cryptologist, he was an expert in games, bridge, chess and Bach music, "a combination that fits together," explains Bernstein. Mott-Smith had written a number of books, including *Mathematical Puzzles*, *Contract Bridge* and *Pencil Bridge*, and was preparing another, *Games for Two*, in collaboration with Albert H. Morehead, another bridge authority, when Bernstein came to see him in 1947.

Ex-OSS man Mott-Smith was as delighted as Bernstein to get back to his old calling and gleefully donned the disguises required by his new mission. Bernstein vividly remembers arriving one evening at Young Israel, where the school's classes in the arcane specialties of espionage were being passed off as innocent courses in Biblical lore. There was Mott-Smith, a black skullcap balanced on his head, swaying forward and back as he tried to explain cryptography in the droning tones of a Talmudic scholar.

Down the hall a former U.S. Army captain was demonstrating the use of knives, piano wires and thumbs at close quarters to his class in "kill or be killed." (A mild-looking chap named Meyer Birnbaum, he later became the successful proprietor of a chain of kosher poultry stores.) In another room a demolition specialist chalked diagrams on the blackboard to illustrate the best method of placing explosives on the girder of a bridge or, with equipment obtained by Bernstein, demonstrated how to connect a primer cord or set a timing device to go off at a specific moment. When he felt his students had learned all they could within the confines of Young Israel's classroom, he took them out on weekend field exercises to get some practical experience with explosives to two upstate New York farms, loaned with no questions asked by Bernstein's brother Gad and Wall Street broker Louis Rocker.

An electronics expert quietly explained the latest techniques in wiretapping, tape recording, the use of microphones and other forms of electronic surveillance. Bernstein himself taught the course referred to in undercover schools by the harmless name of "police methods": i.e., lock-picking, safe-cracking, surreptitious entry, living under cover, tracing automobile tracks, following and eluding the enemy.

In all, the school turned out some fifty or sixty graduates, who were promptly nicknamed Shoo-Shoo boys, the Hebrew slang for secret agent. The final examination at the end of each six-week course was a field test, given under conditions similar to those the OSS had insisted on for its trainee operatives.

Each student was given a specific objective and sent out on a mission to break "enemy" security. They were given access to printing presses that could forge identification papers and other things usually available to secret agents. Beyond that they were on their own. After a week in the field each filed an intelligence report on what he had been able to discover. The best report was read aloud by its author at the school's "graduation" ceremony.

At one such ceremony the honor graduate reported that he had infiltrated the New York offices of the Jewish Agency and discovered that a certain Mr. Rabinovich who had an office there was not really an Agency man but a high officer of Haganah who was in the United States on a secret mission, about which he had amassed considerable information.

As the student went on, a stocky man who had been sitting quietly at the back of the room jumped up. He sputtered and fumed as he introduced himself: Major Shlomo Rabinovich. With elaborate sarcasm he congratulated the young man on his excellent report. If he himself was now blushing, Rabinovich explained, it was not in embarrassment. He was crimson with anger. The report proved what he had been saying for weeks: His mission's security was terrible.

XIV

W2OXR

The school's cryptology department was soon asked to take on an extracurricular activity. The underground needed a code, an absolutely foolproof code for use in sending secret radio messages to Palestine.

Bernstein consulted with Mott-Smith, who advised him that the "five-letter one-time-pad" system which an American had invented, and the Germans and French had improved upon, was believed to be "as unbreakable as any code yet devised." Mott-Smith had been teaching its rudiments to his students and, with the cryptologist's yearning for the perfect code, he was eager to have it translated into Hebrew and try it out.

A few days later a young courier who called himself by the Hebrew name Zvi, although he was obviously American, boarded the Staten Island ferry in downtown Manhattan, sailed past the Statue of Liberty, got off in Staten Island and went directly to a hilltop house at 282 Franklin Avenue in the town of West New Brighton. There he delivered the first messages phrased in the new code to the owner of the house, a thirty-two-year-old attorney named Reuben Gross.

Zvi knew the route well; he had earned his sea legs on the Staten Island ferry. Three afternoons a week he came to Gross's house to deliver outgoing messages; three mornings a week he returned to pick up incoming messages. For Gross was the underground's radio contact with Tel Aviv, transmitting and receiving messages considered too urgent or too secret to go by commercial cable. A lawyer by day, at night he traveled amid the grunts and whistles of the short-wave band, pursuing his hobby of ham radio operator on a first-class radio telegrapher's license, tapping at the key of his station W2OXR on what he regarded as essentially a mission of mercy. A chunky man with the blue-jowled face of a cherub who must shave twice a day, Gross, a graduate of Harvard and a World War II Army veteran, had walked unsolicited into the New York offices of the Jewish

Agency almost a year before and offered his services. Although he was a family man, struggling to rebuild his practice after his Army service, his conscience was troubled by accounts of the greater uncertainties faced by his co-religionists in Europe and Palestine. A religious man—a rarity among educated Jews of his generation, he observed Orthodox dietary laws and rituals—he wanted to do something to help. The agency sent him to a hotel on East 60th Street to meet a woman named Minna Rogers, whom he had taken for British —she had been a captain in the British Army's ATS. For a fleeting instant he had felt double-crossed, but Captain Rogers's welcome quickly reassured him: "You're like something from heaven."

She confided to him that several attempts to establish radio communication with Tel Aviv had failed. A plan to set up a station in New Brunswick, New Jersey, had been abandoned when they were warned, "The FCC will be on to you right away. You can't use the airwaves of the United States without being investigated from head to toe." Captain Rogers recognized that in Gross, an established licensed amateur operator, she had stumbled onto a prize and arranged for him to get a surplus long-range BC-610 transmitter.

Neither Gross nor his brother, a wartime Navy radar officer who offered to help him on the project, were engineers, but there was no one they wanted to call upon, so in February 1946 they took a day off from work to install the new equipment themselves and to erect an antenna around a tree in Gross's windswept backyard.

"It was so cold we couldn't stay out very long," Gross recalls. "We'd put on gloves, climb the tree, take off the gloves, and work on the antenna for about fifteen minutes; then we'd have to come down, go through the whole business with the gloves again." But they got the antenna up and working in time to begin a prearranged schedule of transmissions. The very first night it was heard in Tel Aviv.

Thereafter, W2OXR operated on a regular schedule. Three nights a week, starting at 8 P.M., Gross would call a station with Dutch call letters, promptly identifying himself. Listening in on the same band, Tel Aviv would answer, disguising itself with Greek call letters.

Gross recognized by the Tel Aviv operator's "fist" that they both had been trained under the same procedures; in the latter stages of the war the United States Army had coordinated its communications procedures with those of the British. "We got to know each other's minds. When he changed frequency, he would not say which one he was going to. I would turn up or down and there he would be, waiting for me."

Gross never saw Captain Rogers again—strange voices on the telephone gave him instructions—he saw only the courier Zvi. Nor did Gross have any notion of the contents of the messages that he sent and received; they were always in cipher. Gross knew that the sending of coded messages was restricted by international treaty, but he already had decided to cross that line. He was troubled, however, by the new code that Zvi delivered to him.

The messages no longer sounded like the ordinary exchange of ham operators; they made no sense. In the previous code each letter of the alphabet had been represented by three words—a noun, a verb and an adjective or adverb. Messages were encoded by choosing among these words so that they formed innocuous sentences. The new code, to which Gross objected, consisted of five-letter groups lumped together at random; and they did not—unless by chance—form words.

Gross protested on the telephone to his unseen controller. "Look, I don't like this system of using letter groups. It sticks out like a sore thumb." The voice had insisted that "our top people have consulted with the experts and there is no better way of doing it."

Shortly after nine o'clock on the evening of September 3, 1947, a black sedan pulled to a stop before Gross's house. The mournful bleating of boats and buoys coming up from The Narrows obscured the muffled sounds of clicking within as three men swung out of the car. At the door of the house they showed their credentials to Gross. Two were FBI agents, the third was with the Federal Communications Commission. "Would you like to come out to our car?" one of the FBI men said. "No," replied Gross; he had heard that FBI cars were mobile recording studios and he preferred to answer whatever questions were ahead in the privacy of his own house. He motioned his visitors to chairs.

The conversation that followed in the Gross living room must have been difficult to boil down into the terse reports the FBI agents and FCC man were required to make the next morning for their agencies' secret files. Gross, assuming that the FBI men were lawyers, like himself, found courage in pretending that he was back in a bull session at Harvard Law School; he turned back questions, theorized, engaged the three men in debate.

At midnight one of the FBI men said, "Mr. Gross, we've been talking for hours and you haven't said a thing that makes sense."

Gross would observe later, "Of course, I knew that. I could tell

from a few things the FCC man said that they'd been monitoring my
station, so they knew a good deal about me already. But there was
something puzzling about the FBI men's line of questioning, something I couldn't quite put my finger on, as if they had found the right
man, but the wrong address. I felt that if I said anything, I might just
incriminate myself." The FCC man had quickly gotten around to the
codes. The random five-letter groups had indeed aroused the FCC's
suspicions. "He wanted to know what those five-letter groups
meant," recalls Gross. All Gross would say was that he had been
communicating with an acquaintance in Palestine. The agents left
after midnight, telling Gross to report at the FBI offices in New York
at ten that morning. Gross was "shaking plenty; I didn't sleep much
that night."

He rose early and went to Manhattan to consult with an older
lawyer friend who advised him to "sit tight" and later notified him
that he had succeeded in postponing the FBI date.

Gross also talked to his Palestinian telephone contact, who said a
conference would be held to consider what to do. He asked Gross to
meet him the following Sunday morning (it was then Thursday) in
Manhattan. After changing subways several times and backtracking
"to make sure we had shaken off anybody following us," they went
to Washington Heights, where they boarded a bus to New Jersey
and wound up at a pleasant summer cottage at Pompton Lakes.

Gross was introduced to a half-dozen men sitting around a table.
One of them was Shlomo Rabinovich, whom Gross now met for the
first time: "We promptly got into an argument." Another was the
owner of the house, Nahum Bernstein, also a stranger to Gross although he knew him by reputation and was reassured by the presence
of so prominent an attorney. Bernstein briskly took charge of the
meeting. He first gave the assembled men a rundown on the codes
Gross had been using.

The random five-letter groups, he explained, represented the one-
time-pad system which the OSS had devised for its agents during the
war. Just before an agent parachuted into enemy territory, he was
handed a pad. On each pad the alphabet was represented by five-
letter groups, typed at random, a different group for each letter. Each
page of the pad had a different code. The OSS man used each page
one time and then burned it. His headquarters had the only copy of
his pad. Bernstein said the one-time-pad was as close to being unbreakable as any code ever devised, since it banished the bugaboo of
letter frequency and changed with each use. It had been prepared in

Hebrew for Gross's use by a group of girls working in an apartment on West 72nd Street. For days on end they had sat at typewriters typing five letter groups at random. Every twenty minutes they switched typewriters so that they would not get used to any one machine and unwittingly repeat themselves. Gross, fascinated to learn at last the structure of the code he'd been using, interrupted to say, "The FBI and FCC asked me again and again, 'Where is the code?' The code is what they are interested in."

"Then we'll have to let them have it," said Bernstein.

Gross and the others looked at him astounded. Was all the secret work of the past months going to be handed over to the FBI? Gross did not know the true contents of the messages he had been sending, but some of the others did. They had concerned the secret acquisition of ships, the movement of immigrants, the search in the United States for materiel and personnel, Slavin's super-secret arms project. They were realistic men; they knew that American intelligence agencies worked closely with the British secret service. Were all of their activities to be revealed to the British too?

Bernstein quickly reassured them. "Using the same one-time-pad codes that the FCC has monitored, we can produce any kind of message we want." One of the girls, an expert in philology, he said, would reconstruct some of the codes, but in such a way that the messages they produced would be innocuous. For instance—he gave a very simple example—the code for a message which had originally meant "Send guns" could be amended to read "Send fans," by simply reassigning the five-letter grouping that, in the original code, had stood for G to F, and the grouping for U to the letter A. It would be much harder, of course, with longer messages, but he was sure it could be done. Having the code for one message would not help the FCC decipher other messages it might have monitored, since the code changed with each one.

The important thing, he emphasized, was to satisfy the FBI and the FCC so that they would not push their inquiries, perhaps exposing the entire underground operation.

That night after the meeting Gross went home. At the appointed hour he tuned in his receiver and heard Tel Aviv calling him. W2OXR remained silent. "I nearly cried," he recalls. "It was like seeing your brother drowning. You want to stretch out a hand. But I had to keep quiet. I only listened."

In due time the FBI was given a sheaf of codes and decoded messages. They carried such mundane communications as "Please contact Joe So-and-So, Detroit, for annual contribution." The FBI was satisfied. As a matter of fact, Gross found out later, the FBI agents had lost interest in him as soon as he mentioned Palestine. His hunch that there had been something out of kilter about their line of questioning that night had been right. The agents who visited him were members of an anti-Communist unit who had been tipped off by FCC monitors that Gross was communicating in code with a mysterious station using Greek call letters; they had even pinpointed its location as the island of Crete. The FBI had feared he was part of the Communist conspiracy that was plunging Greece into civil war.

Gross never heard from the FBI again. The FCC suspended his license for violating the international treaty restrictions on the use of codes. Gross appealed, won a hearing, and got the suspension reduced to six months.

When Gross later left family and law practice behind to go to Palestine as a volunteer radio operator with the Air Force, he tried to find the operator with whom he had felt such close aerial affinity all those months in Staten Island. He vividly remembers the day a young man about twenty-five years old—Gross was then thirty-five—walked into his office and introduced himself as "SV9CD"—the call numbers of the Tel Aviv station.

"He's very happy to see me," recalls Gross. "He drives me to the outskirts of Tel Aviv and we walk up an alleyway between two apartment houses. We go into a rear door and into a one-room basement apartment, furnished with only a cot. He goes into the little bathroom, leaving the door open, and sits down on the toilet. I'm embarrassed. But I see he's lifting up the toilet tissue holder. From inside the water closet he takes out a big key—almost a crank—and inserts it into a hole behind the paper holder. He turns it, a slab of wall starts moving—the wall is decorated with wooden slats—and he gets down on his hands and knees and crawls in. He waves to me to follow. We make a turn and we're in a little chamber about six by six. He repeats the process with the key and another wall moves away and we come to another room, fairly big. There's an old table there and a pipe coming out of the cement floor. He explains that his equipment was just a crude elementary transmitter—just crystal control—but it did the job. Into the pipe came the power supply and out of it went the antenna, underground, and into the next building and up to the roof where it was disguised as clotheslines. So if the direction finders came they'd start searching the next building and, in the meantime, he could walk down the alley and get away."

XV

F.O.B. ANYWHERE

All through the summer and early fall of 1947 the comings and goings in the lobby of the Hotel Fourteen reflected the seesaw political situation in Palestine.

In August the United Nations Special Commission on Palestine called for an early end to the British mandate and recommended dividing Palestine into three parts: Jewish, Arab and an international enclave in Jerusalem. The British avowed they were determined now to get out of Palestine but hedged on implementing the UNSCOP plan.

The Arabs tried to assess British intentions, sparred with one another and issued threatening statements from their meetings in Cairo and Lebanon.

Jewish leaders in Palestine continued to debate the size and configuration of the military struggle ahead. They must prepare themselves, on that everyone agreed, but for what? A skirmish or a war? It was still unclear.

At the Hotel Fourteen Rabinovich tried to do a little of everything. His operation outgrew the tidy controllable boundaries he preferred. Shoo-Shoo boys from Nahum Bernstein's spy school streamed through the lobby reporting on people and checking out leads. More Palestinians arrived—some to stay at the hotel for a few days, then move on to other assignments, others to remain for weeks or even months. More Institute members were drawn into the underground's activities.

Branch efforts sprang up in other parts of the country or were improvised according to the opportunities.

A young Viennese refugee named Harry Weinsaft, who traveled around the United States making fund-raising speeches about his experiences as a sailor on the refugee ship *Exodus*, reported back to

Rabinovich that wherever he spoke he was offered not only money, but often weapons as well, guns and pistols brought home as souvenirs by American GIs. He had even shipped a few of them to his New York apartment. His experiences weren't unique; almost every fund raiser had been approached, stealthily at first, more and more boldly as the headlines about Palestine grew larger, by former GIs or their families who had, or knew someone who had, a souvenir German Luger or an Italian Beretta, or even a Schmeisser machine pistol. The fund raisers often were nonplused by the kinds of things GIs had brought home in their barracks bags: mortars, bazookas, even live hand grenades.

Mild-mannered people would sidle up after a speech to say they had collected on their own initiative old Army field jackets or overcoats or helmets. No one knew how many closets and basements from Asbury Park to San Diego, smelling of moth balls and GI soap, were filled with olive-drab haberdashery and deadly hardware. The fund raisers took them out of nervous hands and, without any organization at first, sent them on to New York. Soon the supply was too great for such haphazard handling; an informal delivery system was devised.*

Since it was illegal to send firearms through the United States mails, volunteer collectors throughout the country were recruited to pack the guns in footlockers, send them by Railway Express to New York, and mail the claim checks to a postoffice box in the main New York postoffice opposite Pennsylvania Station. Weinsaft was given the job of picking up the checks, claiming the footlockers, and lugging them by taxi or borrowed car to a warehouse for sorting, cleaning, repacking and shipping to Palestine.

As word of this endeavor got around, the unexpected pool of souvenir firearms became one of Rabinovich's steady sources of small arms; thousands were collected from all over the United States.

Weinsaft answered one rush call to New York's Little Italy. It was an Italian funeral parlor on Mulberry Street; a surly attendant opened a casket and wordlessly handed Weinsaft several pistols. From Spartanburg came a .30-caliber machine gun labeled "playground equipment."

---

* American supporters of the dissident factions in Palestine, principally Irgun Zvai Leumi, also collected weapons. On April 27, 1948, New York police arrested two young men—one the son of Louis Untermeyer, the poet—in a West 28th Street fur loft and seized 144 machine guns, 203 rifles, 268 pistols, and assorted ammunition. The youths were acquitted on May 28 of illegal possession of firearms on a motion by one of their attorneys, Paul O'Dwyer.

An Institute member was surprised to receive a visit from a pregnant woman who darted into his office and from beneath her skirt produced eight pistols. Harold Jaffer, manning the Institute's supposedly secret office at 250 West 57th Street, began to shudder whenever a stranger appeared with a heavy briefcase.

Out in Denver, Colorado, a highly efficient operation was developed by one of the city's leading attorneys, Sam Sterling, a graduate of the University of Denver and a retired Army major. Sterling had stood up at a fund-raising meeting one evening to announce his donation, then, on impulse, had added, "And one case of guns which I'll pick up myself." Everyone had laughed, but a few weeks later Sterling got a telephone call: Was he seriously interested in seeing that some of the necessary materials got to Palestine? He was, he replied. Would he be willing to discuss it with someone right away, that night? It was 10 P.M., but Sterling agreed. A few minutes later he was sitting in a parked car outside his apartment getting instructions on how to collect, pack and ship souvenir guns. The young man talking to him was Elie Schalit, who in addition to his duties as the underground's shipping expert had recently taken on another job in which he hoped to enlist Sterling's aid. Schalit was trying to amass gunpowder and blasting caps for Slavin's secret armament plants. Since their sale was closely regulated, he had hit upon the device of buying small quantities wherever he could from sporting goods stores. "It should be fairly easy in the West, where hunting is a popular sport," Schalit explained to Sterling.

Sterling undertook this new mission with his usual aplomb. He made the rounds of the local sporting goods stores and bought all he could. Then he began making trips out of town to Pueblo, Colorado Springs, as far away as El Paso, 800 miles to the south, and Las Vegas, 1,000 miles to the west, returning with several hundred pounds of powder and cartridge caps in the trunk and on the floor of his dark brown Plymouth sedan. He might have been picked up as the fastest gun in the West except that he always traveled with his wife and two children. With a lap robe covering their legs—and the ammunition—they looked like any vacationing family.

Back in Denver, Sterling hid the ammunition—along with the guns which he was also collecting—among the winter clothing in a big cedar storage closet. On Sunday mornings he and a group of friends gathered in his basement workshop to pursue a new hobby: sorting and packing arms in carefully disguised containers. The half-dozen men, all well-placed professional and businessmen like Sterling, became very good at it. They usually used oil drums. Each drum would be carefully filled to eight inches from the top, then put on a scale. If it didn't weigh as much as a full barrel of oil, lead (useful in making bullets) would be added. The busy hobbyists then covered the hardware with heavy tar paper and poured two inches of plaster of Paris on top. When the plaster of Paris was set, they filled the remaining six inches with petroleum. In a few months this Rocky Mountain Lavender Hill Mob shipped over a ton of powder, half a million caps and several cases of small arms.

Another indefatigable collector of souvenir guns was Zimel Resnick, proprietor of the giant amusement park in Asbury Park, New Jersey, who had received one of Fannie's early letters, written for Dostrovsky, and, unlike many other recipients, had responded with a firm offer to help. He collected guns from friends, relatives and, more and more boldly, from veterans' organizations throughout New Jersey. At the height of his activities he was storing them in the basements of some twenty friends. He estimates he collected more than ten thousand guns. Whenever he had a "load," he would call Rabinovich, and a car or a truck would pick them up. When he wanted assured privacy for a conference with someone from the Hotel Fourteen, he led them to the ferris wheel at the amusement park and into one of its gaudy carriages, where, swinging round and round above the seaside resort, they could talk without fear of being overheard.

"Fannie's friends," groaned Ruby, when he heard about Resnick and his ferris wheel. It sometimes seemed to him his hotel had taken on the aspect of an amusement park with distorting mirrors, a spooky house of mystery, thrilling roller-coaster rides and a tumbling barrel that at any minute would toss everybody into a heap. Hebrew had become the second language of the hotel's corridors. "Do you think," Ruby demanded of Rabinovich one day, "that Hebrew is some unbreakable code that if J. Edgar Hoover wants to know what you are doing he can't find someone who is speaking Hebrew too?" To make matters worse, the hotel was not doing well. But Ruby despaired of interesting anyone in his pecuniary problems. The Palestinians, he bitterly observed, didn't even eat in the Burgundy Room; they went out to a delicatessen for pastrami sandwiches.

Occasionally Phil Alper and Elie Schalit came to the Hotel Fourteen to consult with Rabinovich, who was now their immediate boss in the United States, but they continued to get their orders directly from Slavin in Palestine. Alper still worked at the apartment on 112th Street. He was so busy he had taken on an assistant, Robert Keller, a tall, lanky attractive fellow of his own age who had grown up in Boston, graduated from the Boston Latin School and the United States Merchant Marine Academy, and served as a ship's officer in the merchant marine during the war. Keller shared Alper's office-apartment, but he lived elsewhere, with relatives of his wife, a Boston girl whom he'd married the year before.

Schalit had his own office downtown. Jules Chender had at last made good his threat to go back to Paris; his place at the Bronx warehouse had been taken by a husky six-foot-three, 185-pound American named "Big Moe" Wolfson, who had spent eleven years in Palestine driving a truck on a collective farm.

The four men were still methodically fulfilling Slavin's original mission: to put together a small-arms industry capable of manufacturing guns, mortars and explosives. In Palestine Slavin patiently checked Schalit's shipments against his card files and production manuals and informed Alper of the gaps that still needed filling; Alper searched for the missing machinery and informed Slavin of what else was available. Slavin already had several small workshops operating, making mortars, hand grenades and other such simple weaponry. One of them, he would recall in a rare moment of humor, was in the basement of a bawdy night club in Tel Aviv whose upper stories were regularly raided by the police. He had received the remaining dies for Ekdahl's gun and hoped to get it into production soon.

In the late fall of 1947 the General Assembly of the United Nations gathered in New York for a special session on Palestine. This would be the decisive meeting after all the fanciful speculations, feverish hopes, political jockeying, military skirmishing, threats, promises, massacres, bombings, retaliations, laborious work and vengeful destruction of the past years. It would be the first important decision of the fledgling world organization.

Every hotel in New York was filled with delegates and staff people; they had spilled over from the Waldorf-Astoria, the Plaza and the Biltmore to fill the rooms and corridors of the city's smaller hostelries. Several rooms at the Fourteen had been taken by members of the British mission.

Rabinovich bore down upon Ruby in the lobby and hustled him outside. There, pacing the sidewalk while he darted suspicious looks over his shoulder, he whispered angrily. He had heard English-accented voices outside his door; what were they doing there?

"Look, Shlomo," replied Ruby frostily, "this is a well-known hotel. All kinds of people are staying here."

Rabinovich was still suspicious. Why the British mission?

"Maybe with the UN sessions they don't have enough space in some of the other hotels. There is no other reason, I assure you."

Unappeased, Rabinovich walked along, hands in his coat pocket, head down. Ruby looked at him with distaste.

"Shlomo," he remonstrated, "here in America you go around with your hat down and your collar up, people will think you're a gorilla, a gangster."

Rabinovich ignored Ruby, deep in thought. "I think all the telephone wires in the hotel are tapped," he said suddenly.

Ruby scoffed at the suggestion.

"Where are they?" Rabinovich persisted.

With a shrug of resignation, Ruby took him into the cellar and showed him a big box on the wall. "Anybody fools with the wires, they're fooling here," he said, then mused, "unless they got contraptions which they can hang on the walls which I've read in the literature. Here, no one is fooling but if you mean, can I protect you against devices upstairs, the answer is no."

In that case, Rabinovich replied, he could not have the British government on the same floor with him. "Either they go or I go."

"With Rabinovich," Ruby told Fannie later, "there is always something wrong. Nothing is a coincidence; it is always a put-up job. I told him, 'Shlomo, you don't like it here—go.'"

Fannie nodded to her husband and agreed that Rabinovich had better live elsewhere.

And so Rabinovich went—to the Barnetts' apartment on West 86th Street, while they, to make room for him, moved to the hotel. In the interests of security, everyone agreed.

XVI

PARTITION

At noon on October 25, 1947, Rudolf G. Sonneborn did what was expected of him, what he had been doing for more than two years, what Ben Gurion, out of the blue, had asked him to do. He went to the Jansen Suite of the Waldorf-Astoria Hotel to preside over yet another meeting. As usual, it was listed on the hotel directory "in honor of Mr. Rudolf G. Sonneborn."

There would be about fifty-five guests from Indianapolis, Cleveland, San Francisco, Birmingham, Baltimore, in all some twenty-five cities. Like the United Nations delegates, out-of-town members of the Institute were distributed in hotel rooms about the city, wherever there was space.

Almost all the invitees—a careful list of key members of the Institute—had accepted, for this was an extraordinary convocation, a weekend of luncheons and dinners, called to consider the implications of the forthcoming meeting of the United Nations. They would be made privy to confidential briefings on the military and political situation by top representatives of the Jewish Agency who were arguing the Jewish case at Lake Success.

Unlike that other fateful meeting with Ben Gurion, more than two years before, this one would be concerned not with vague possibilities but immediate realities.

Sonneborn began with a brief review of the Institute's history and accomplishments. "I am talking to you intimately and frankly," he said, yet even today his words were guarded. He spoke of "the shipping program," of "general defense work," of "certain types of tools and machinery."

He looked around the horseshoe table, at the faces intent over their plates of melting Frozen Soufflé Alaska, and assured his listeners they were the elite of what had grown to a substantial group. "We have today at least one person in virtually every community in America . . . there are perhaps eight or ten thousand of us throughout the country and we represent here the energizing force. None of us knows the full complexity of our work, but all of us realize what it represents and recognize its significance."

With events moving so rapidly, he continued, it was urgent that they take stock and plan immediate and appropriate action. Significantly, this first session would be devoted to the military situation. The first speaker was an impressive man of whom some of them already had heard: Major Aubrey Eban,* a Cambridge graduate and former Cambridge don, former major in the British Army, now assigned to the Agency's political department at Lake Success.

In a candid flow of eloquence, designed to jolt the complacency of any who thought that only a favorable vote at the United Nations stood between present uncertainties and a Jewish state, Eban took the assembled men backstage to the committee hearings and the confidential conferences at Lake Success. Again and again he made the same point: There would be no Jewish state—not even a favorable vote for a Jewish state—unless the Jews of Palestine were in a position to defend it themselves by their own force of arms.

UNSCOP, the committee of eleven neutral states which had been studying the Palestine situation, had recommended the establishment of a state. But, said Eban, "the Swedish president of the committee came to us after the discussion and said, 'However deeply we may be convinced of the justice of your claim, we shall not advocate that claim unless we believe that you yourself can make it good. We will recommend no state which you cannot defend.'"

The same situation now prevailed at Lake Success, Eban continued. Both of the great powers, the United States and—quite unexpectedly—the Soviet Union, had declared themselves in favor of a state and it was "quite certain" that a majority of the Assembly would support it. But, "to put it to you very concretely, there are several states, whose names I am not mentioning, who say that 'we will support the proposal for the creation of a Jewish state if we see that we are not called upon as states or as the United Nations to make any physical sacrifices on its behalf.'" The neutrals and small nations did not want to become involved, he explained. And both of the great powers, the Soviet Union and the United States, were too fearful of seeing the other's forces in the Middle East to sanction any sort of

---

* Later to become better known as Abba Eban.

armed intervention by either. Despite some vague talk of an international volunteer force, careful soundings among the UN delegations had convinced Agency representatives, Eban continued, that "the question of international agreement upon some external force for the maintenance of the order of Palestine is fraught with such dangers that if we make the implementation of this scheme dependent upon external support, the whole scheme might fall through for lack of that support." To ensure support for statehood, the Agency had taken the only alternative position. It had assured the nations of the world that "the Jewish people will provide for the defense of themselves and their frontiers with their own resources." Only on those conditions could they muster the votes they needed. Eban continued gravely: "We are going to be taken at our word."

He then went on to outline the conditions the new state might face. British withdrawal, he felt, most probably would begin with the inland regions, where the Arabs were predominant, and move slowly toward the coast, where the Jewish population was concentrated. "During that time lag the Arab section of Palestine will be able to organize and to reinforce their defensive capacity while we ourselves will be still under the same limitations under which we have languished for so many years." The Arab armies, he reminded his listeners, were "open and aboveboard. They receive arms from foreign missions, they can train openly . . . Our own force in Palestine, which I do not underestimate, is, however, a force in potentiality rather than in fact." The Arabs, he predicted, would attack quickly, while the Jews were still weak; they would not be deterred by a United Nations declaration. "They will attack the Jewish state and face the music at the United Nations later, knowing that in international diplomacy there is no stronger force than the force of the accomplished fact."

Gideon Ruffer, a representative of Haganah, followed Eban with a detailed view of the Arab military situation. "The Arabs," he said, "have an air force, although a tiny one; they have airplanes. The Arabs have tanks, the Arabs have field artillery, and next to our borders is a very fine force, the Arab Legion of Transjordan."

When he finished, the room was quiet for a moment, the assembled men no longer soared on the euphoria of an impending, probably favorable, UN vote on partition.

Sonneborn opened the floor to questions. The first one expressed the bewilderment of many: "I would like to ask how it is possible for American Jews to get over heavy artillery and tanks, assuming we have the money?"

Sonneborn's answer brought a round of applause. "I think that is going to be a very, very difficult question to answer, even in the intimacy of this room. May I tell you that it will be done."

Question: "Doctor Eban, one of the main points you make in your talk is that the United Nations . . . would only possibly grant this new state if you can give them assurance of your ability to protect the military aspect. How, in the absence of any government until now and the absence of any army until now, how do you proceed to give them that assurance?"

Eban: "We give them that assurance on the basis of the willingness of the Jews abroad to provide for their finances and their equipment."

As questions and answers bore down on military problems, one of the guests suggested the meeting adjourn: "I think we are getting in a dangerous area."

Another million dollars in cash was needed from the United States immediately—in the next two months—to make the necessary purchases for the crises ahead.

Sonneborn reminded them that the Institute's money-raising activities always had been carried on quietly, on a man-to-man basis, with no committees, no letterheads, no fanfare, neither "in competition nor in partnership" with any other organization. Its activities could not impinge on the collections of the official Zionist organizations or the juggernaut United Jewish Appeal—which every year raised well over $100 million for local and foreign philanthropies—or compromise the semiofficial Jewish Agency, which had to deal clean-handedly with the United Nations and foreign governments. The Institute's funds were used for purposes which could not be publicized or even fully disclosed.

Sonneborn explained. "The responsible leadership of Haganah has said to us, in effect to you and to me, we need funds; we need free funds, we need these funds for these obvious purposes."

During the question period the men clamored to know more; how much, they demanded, could they disclose to the friends whom they would be approaching for contributions? The more they could tell, the bigger the checks would be.

"Nothing," said one, "has so excited the interest of the Jew on the street . . . Men who are unaffiliated with Zionist organizations are ready to give substantial contributions . . . men who do not give to the United Jewish Appeal."

A gentleman from Philadelphia agreed. "Haganah is the biggest romance, it is the greatest thing certain Jews have had happen to them in this country. I have known Jews all my life who were waiting for the day that they could point to another Jew that carried a gun and say, 'He represents me.' Meaning not a gangster but a hero, and in the last few weeks the papers have come forth and they mention Haganah with respect."

Sonneborn, nodding, steered the discussion to fiscal realities. How much could the Institute count on from each of their communities? Purchases had to be made immediately, contracts signed, commitments undertaken. Each man canvassed the situation in his area and gave his appraisal.

The men had been listening and talking for two days. Their heads reeled with the arguments, figures, revelations, requests that had bombarded them. It was 3:30 P.M. Sunday and most of them had planes to catch, journeys to make, in order to be back at their desks in the workaday world on Monday morning. Sonneborn adjourned the meeting by urging them to translate their pledges into cash by the end of the year, cryptically adding, "As to our share of the much larger tasks which we will be called upon to fulfill, we will be informed when it is clearer just what we must do."

One month and three days later, on November 29, 1947, the United Nations General Assembly, meeting in a former war plant on Long Island, voted 33 to 13 to partition Palestine into two separate countries. One would become a new Arab state; the other, only one-eighth the size of the homeland envisioned in the Balfour declaration and the mandate, would be the first Jewish commonwealth to exist in two thousand years.

Two weeks later the British announced they would "probably" withdraw from Palestine in six months—by May 15.

PART
THREE

XVII

YEHUDA ARAZI

Yehuda Arazi, alias Alon, alias Joseph Tannenbaum, alias José de Paz, alias Rabbi Lefkowitch, alias Dr. Schwartz, alias Mr. Oppenheim and, most recently, alias Albert Miller, stepped into the lobby of the Hotel Fourteen and coolly appraised its baroque décor, its modest bank of elevators, its Burgundy Room and—for all Ruby Barnett knew—his dwindling bank account and increasingly red-inked ledger.

A tall gray-haired man of indeterminate but definitely foreign appearance, Arazi, at forty, was a living legend, a swashbuckling secret agent who had been turning up weapons and information for Palestine in improbable places for more than half his life. His arrival at the Hotel Fourteen marked the beginning of a new phase for the underground. He came with a mandate from Ben Gurion "to make as widespread purchases as possible . . . of the types of weapons which Haganah has not yet been able to obtain during its whole history . . . aircraft, artillery, tanks and other forms of heavy equipment." It was the kind of operation Arazi had always dreamed of.

He had begun his underground career at nineteen when, on orders from Haganah, he joined the British mandatory police force and rose from the ranks to become an inspector of the CID in Jerusalem, its chief investigator of Communist activities. He had been dismissed when the CID discovered that he was also supplying Haganah with the names of police informers within its ranks and leading it on raids of Arab arms caches that the police had learned about. He studied law for a while, then went to work in the port of Haifa, where he learned from the inside the technicalities that would benefit him most in his next assignment: buying arms secretly in Europe and smuggling them into Palestine. Like a moth attracted to flame—but always managing to avoid the fire—he went to Poland, where he dealt successfully with the Army's anti-Semitic high command by pointing out (in Polish—he spoke six languages) their mutual interests: *They* wanted to get rid of their Jews; *he* needed arms to win a homeland for them. In Rumania and Hungary he played cheek to cheek with the military while buying rifles and ammunition. As the war closed down his European markets, he returned to Palestine and worked with British intelligence until they learned he was acquiring British arms on the side.

A price was put on his head. Barely escaping arrest, he donned one of his many disguises. He grew a beard and became, for the next two years, Rabbi Lefkowitch.

Before the war ended, he slipped out to Italy disguised as a Polish air force pilot to work with members of the Jewish Brigade of the British Army, who as a sideline were accumulating surplus arms jettisoned by the Allied armies. Under Arazi's direction the young soldiers scoured the salvage dumps of Europe for guns and ammunition and hid them in small caches in France and Italy. When the British decided to demobilize the Jewish Brigade and ship it home, Arazi switched his attention to illegal immigration, helping more than 11,000 refugees reach and cross the Mediterranean. At one tense interval the Italian government balked at releasing a group of DPs interned at the port of La Spezia; Arazi smuggled himself into the camp and led a stormy demonstration which won their release. Then he too left for Palestine—secretly, since the British were still looking for him—to rest and await his next assignment.

It came soon.

Even before the UN General Assembly gave its final approval to partition, Ben Gurion called Arazi in to discuss the situation now facing them.

For political reasons—to convince the world they could not be ignored—the Jews of Palestine had built up an image of strength. So persuasive was their propaganda, even the Arabs had been fooled; the Arab League estimated their strength at fifty thousand mobilized troops, not including reserves, with artillery, armor and even an air force. An occasional ingenious and daring Haganah raid reinforced the picture. It was a posture that had operated to the advantage of the Jews, particularly at the UN, where the crucial decision to create a Jewish state was being made less on humanitarian grounds than on a realization that, given Jewish strength and obstreperousness, nothing else would work and that the Jews themselves would be able to defend their state.

It was effective political sleight-of-hand, but the reality, as Ben Gurion and a handful of Haganah leaders knew, was pathetically different.

The only fully trained organized force was Haganah's special striking force, Palmach, and it consisted of three thousand troops, a few hundred of them girls. Haganah had four hundred full-time officers who had managed to give varying degrees of military training to a reserve of some fifty to sixty thousand men, half of them men over twenty-five, who at best could constitute a sort of home guard. None of the troops had been trained to operate at anything larger than small battalion strength. Haganah had just begun to mobilize. It had weapons for less than a quarter of its men. Its total arsenal at the moment consisted of "some 8,300 rifles, 3,600 Sten guns, 700 light machine guns, 200 medium machine guns, 600 two-inch and 100 three-inch mortars, all of different types. There was sufficient ammunition for only three days' fighting."

Haganah's few thousand guns—which had been laboriously bought, captured, stolen, or manufactured over the years—were thinly scattered through the country. Most of them "belonged" to the various communal farm settlements; the kibbutzim had paid for them, Haganah then using the money to finance further acquisitions. But the usual sources—British surplus arms dumps in North Africa and Palestine—were now exhausted. The shipments from America brought a smattering of souvenir guns donated by ex-GIs, but most of the big crates from Alper and Schalit were laden with machinery to *make* arms, a promise for the future rather than a reality for today. Slavin's clandestine production was still small and sporadic and could not be expanded until the British left and he could come out of hiding.

Haganah had no heavy armaments of any kind—no heavy machine guns, no artillery, no antitank or antiaircraft guns, no real armored cars. Nothing whatever to use in the air or on the sea.

With statehood—and probably war—looming only a few months away, Ben Gurion told Arazi, they must begin immediately serious and urgent efforts to provide Haganah with the modern armaments it would need to face a half-dozen Arab armies.

As Ben Gurion would recall years later: "You cannot hide a plane in a basement, nor a tank in an attic closet. What we had to do therefore was to try to buy them overseas, which was also not an easy task, and hold them until the British troops would leave."

Ben Gurion still had not convinced many of the other Palestinian leaders that armaments deserved top priority; money was always short and achingly needed in a dozen other urgent causes. But he assured Arazi he would find the funds somehow—in this battle the Sonneborn Institute was his secret weapon.

He was sending several trusted Haganah aides to Europe to see what could be obtained there. To the United States, which had been the arsenal of the free world, which possessed in overflowing abundance the diversity of weapons he so badly needed, he would send the "old man," Yehuda Arazi.

Ben Gurion had high hopes for the United States. It was selling its surplus weapons to most of the countries of the world, including the Arab. He hoped that the American government, which was supporting partition at the United Nations, would soon also approve arms purchases by the Jews.

To Arazi, a new country meant a new name.

As Albert Miller, he sublet an apartment on Central Park West, where he passed unremarked as one more transient gentleman of some means (he was always a big spender), a bachelor apparently (he had an eye for women), of some indefinite Central European background (he spoke with an accent and "looked distinguished"), in the United States on some sort of business (there were many like him) from some country or other (Latin America, it seemed to be at times). He was an attractive man, as a lonely widow or two and some who were not yet widows noticed. He stood one inch short of six feet; he was broad-shouldered and narrow-waisted and walked with a limp. Prematurely gray, he looked older than his forty years. He dressed to emphasize his most striking features: gray suits to go with his hair, blue shirts to heighten the color of his cobalt eyes.

He visited the Hotel Fourteen frequently but he never lived there. Arazi was a loner; he had his own mode of operation and it did not meld with others. "He couldn't work in a group," one of his colleagues from the prewar gun-running days in Rumania recalls. "He never did what he was told. There were no roadblocks in his way. To live for the cause, to die for it, this was in all of us. But his determination overwhelmed everyone. He swallowed others up. There were very few who could withstand him. He had terrific charm, but to give you the back of his hand was nothing to him."

Arazi's personal life also might have been hampered at the Hotel Fourteen. He seldom wrote to his wife and children back in Tel

Aviv. There wasn't much he could tell them about his work—or his play.

His taste in women ran to height and full bosoms. In the United States he found no shortage of these. At one point he had two sturdy young women ministering to him. Al Robison, the gentlemanly textile man who became the Institute's liaison with Arazi, once found both women fussing over him in his apartment. Robison's logistical turn of mind as well as his sensibilities were offended. "The least you could do," he scolded, "is to have one come on Mondays, Wednesdays and Fridays and the other on Tuesdays, Thursdays and Saturdays."

A tall deep-chested young woman named Rachel Nachman, a researcher for *Life* magazine, along with her Air Force veteran, law-student husband, a member of an intellectual Greenwich Village Zionist group, occasionally was pressed into service carrying messages to Arazi in sealed manila envelopes. Each time she called at his Central Park West apartment, "he would embrace me madly, his hand would linger." The young wife asked to be relieved of the assignment.

When Elie Schalit heard that Arazi had arrived in the United States, he hurried uptown to pay him a visit, both because Arazi had been "the hero of my Haganah boyhood" and because he feared that if he didn't get there first, Arazi might come to *his* office at 2 Broadway near the Battery "in a fleet of Cadillacs, trailed by bodyguards, riding the length of Broadway through all the red lights."

"Arazi did amazing things in Europe by being flamboyant," Schalit recalls, "by throwing around money and daring to charge into the lion's den." Schalit didn't think it would work in the United States. He himself still carefully adhered to the principles he had outlined to Slavin two years before, working as discreetly and above-board as he could through legitimate channels, attracting as little attention as possible. When Arazi peremptorily informed him, "Elie, as of today you are working for me; I need a good man to handle shipping," Schalit politely but firmly declined.

"Yehuda," he assured the older man, "you've been like a god to me; I've walked in your shadow. But I have an assignment and I can't just drop it." Arazi insisted and the question was submitted to Tel Aviv. The cabled reply directed Schalit to continue his work for Slavin and to keep his operation separate from Arazi's. Schalit advised Phil Alper to do the same.

Arazi soon recruited his own lieutenants: a tall, tough, taciturn redhead named Joe Eisen and Danny Agronsky, a big, loquacious American whose father, Gershon Agronsky, published the *Palestine Post*, the country's English-language newspaper. Agronsky had worked with Arazi during the war, liberating arms from British and Axis dumps in the western desert. When he came to the United States, ostensibly to buy printing equipment for the *Post*, Arazi quickly pressed him into service.

In the bar of the Hotel Fourteen Arazi pursued his two interests, his eyes roaming from the curve of a woman's breast to a brochure from the War Assets Administration.

There were in the latter many of the items of heavy equipment he was looking for. He could feel his muscles tighten with frustration as he read the lists. Everything he needed was in the United States, but none of it was available to him.

On December 5, 1947, less than a week after partition had been approved by the United Nations General Assembly, the United States government, suddenly and inexplicably, had announced an embargo on the sale of all arms to the Middle East. The embargo extended to the Arabs as well as the Jews, but the Arab armies already were equipped. They had bought more than $37 million worth of surplus American arms abroad through the Office of Foreign Liquidations Commission. They long had been supplied by Britain and would continue to be. The British had explained they would not follow the U.S. lead and impose an embargo, because they had "contractual obligations" to the Arab states.

The Jews were starting from scratch and the embargo, in effect, kept them there. Contrary to expectations, the United States had not followed up its support of partition by selling them the arms they needed to defend their new state, but by denying them arms. It was a major blow to all of their hopes and calculations.

Arazi felt the fury and impatience well up within him. He had planned to buy artillery, tanks, armored cars and airplanes on the open market in the United States. The embargo had slammed that door in his face. Once again he was working the dark side of the street, listening to anyone who had a lead, anyone who knew somebody who might have something.

Men appeared with offers: men just over from Dublin with a list of available arms, written in French; a group down from Montreal that claimed it could furnish anything short of the atomic bomb; other anonymous and swarthy gentlemen who seemed to be wearing the artillery they offered for sale under their pin-striped suits. There were Americans with contacts in South America, and South Americans with contacts in the United States. Arazi checked out every possibility.

One morning Al Robison arrived at Arazi's apartment to find him talking to two hard-looking individuals. "As I walked in," Robison recalls, "he said 'I'll see you tomorrow, Al.' I realized he was having a conversation with somebody he didn't want me to meet, so I took the hint and left. The next day he apologized. 'In my business, Al, we can't be too fussy about who we do business with. Sometimes they're not nice people. You're a nice American fellow, with a good standing in your community. I don't want you to meet some of the people I have to deal with. This is an organization that comes out of Brooklyn. I think they're called Murder, Limited.' "

The British-oriented Arazi had made an understandable error in the title of "Murder, Incorporated."

The Institute checked out a rumor Arazi had heard that the Mafia had hidden a vast stockpile of arms and ammunition under the sea in waterproof containers off the Dutch Antilles island of Curaçao. So widely believed was this story that even some law-enforcement agencies had reported that the Mafia had used its "muscle" in the waterfront unions during the war to divert part of the military cargoes bound for bases in the Caribbean for its own postwar plans. The Institute got the Jewish community on Curaçao to investigate; the alleged cupboard was bare.

None of Arazi's underworld connections came to anything—prices were too high or the offers phony.

Arazi made a quick trip to Canada and found what he wanted, available and priced right. But, as in the United States, it was impossible to get the necessary licenses and export permits. He would have to look elsewhere. A New York attorney introduced him to Count Stefan Czarnecki of the same Polish nobility with which Arazi had worked so successfully a decade before. A short elegant man in gold-rimmed spectacles, Czarnecki was in the United States as head of a helicopter development company. But he had been an arms dealer and he ticked off to Arazi the situation in each country of Europe, "where the merchandise which interested him could be bought and . . . certain sources in these countries to whom he must address himself." Arazi proposed that Czarnecki accompany him, and they made plans to meet in Europe in a few weeks.

Latin America was another possibility. Among the many full-

and part-time, professional and amateur, arms dealers Arazi had met during his brief stay in New York was an American who claimed to have interesting contacts south of the border.

Larry Ives was a robust, engaging fellow, handsome as a movie actor, the kind that plays tough guys, ex-Marines and international adventurers. He was, in fact, a familiar figure in Hollywood, in the places where the big names and the big spenders congregated; he was mentioned in the Hollywood columns. But instead of playing adventurer on celluloid, he was doing it in real life. He had been a Marine major during the war. Afterwards he had gone down to Mexico City.

Ives was a familiar type, the legitimate arms dealer with government connections; every government needs them, the middlemen to do the things it cannot do itself without becoming involved in complicated questions of foreign policy. If certain government officials managed to line their own pockets along the way, that was all part of the game. Everyone understood, certainly Arazi, who was used to playing by those rules. Through his connections in Mexico, Ives told Arazi, he could get rifles, Thompson submachine guns, ammunition, heavy .50-caliber machine guns, and 75-mm. artillery. It would be American lend-lease equipment that had been furnished to Mexico in exchange for its declaration of war against the Axis.

Arazi gave Ives a down payment of $70,000, and the American returned to Mexico City to make the deal.

Arazi was told of another American who claimed he could get airplanes in Mexico—crack P-51 "Mustang" fighters. To Arazi, nothing was too far-fetched to try—he would worry later about pilots, mechanics, armament. He asked to be introduced to the American and, for the meeting, adopted a new alias—"Mr. Green." He looked startled when the American, in turn, was introduced as "Mr. Brown." But Arazi went ahead. He commissioned "Brown" to look into the prospects.

On December 11, seventy-two members of the Sonneborn Institute attending the regular weekly meeting were told that by the end of the year the Jewish Agency needed an additional five million dollars "to meet its commitments."

"No one has that kind of money," admitted the usually sanguine Sonneborn. "We haven't it, nor even under the most optimistic conditions can we hope to raise five million dollars in two weeks." The Institute already had raised more than two million dollars during 1947. Nevertheless, he said, the Jews of Palestine had to have the money if they were not to be "left unprepared to meet this emergency. This group remains the only group on whom the Agency can call."

If it didn't have the cash, suggested Sonneborn, it had the credit. He asked that individual members join with the Agency in borrowing five million dollars "adding our names as endorsers for limited liability."

Present that day was Yehuda Arazi. Part of the emergency credit was for him. He sat next to Leonard Weisman, one of the newer members of the Institute, whom Arazi had met for the first time a few days before, in an encounter which would be fateful for both.

XVIII

THE *ATTU*

———————————

Leonard Weisman was a thirty-two-year-old former Pittsburgher who described himself as an "opportunistic trader." He had made a postwar pile in scrap metals and surplus construction machinery, bought a Southern Colonial mansion in Mount Vernon, New York, that occupied an entire blockfront in that fashionable Westchester suburb and, from a suite of offices on the busy corner of Madison Avenue and 42nd Street, ran three companies, none of which had "scrap" in its name: Materials Redistribution Corporation, Pratt Steamship Lines, and Paragon Design and Development Corporation. He also had an inactive corporation in his portfolio: Foundry Associates, Inc., originally set up to buy a foundry in Maryland.

"Glad to help," he had said, flattered to be asked, through the Institute, to buy some field telephones. It had been "no trouble at all" for him to get other communications equipment, ammunition belts, first-aid supplies. These were all things he dealt in every day; he knew the ins and outs of the war surplus business.

"It's easy for us," he had said when Albert Miller dropped into his offices and, after mentioning some mutual friends, asked about TNT. Weisman had simply flicked his intercom and asked one of his thirty employees, Samuel B. Nattis, to telephone Hugh B. Knight, chief of the chemical section of the WAA in Washington. Knight was sorry, they were fresh out of TNT, but "we have demolition blocks." The WAA was selling 6,000 tons of surplus M-3 demolition blocks at ten cents for each 2¼-pound block. No special license was required to buy it.

It was December 5, the day the State Department had announced the embargo on arms shipments to the Middle East. Arazi had walked in feeling desperate, but the ease with which Weisman operated cheered him. Demolition blocks were not tanks and artillery, but they would be useful. His American friends would find a place to store them until he got to know the ropes in the port of New York. Schalit had refused to work with him, so he would smuggle them out himself. Tel Aviv would know Arazi was still in business.

He and Weisman talked it over. They decided to buy 200 tons of demolition blocks. Weisman sent Nattis to the WAA to place the order and hand over a check for $1,777.78 drawn on Foundry Associates and was told the goods would be ready for delivery in about thirty days. Arazi was elated. This was what he had expected America to be: a land of plenty, of mass production, of telephone calls and over-the-counter service. Weisman expanded under the older man's praise and invited him to come around again. He would turn over the inactive Foundry Associates to him to use as he pleased.

Arazi spent more and more time at Weisman's offices, talking to him about the sales that were coming up, the merchandise that would be available, tantalized by the variety and quantity of surplus goods the American government was selling. One day he picked up a brochure which announced the availability of a number of aircraft carriers. He was mesmerized. He asked Weisman a dozen questions: How big were they? How much did they cost?

Weisman answered as best he could. They came in two sizes (everything in the United States did, Arazi observed); the smaller ones were called "baby flat-tops" (Arazi liked the typically American catch-phrase for so deadly a weapon); these were escort carriers, smaller, shallower and more maneuverable than the big ones. Even so, they were enormous craft. They were going very cheaply, for scrap.

"I have to have one," Arazi said quietly.

Weisman stopped talking, not sure he had heard correctly.

"I must have one," Arazi repeated.

"You must be crazy," Weisman said finally. "What are you going to do with an aircraft carrier?" He didn't bother to add the obvious—that the Palestinians didn't yet have an army, let alone a navy and an air force that would require an aircraft carrier.

But Arazi had another idea for it. His mind had been ranging ahead to the time not far off when whatever armaments he and the Haganah emissaries in Europe had managed to buy would have to be shipped to Palestine, on a split-second schedule that would get them there at the very moment they were needed—and could be safely taken ashore. This could be neither too soon—while the British were still there to confiscate them; nor too late—after the Arabs already had overrun the land.

The British would begin their withdrawal from Palestine before their announced date of departure—May 15. But they would leave by stages, withdrawing, not retreating, and not surrendering any port. As the Union Jack was struck above the British police stations on the inland hills, the Arabs could be reinforced overland from neighboring Arab countries. The Jews, fighting to hold their coastal strip, could be reinforced only by sea—but not before May 15.

On that day, precisely, enough equipment must reach the shores of Palestine to repel an Arab invasion—an Allied invasion of Normandy on a smaller scale and without the direct connections to assembly lines spewing out replacements and without superiority on the sea and in the air. On May 15 there could be no delays, no breakdowns, no mistakes, no excuses, for everything that counted would be wrapped up in one package—all the work, all the money, the time and the planning. General Eisenhower had said that if the Allies had been thrown off the Normandy beaches on D-Day, the consequences would have been "almost fatal." For Palestine they could be fatal.

A fleet of small ships might be sent from Italy. But could they arrive on time, all at once, and withstand Arab raids while they waited like sitting ducks to be unloaded in the open roadstead off Tel Aviv?

There was one kind of ship that could carry everything, and provide its own protection: an aircraft carrier.

It would be fast and large. Heavy cargo—armored cars, artillery, even tanks—could be stowed on its hangar deck; there would be elevators to bring it up and cranes to lift it over the side. There would be bays on the sides through which smaller cargo—ammunition— could be unloaded quickly. It would carry airplanes to defend it when it was most exposed, lying off Tel Aviv within range of Arab aircraft.

Arazi had not made his reputation as an arms smuggler by thinking small—or of the obvious. He pressed Weisman for more details; could he really buy a baby flat-top?

"I can *buy* one easily enough," Weisman replied, "but that is only the beginning. How are you going to get it out of the country? There are rules to comply with and we'd be watched every step of the way. There's a fifty-fifty chance the whole deal would go haywire."

Arazi smiled. That was American optimism for you; he liked odds like that. "Think about it," he said.

Weisman looked into the regulations, and so did Arazi. In the Institute they had all kinds of experts to whom an idea could be quietly passed and the ramifications fed back.

The United States government insisted that aircraft carriers which were sold as surplus be demilitarized—chiefly by having their flight decks cut down, removing the cantilevered overhang at either end. With overhangs off, there was no longer a flight deck long enough for airplanes to take off or land. But planes still could be launched from the catapult. Government regulations specified that it be removed also, but there was no reason why, once the ship left an American port, it could not be replaced.

"The planes are no problem. We can buy Grumman Wildcat F4Fs for about three hundred dollars apiece," Weisman said. Carrier planes, designed for so special a purpose, were going for less than scrap value.

One day Weisman telephoned Arazi. "I've got a baby flat-top for you."

The escort carrier U.S.S. *Attu,* named for the southwesternmost of the Aleutian Islands off Alaska, closest to Japan and the scene of a Japanese invasion during the war, could do eighteen knots. She had slid off the ways on May 27, 1944, one of thirty-four ships of the Casablanca class. Five hundred feet long, eighty feet wide, she displaced 10,200 tons fully loaded, with her thirty-two antiaircraft guns, twenty-one planes and a complement of eight hundred men. But she had never seen combat. A private investor had bought her after the war, intending to convert her to peacetime use, but he had done nothing to her. She lay moored in a Navy anchorage upstream from Norfolk, Virginia, all dressed up with no war to go to.

"I must see it for myself," Arazi had said. Weisman and "Mr. Miller" had flown down to Norfolk, put up at the best hotel, and sped out to the anchorage in a hired car.

The watchmen had been notified to allow them to come aboard. They walked the flight deck, looked over the cantilevered superstructure. Excited as small boys in the presence of so much power, the problems in their minds diminished as their enthusiasm mounted.

"We have to get this," Arazi exulted.

"It's an awfully big boat to take out of the country," said Weisman, "but if you want to, I'll try."

Back at the hotel Arazi paced the room and nodded impatiently as Weisman ticked off the possibilities. They had been told that a cargo of locomotives was to be shipped to Turkey under the Truman

Doctrine early in 1948. A heavy-lift cargo ship would be required. Someone knew the freight forwarding firm that had the inside track on the locomotive contract. The job might come their way. It might provide an excuse for the purchase of the *Attu*, its conversion to carry heavy equipment, its departure from the United States, and its appearance in the Mediterranean. Once the locomotives were discharged in Turkey, the *Attu* would be free for other cargo—and that desperate dash in mid-May. But there was a lot of expensive work to be done between now and then. Elevators would have to be strengthened, bays enlarged, the flight deck altered and probably covered to provide additional cargo space . . .

The *Attu* was bought for $125,000. "There should not be much attention paid to this one by the Navy Department, since we're buying it through private channels," Weisman explained to Nahum Bernstein, who was asked to draw up papers for the ship's transfer to Pratt Steamship Lines, another of Weisman's companies.

"Isn't it too much to handle?" Bernstein asked.

Arazi and Weisman, landlubbers no more, assured him it was not. A firm of naval architects in Washington had drawn up blueprints for the conversion; at the bottom of each sheet they had lettered in the ship's new name: S.S. *Flying W*, as in Weisman.

Weisman was soon commuting to Norfolk, where the conversion ran into immediate complications. Removing the overhangs meant that steel plates had to be acquired during a time of shortage; the twin reciprocating engines required two separate engine rooms; how far could the disguise be carried out without making the ship useless for Arazi's real purpose?

When Weisman's nerve faltered, there would be Arazi's blue eyes, over a drink, urging him on. Arazi would talk about some of his European feats, things that made the aircraft carrier seem not so big after all. He would casually mention the time he and his "boys" had smuggled an entire railroad train across a frontier. Or the time he had organized an "Allied military convoy"—drivers in Allied uniforms, an escort of military jeeps, travel orders and requisitions which allowed them to gas up at Allied petrol dumps and draw rations from the quartermaster depots—identical in every detail to the real thing except that it was operating under his command to take DPs to Italy to board ships for Palestine.

Weisman drank it all in, "like a small boy who has been watching cowboy movies and suddenly I'm riding with Tom Mix."

XIX

SCHWIMMER

Undaunted by Rabinovich's initial rebuff, Adolph Schwimmer, the young TWA flight engineer, had been dropping in at the Hotel Fourteen all through the summer and early fall of 1947 to renew his proposal that airplanes "might help." Like so many young airmen schooled by World War II, Schwimmer dreamed of running his own airline and he knew just how he would do it. He saw the future as the age of the air. With airplanes you could do everything, and quickly: move cargo, move men, soar over blockades—fight.

Rabinovich still found the idea farfetched. As he continued to point out to Schwimmer: Where would the Jews get pilots, mechanics, airstrips, weather stations, spare parts, maintenance shops? For that matter, where would they get airplanes?

Nevertheless, he was impressed by Schwimmer's persistence and he asked the Shoo-Shoo boys to check up on him in his hometown of Bridgeport, Connecticut. Their report came back: "Nothing bad, nothing good." Rabinovich mused. Schwimmer's father had a small soft-drink-bottling business, his parents were hard-working, decent people, Jewish but with no Zionist background.

Of Schwimmer's aeronautical credentials there could be no doubt; they were first rate. At thirty he was already a veteran of aviation, a licensed mechanic and pilot as well as a flight engineer. In the classic American fashion he had tinkered as a boy with flivvers, hung around the Stratford airport and, while still in high school, gone to work in the nearby Sikorsky plant, which was pioneering in the manufacture of helicopters. From there he had gone to the Glenn L. Martin plant in Baltimore, which was making the B-26 bomber, ominously known as the Martin Marauder. He had pushed on to California, where he had worked in Lockheed's flight test department at Burbank, then joined TWA in 1942, just as it won a contract with the Air Transport Command to fly military personnel and priority cargoes all over the world. As a civilian in uniform with the assimilated rank of captain, Schwimmer had ranged the world for ATC, flying to China, over the Hump, to the Middle East, including Palestine, to Africa. He had been the flight engineer on one of the airplanes that took President Roosevelt and his party to the Casablanca Conference with Churchill and de Gaulle. He had been cited for saving plane, crew and passengers when fire broke out on a flight taking General Pat Hurley to China.

After the war he had stayed with TWA as a flight engineer, a relatively new specialty at the time; Schwimmer was one of the first to be licensed by the Civil Aeronautics Administration.

Cautiously Rabinovich had begun to draw on the young American's experience and information. Messages from Ben Gurion were getting more pressing; the situation in Palestine was worsening; new approaches were vitally needed. Ben Gurion had asked Rabinovich to find out about a remote-control pilotless drone that a former Palestinian, now living in New York, had developed.

Ben Gurion was fascinated by its possibilities. Perhaps these drones, which were about one-third the size of a Piper Cub, could be filled with explosives and sent to specific targets, thereby furnishing, in some measure, the air power which he knew any modern military establishment needed but which he saw no possibility of acquiring.

Rabinovich asked Schwimmer what he thought of the idea. Schwimmer was doubtful. Drones were too limited. They were unreliable. Airplanes would be better. He urged Rabinovich to press the idea.

After that their conversations always ran about the same:

Schwimmer: "Shlomo, anything new?"

Rabinovich: "No, Al, nothing new."

By November, with partition pending at the United Nations, everything was new. Rabinovich had gone to Palestine to get new orders for the American operation. Just before leaving he asked Schwimmer to talk with a new arrival in the United States: Yehuda Arazi.

"My first take of him," Schwimmer remembers, "was that he was wearing suspenders *and* a belt. A guy even more cautious than Rabinovich." But a few minutes' talk convinced him Arazi was as willing to take chances as he. Pacing the room with his slight limp,

Arazi excitedly asked Schwimmer about the best types of airplanes to carry immigrants and cargo, what they might cost, how long it would take to acquire them, what other uses they might be put to, their range, their military possibilities. Fighter planes were ruled out for the moment by the U.S. arms embargo. But cargo planes could be exported. Schwimmer had "most of that in my head already; I'd been over a lot of the same ground with Rabinovich."

Less than two weeks later Arazi called Schwimmer to another meeting. He dug his hand into his trousers pocket and yanked out a thick roll of currency. "For immediate expenses," he said, peeling off several bills. "I'll be sending you more." It was agreed that Schwimmer would go immediately to California, the country's aviation center, to see what was available. He hurriedly quit his job with TWA and by early December was already to leave. Reviewing the hectic turn of events on the plane, he suddenly burst out laughing. "Remembering Arazi and that dog-collar wad of bills, it suddenly hit me—no wonder he wore both a belt and suspenders."

Schwimmer had asked an old friend, Reynold Selk, to go to California with him. Selk, a husky, good-looking young man, had been an Air Corps mechanic. He and Schwimmer had known each other in Connecticut and in California before the war; they had talked about operating a small airport near Lake Arrowhead someday, living the quiet life. They both laughed as they recalled it now. As soon as they had checked into the Hollywood-Roosevelt Hotel, they hired a car and drove past the Lockheed plant, where new Constellations were coming off the assembly lines. Schwimmer could see their distinctive triple tails and long sleek silver bodies glittering beneath the greenish-white fluorescent lighting of the open workshops. He walked to a corner of the field and looked over a group of "surplus" Constellations there, about fifteen of them, shabby in their peeling wartime paint, and yet the same plane that was the postwar glamour ship of the airlines. No plane since the war had so captured the public's imagination. Howard Hughes, the owner of TWA, had helped design it. Other airlines had ordered them since TWA flew the first one commercially in 1946. The Constellation could carry up to 100 persons, fly over 300 miles per hour, at 16,000 feet. Schwimmer gazed at them like a young man in love. In the next few days he found out everything he could about them. He flew East to report to Arazi. Selk had to stay behind—they had run out of money and couldn't pay their hotel bill. Taut with suspense, he walked around the lobby pretending to be an Eastern tourist out for the Christmas holidays; when he got bored with that, he went across the street to the forecourt of Grauman's Chinese Theater and studied the movie stars' footprints.

In New York Schwimmer found himself describing the magnificent potentialities of the Connies, not to Arazi, who had gone to Europe, but to Nahum Bernstein. He was learning where that wad of money had come from. Arazi was the idea man, but there were others who approved the ideas and paid the bills.

"We started in the early evening and went on until the wee hours of the morning," Bernstein remembers. "Schwimmer is a reticent man but he gives the impression of knowing his field very well, of being able to accomplish without fuss or feathers tasks which seemed to us laymen almost impossible to attempt." The Constellations could be bought, Schwimmer said, for only $15,000 apiece. Lockheed could modify them to meet postwar CAA requirements of airworthiness, but that would be expensive: $200,000 per plane. Schwimmer felt they should buy at least three Connies to make the project worthwhile, and several other smaller planes as well.

"I was stupefied," Bernstein says; "$600,000 for the three Constellations and then there were going to be ten C-46s. It would require a budget far beyond anything we could raise." He told Schwimmer that, shaking his head in disappointment. But Schwimmer demurred.

"Al said to me," recalls Bernstein, " 'You know, I think I can get together a group of mechanics and if only I can get Lockheed to give us the technical know-how and give us some space in Burbank, we can do all that work ourselves at only a fraction of the $600,000.' "

Listening to Schwimmer, Bernstein reconsidered. "Al had that quiet confidence that made you stop worrying. If that's what we wanted him to do, he'd find the means, he'd find the people and it would get done."

With a check for $45,000 in his pocket, Schwimmer went to Washington, saw Thomas Wadden at the War Assets Administration headquarters, and paid for three Connies to be delivered in California. Back in Los Angeles, he and Selk paid their hotel bill and took a small two-bedroom apartment in a motel near Lockheed Air Terminal. Schwimmer opened a bank account in his own name at the Bank of America branch near Hollywood and Highland Avenues with a $20,000 cashier's check; later he regularly deposited other checks, drawn on a number of companies, which were sent to him by Nahum Bernstein. Lockheed Air Terminal rented him an office and some space. On the office door he put up a sign: "Schwimmer Aviation Service."

Airports, in those days of early 1948, were full of young men like Schwimmer and Selk, dressed in scuffed leather flight jackets they had brought back from the war, climbing borrowed ladders to paint pretentious company names on the fuselages of airplanes they had bought at government surplus sales. As everyone kept saying, they were getting in on the ground floor of an era that would take to the sky. The government was doing everything to help them, short of filling out the papers. The usual plane they bought was a DC-3, which had cost Uncle Sam $250,000 new and which now, still new but slightly shopworn, was selling as surplus for $15,000. An ex-GI need pay only $750 down. There was nothing unusual about what Schwimmer was doing—except in the way he was spending money. Airports being gossipy places, the new operation drew its share of rumors: it was obviously thinking of bigger things than most.

The Constellations came cheap, but they were expensive to bring up to the latest civilian standards. Furthermore, Schwimmer was buying more aircraft from the WAA. He and Selk had paid for five C-46s, the Curtiss Commando, a powerful thick-bodied twin-engined transport that had been used to fly cargo over the Hump into beleaguered China during the war. The first planes already had been turned over to Schwimmer at the CalAero airport in Ontario, California, and he had asked for five more.

Schwimmer Aviation was also hiring a lot of mechanics and paying $1.95 an hour, the top rate, to ensure getting the best. The men were put briskly to work under Selk's direction modifying the big Constellations; it was a company in a hurry. The men worked willingly enough. The money was good; some of them also saw a future with the bustling young company—if it was really going to operate across the Atlantic with a base near New York and another in Rome, as they had heard. Everyone dreamed of getting in with an up-and-coming airline.

Walking through the terminal one day, Schwimmer spied a familiar figure, a lanky man with a lantern-jawed face whose keen blue eyes looked out from behind silver-rimmed glasses. It could only be Ernie Stehlik, a veteran mechanic who had been with Lockheed as a field service representative all over the world. He was "Mr. Constellation" to the TWA crews on the North Atlantic run. Ever since the plane had begun flying commercially in 1946, Stehlik had traveled around like a country doctor examining ailing airplanes. What he knew about the Constellation wasn't even in the maintenance manuals. Airplanes were his life. A bachelor, he lived in a furnished room, worked all hours. The son of Czech immigrants from Elk Creek, Nebraska, he had been in aviation from the early barnstorming days.

Schwimmer broke into one of his rare grins and hailed Stehlik. "Howdy," Stehlik replied. He remembered Schwimmer as a young fellow around TWA.

Schwimmer, a laconic type himself, blurted out, "How would you like to come to work for me?"

"What for?" asked Stehlik.

"We're starting an airline," Schwimmer said, "going to fly refugees out of Europe." He waved toward the field. "We've got those Connies over there; gonna modify them and use them for transport."

Stehlik squinted at the younger man: "That's kinda down my line. I know a few things about them."

On a quick trip to New York, Schwimmer took on another man, short, fat, comical Willie Sosnow from Brooklyn. Sosnow was an expert flight engineer and mechanic. He had seen Schwimmer around when both were working for TWA, but he had taken him for a German and prudently kept away. A mutual friend had told him that Schwimmer was starting an airline; overcoming his reluctance, Sosnow looked up "the Dutchman." When he heard what Schwimmer was up to, he joined, even though Schwimmer could promise him only expense money. As Sosnow so often said, "When you grow up in Brooklyn, you know you're a Jew."

On the way west he and Schwimmer stopped at Walnut Ridge, Arkansas, to look at some airplanes. Sosnow had heard about the Connies and the C-46s, but he wasn't prepared for the plane Schwimmer examined at the WAA surplus depot in Walnut Ridge. It was a P-51 fighter, the North American Mustang, considered the "perfect pursuit plane." It flew at 437 miles per hour, went as high as 41,000 feet, and carried four to six 50-mm. machine guns or a ton of bombs; it was the plane that had delivered the death blow in the air to the German Luftwaffe and had the added advantage of a cruising range of 2,030 miles. "Just looking," responded Schwimmer to Sosnow's look of inquiry as they flew on to Los Angeles.

From New York Schwimmer had brought back the names of

two more prospects for Schwimmer Aviation. They were pilots; it was time to start thinking of flight crews. Schwimmer had known of one of them, Sam Lewis, as a TWA captain during the ATC days and as one of the first pilots to qualify on Constellations after the war. The second name, Leo Gardner, was new to Schwimmer, but he knew that Gardner had been a civilian flight instructor and a wartime ATC ferry pilot delivering bombers overseas.

The two men, both of them based in Los Angeles, had drafted a letter proposing an airline to fly DPs out of Europe; they had sent it through the channels of a philanthropic organization—apparently to nowhere. They had never received an answer. Lewis, on a New York layover, had gone looking for it and, going from office to office, had met someone who had passed on his name and Gardner's to the Hotel Fourteen.

Schwimmer could understand Lewis and Gardner's dream of starting an airline; it was one of the things that had kept him coming back to Rabinovich during those eight long discouraging months. But would they be willing to forgo their own dream to share his? He spent an evening with the two of them at Lewis's home. "You're a Connie man," he said to Lewis. "We have three Connies—our own."

Gardner, an excitable young man, bored with his family's jewelry and loan business, listened to Schwimmer describe plans to airlift refugees and cargo and dreamed: Six months or so and this job will be done and we'll have something out of which could come an airline. Both men agreed to come in. Afterward, Lewis would recall, "The main thing was the Connies. They were beauties." To Gardner it was, Now or never, put up or shut up.

Selk pushed ahead the work on the Connies. The five C-46s were still at the CalAero airport. They had been sold "as is"—and they had been sitting out in the weather for a long time. One of the mechanics, Robert Frieburg, had been sent to Ontario to get them into shape. He rubbed them down with penetrating oil, day after day, to remove the rust and stop corrosion. As soon as they were flyable, Lewis and Gardner would ferry them to Burbank. The airline they all had dreamed about was shaping up.

YAKUM PURKAN

Arazi had slipped out of New York late in December, met Count Czarnecki and, with him, made a quick tour of Czarnecki's European sources. French arms dealers would sell artillery and small Renault tanks; the Swiss would sell some of their excellent antiaircraft guns; in Belgium, Sweden and even Spain arms were available. There was one catch—everyone insisted the transaction be handled indirectly, through a neutral "cover" country, willing to lend its name as the buyer of record. Arazi felt he could handle that; he had bought Polish arms before the war on the same basis through the Central American republic of Nicaragua. One of the tools of his trade which he still held was a "diplomatic" passport from that country.

Arazi went on to Italy, where he had operated before, to look for a base for Schwimmer's airplanes. Italy was the obvious midway point for the airborne supply operation he was envisaging and, furthermore, the Italians were sympathetic. Both the government and ordinary civilians had demonstrated their cordiality in their quiet support of illegal immigration. Arazi found an airfield available at Castiglione del Lago near Perugia, owned by Luigi Ambrosini, who had manufactured airplanes for Mussolini's air force but was now engaged in the more peaceful production of accordions.

Traveling through Italy, Arazi stopped off at one of his old haunts, a transit camp for DPs at Magenta, west of Milan. The camp was still crowded with new streams of refugees fleeing postwar outbreaks of anti-Semitism in Poland, Hungary and Slovakia. Beneath its bustling activity it also sheltered Haganah's principal arms cache in Europe—forty tons of small arms and ammunition which Arazi, along with members of the Jewish Brigade, the all-Palestinian unit that had served with the British Army during World War II, had collected and secreted in small caches in France and Italy.

The arms were now being recovered from their hiding places and smuggled into Magenta, where a group of hand-picked DPs was packing them in the Alper-Schalit "American manner," hidden in the disemboweled innards of "used industrial machinery." An old colleague of Arazi's in underground Haganah operations, Eliahu Sacharov, had been sent from Palestine to direct the project. Sacharov had good reason to respect the Alper-Schalit techniques; he had been in charge of "receiving" their shipments in Haifa. They were "gigantic," he would report to his superiors, "without precedence in the undercover and secret shipments of Haganah," yet so well camouflaged he was able to shepherd them without detection through British customs. He hoped to do the same with the arms at Magenta.

As weapons went, they were a motley assortment—British, German and Italian rifles, tricky Sten submachine guns which had been dropped to partisans, half a million rounds of ammunition—but if they got to Palestine quickly enough, they would make a difference against the waves of Arab terrorism sweeping the country. No other arms were coming in from anywhere.

Forty tons could arm a holding operation until Arazi and other Haganah agents arranged for real help.

Sacharov oversaw the packing in neatly cut crates with destinations precisely hand-lettered to resemble the stenciling of the New York shipments; he filled out shipping documents as meticuously as Schalit. A Danish ship would carry the shipment of "used industrial machinery" from Genoa to Haifa; the arms should be in Palestine by early January. Sacharov, carrying the consignment documents with him, flew triumphantly back to Palestine to count the days until the ship arrived.

Arazi also went on to Tel Aviv, where he was invited to sit in on Ben Gurion's meetings with the Haganah's high command as they reviewed the intensive search for armaments which Ben Gurion had inaugurated two months before.

Ben Gurion had received a coded message from Europe: The only country ready and willing to sell the Jews arms was Czechoslovakia, that small highly industrialized nation still struggling to maintain its independence as a Westernized democracy in the center of a Europe whose fulcrum had shifted east.

The possibility of buying arms in Czechoslovakia had come to Ben Gurion during a gloomy tour of Jerusalem's inadequate defenses in the fall of 1947. He had fallen to talking with the second-in-com-

mand, Michael Felix, a Czech-born engineer, who told him that his
brother Otto, a lawyer, had made an interesting discovery during a
recent trip to Czechoslovakia. He had found that many of his old
school friends from Charles University were now important government officials; some were in the Czech ministry of defense, a few were
even generals. The Czech arms industry was one of the best in
Europe. The Skoda works in Pilsen made artillery and tanks; the
Czechoslovak Arms Factory at Brno produced rifles and machine
guns. The arms were readily available, for the German occupation
had impressed Czech heavy industry into its service. Since the war the
Czechs had been selling surplus arms to any reputable customer, including the Arabs. Why not the Palestinian Jews?

Ben Gurion thought for a moment, then looked up at Felix from
under his heavy eyebrows. "Is your brother religious?" Felix shook
his head no. Ben Gurion grinned at his bewilderment. "Then let him
come to see me at my home on Yom Kippur."

Yom Kippur, the day of atonement, was the most sacred holiday
in the Jewish religion and the one day on which Ben Gurion was sure
of being left alone.

A few weeks later Otto Felix returned to Prague to find Czechoslovakia in the throes of an internal revolution as the Communists
consolidated their power. Avoiding the uneasy top echelon of government, he concentrated on officials of the second rank—generals,
factory managers and deputy directors of government bureaus who
still had a measure of autonomy.

By December he had negotiated the Jewish Agency's first sizable
purchase of arms: 4,300 rifles, 200 medium machine guns, and ammunition. And there was a promise of more.

There remained the ever-present haunting question of how to
get the arms to Palestine from a landlocked country in the middle of
Europe.

Arazi made his report to the men assembled in Tel Aviv. He
warned them that the United States was unlikely to lift its arms
embargo before May 15—if then. However, he hoped to buy substantial quantities of heavy equipment in Mexico, and he had turned
up some promising new sources in Western Europe with Czarnecki.
Most important, he had a plan for transporting the arms to Palestine,
a problem which often proved more intractable than obtaining them.

There were raised eyebrows when Arazi mentioned his most
cherished project, the *Attu*. Did he expect to sail an aircraft carrier up

the Yarkon River, through Tel Aviv? one colleague facetiously inquired. But the men were excited by his description of Schwimmer's Constellations, "the big birds," as Arazi called them.

The Constellations would not have to wait for British ports to be vacated on May 15. They could fly *over* the Royal Navy blockade to secret airstrips inside Palestine, each one carrying ten tons of supplies on each trip. The American Air Transport Command, in which Schwimmer had served during World War II, had proved it could be done. China had been kept alive by air, over the Hump. Russia had received fighting planes and other supplies by air, via the Arctic. Britain had gotten bombers and fighters across the North Atlantic. Men and goods had been flown to all theaters of the war: across Africa, to the Middle East, down the chain of islands in the Pacific . . .

There were young men in Haganah who had served with the Allied air forces during the war; Ben Gurion put several of them to work on plans for the airborne supply operation. It would be called "Yakum Purkan," from an ancient Aramaic prayer: *"Yakum purkan min shemaya . . ."* (Salvation would be forthcoming from heaven). Or, in its present anxious context: Delivery would come from the skies.

XXI

S.S. *EXECUTOR*

S lavin cabled Alper and Schalit to send him explosives. He hadn't
yet been able to start making his own with the processes and
formulas he had learned in the Chemists' Club Library from Grageroff. He needed more smokeless powder for the ammunition and
small mortars he was manufacturing. And he needed TNT.

Haganah had devised an ingenious means of making up for its
lack of artillery. Haganah sappers, carrying TNT on their backs,
made their way right up to enemy positions and planted it by hand. It
was formidably dangerous and the results often were unsatisfactory,
but it was the only makeshift available to them.

For some time Schalit had been accumulating stockpiles of smokeless powder piecemeal. A Texas oil firm contributed some; so did
several mining and construction companies in Iowa and Illinois; Sam
Sterling, the Denver attorney, stepped up his family tours of the
West's sporting goods stores. To collect these assorted offerings Schalit
employed the most direct and uncomplicated means he could think
of—he sent two young men, whom he recently had taken on as
assistants, to pick them up in a rented car.

Schalit's new assistants, who were even younger than he, were
both dark, both slight, both silent and seemed to have slipped out of
some Palestinian desert onto the sidewalks of New York. They were
known as Moosik-and-Shapik or Shapik-and-Moosik, their nicknames
being as interchangeable as their looks. The pair got around so
widely, usually in the dead of night, to pick up a package or pass on a
message, that there were people all over America who were never
sure whether they had dealt with one man or two or which was
which. Crisscrossing the country on their mysterious errands, Moosik-
Shapik tested several makes of rented cars and finally settled on a

Cadillac, thereby bestowing on it a new kind of testimonial: It was the only automobile that could carry two tons of gunpowder without betraying its heavy load to the police.

Schalit finally found a major source of explosives in Mexico. The Mexican department of national defense operated a modern smokeless powder plant on license from Du Pont. Friends in Mexico City had found someone at the top who was willing to meet the young man from New York. Schalit said he could use five and a half tons of smokeless powder, which would come to 210,000 pesos ($42,000) at the official price. The government official said he could use 15 per cent of the total, or an additional 41,500 pesos ($8,200) as his *mordida* —bite. "A pretty cheap deal for 15 per cent," Schalit cabled Slavin. The code word for the powder was "cornflakes."

Mexican Army trucks delivered the merchandise to a warehouse Schalit had rented in the industrial outskirts of Mexico City. The delivery had been carefully planned by Schalit and each step was executed with military precision. As soon as a truck had finished unloading, it sped away; the government official had guaranteed only one hour's safety from interference by local police. Schalit was waiting in the shadows with two young Mexicans. They began slapping blue labels marked *"fertilizantes"*—fertilizers—on each canister of smokeless powder. As the last Army truck vanished, the first of five trailer trucks drove in and began loading the canisters. Their drivers, vouched for by Mexican friends, headed for a dairy farm in the hills outside Mexico City owned by a sympathizer who had guaranteed peace and quiet—and an empty farm. Waiting at the farm was David Glassman, a Yale student and former Navy officer who had been working in the Bronx warehouse. He had gone ahead with several young assistants, a portable welding machine and a truckload of fifty-five-gallon drums.

Schalit had learned that a common export from the Mexican Gulf port of Tampico was refractory clay, which resembled smokeless powder. He had bought one gray-enameled drumful from a refractory clay plant and had had stencils made to duplicate the markings. But then he had run into a serious snag; metal drums were in short supply and he was not able to buy any. Urgent inquiries turned up a sympathizer in Los Angeles who was willing to give him secondhand gasoline drums which were reasonably similar to those customarily used for refractory clay. These were sent to a manufacturer of metal beds—another sympathizer—to be sprayed with gray enamel and stenciled. Arriving to supervise the operation,

Schalit's eye caught a familiar name; the drums had come originally from Rudolf Sonneborn's chemical firm.

At the farm Glassman and his helpers worked silently and rapidly; only a few hours remained before sundown when the trucks would have to move on.

They wrapped each canister of powder in asbestos before putting it into a drum. Then they filled the empty space with refractory clay. Glassman spot-welded the rim that held down each drum's lid. Schalit had decided on spot-welding so that a little telltale refractory clay could escape.

At dusk the trucks roared out, with Schalit, Glassman and the two Mexican assistants leading and bringing up the rear in jeeps. They took back roads, raising clouds of dust, slowing down through villages, in which faint lights gleamed through the glassless windows of thatched-roof houses, and grinning brown children stood in the doorways and stared round-eyed as the convoy clattered past. The trucks went on. In the villages the children disappeared and were replaced by pie dogs that yelped alongside the wheels; the sun rose menacingly, and the children came out into the doorways again, grinning.

The trucks drove all that day, making only the most necessary stops, once doubling back when they came to a bridge that couldn't carry their weight. (At just about the same time, another group of trucks was twisting down the hills of northern Italy carrying the Italian arms from Magenta to Genoa.) At dusk they reached Tampico, where the drums were loaded onto railway cars to be taken to the docks.

Schalit flourished what appeared to be a genuine invoice from Refractaria de Mexico, S.A., for 132 drums of refractory clay, total cost 4,125.66 pesos ($825), to be shipped to the Union Portland Cement Co., Ltd., Capetown, Union of South Africa. Since few ships for Capetown called at Tampico the cargo would have to be transshipped; accordingly it was manifested for the foreign trade zone in the port of New York. Schalit handed over the invoice to a customs official who had been primed in advance. The man pounded a rubber stamp on 68.08 pesos' ($13.61) worth of tax stamps and the shipment was licensed for export.

As soon as the ship had sailed, Schalit and his three aides got into one of the jeeps and raced north for the border. In Brownsville, Texas, they celebrated by buying new clothes, and that evening in Houston Schalit and Glassman boarded a plane for New York.

The Institute, that cornucopia of goods and service, turned up another important source of explosives in the portly, garrulous person of a coal broker from Pottsville, Pennsylvania, named Abe Cramer, who agreed to buy thirty tons of TNT from the Philadelphia office of the War Assets Administration, ostensibly to use in strip mining.

Alper jubilantly notified Slavin of the lucky find and asked how to pack and ship it; with Schalit in Mexico, the job would fall to him.

Slavin, as usual, replied precisely and in detail. He wanted the WAA's small one-pound tins of TNT to be packed in boxes filled with sawdust; these boxes were to be put in fifty-gallon steel drums and the drums filled with water; finally, the sealed drums were to be bolted into large wooden crates bearing the usual label of "Used Industrial Machinery."

Alper pondered the instructions; they would be complicated and time-consuming to execute and time was short. The next ship heading for Palestine was the American Export Lines' S.S. *Executor*, scheduled to leave New York on January 3. Alper already had space reserved on it. If the TNT missed that ship, no telling how long it would have to wait for space on another; not many ships were stopping in the troubled waters of Palestine these days. Daily cables from Tel Aviv urged him to make the sailing at all costs.

Slavin's elaborate packing plan might have been possible at the Bronx warehouse, where there were equipment and experienced personnel. But Alper did not want to risk taking TNT to the warehouse, in view of the new arms embargo. If discovered, it could jeopardize the other large shipment he was getting ready to go out January 3 on the S.S. *Executor:* machinery (including two Waring blenders for destroying secret messages); brass stripping (used in making cartridges) and several hundred thousand blasting and primer caps (for detonating the TNT). Rushed, jittery and more concerned with the security of the warehouse and its contents than anything else, Alper considered what to do.

He knew that TNT was stable material. The Army had demonstrated that it would not explode even if burned in an open fire; it could be dropped or chopped up into pieces without danger; only a very sharp impact, usually with a blasting cap, would detonate it. Slavin's elaborate safety precautions seemed—well, typically Slavin. What was good enough for the United States Army should be good enough, Alper reasoned.

Besides, it was snowing. It had started Christmas night; by

December 27 a record twenty-six inches had fallen and the entire metropolitan area was smothered in one of the worst blizzards in history. The snow could snafu everything. To make the *Executor* sailing, Alper had to move fast.

He had some strong wooden cases prefabricated at the Bronx warehouse and moved to a vacant summer camp, Camp Galil near Pipersville in Bucks County, which he had arranged to use for twenty-four hours. He and his warehouse foreman, six-foot three-inch Big Moe Wolfson, went up with half a dozen young men from a Zionist training camp. A trucker with a permit for explosives was hired to haul the TNT from the WAA depot to Camp Galil. As soon as the trucks arrived, their cargo of wooden crates, each one containing five one-pound tins of TNT, was rolled off on conveyors—steel rollers on a narrow track which Alper and Wolfson had brought with them to speed the job. The trucks pulled out and the boys went to work painting the boxes black, with big splashing strokes, to cover the TNT markings. Phil and Big Moe stacked them into the large prefabricated crates from the warehouse, fifty to a crate, and closed them with steel strapping. It was hard, heavy work in the biting cold, but by the end of the day everything was wrapped up tight; twenty-six crates lay hidden among the hay in the barn. Next morning other trucks would load them with winches and haul them to the dock—Pier F in Jersey City.

Driving back to New York, Alper's old 1936 Chevy—the car he had persuaded Slavin to buy—skidded on the icy roads; it was snowing again.

By morning Alper had run into a new embargo. All but essential traffic was barred in New York City. Even trucks needed special permits to be on the road. The Hoffman Trucking Company, which usually made dockside deliveries for Alper, doubted that its trucks could get through, either to pick up the crates in Bucks County or to take the large shipment, ready and waiting in the Bronx warehouse, to the Jersey City dock.

Alper telephoned Bob Keller to bring heavy duty tire chains for the trucks to the Bronx warehouse. He called attorney Nahum Bernstein, who arranged to get special permission for the trucks to travel. The New York police teletype would say they were carrying medical supplies. The snow stopped. Reluctantly, the trucker agreed to make the trip. Alper was a good customer.

It was 2:30 P.M. on December 29 by the time the three trucks detailed to Pennsylvania reached Pipersville and, as instructed, went to the Pipersville Inn. There they were met by Big Moe, who guided them along Route 611 two miles east of Easton, where they turned off on a narrow country road; there a snowplow attached to a jeep was waiting to clear the road ahead of them. Even so, it was slow going; they had to ford a twenty-five-foot brook. It was 11 P.M. by the time all of the heavy crates had been loaded. Trucks and crew spent the night in Pipersville and next day drove on to Pier F in Jersey City.

Phil was there waiting. With a sigh of weariness and relief he watched the crates being unloaded and set down beside the others which already had arrived from the Bronx warehouse. He checked them off on his list. All seventy-seven crates were marked "Used Industrial Machinery." The twenty-six crates of TNT carried the stenciled markings: from the Oved Trading Company to Haboreg, Ltd., of Tel Aviv. The other fifty-one crates were stenciled: from the Mar-Tech Trading Company of New York to the Palestine Glass Works in Haifa. All were standing in the open; they wouldn't be loaded onto the ship for two or three days, but they were there, ready to go. Phil blew on his icy fingers, rammed on his gloves and left.

Elie Schalit was relieved as he sloshed through the snow on lower Broadway. The 132 drums of "refractory clay" had arrived from Mexico in the port of New York's free zone on Staten Island. He had routinely changed their destination from Capetown, South Africa, to Palestine and added a rotary kiln to the shipment, a last-minute idea he was rather proud of. The consignee now was the Palestine Portland Cement Works, "Nesher," Ltd., Tel Aviv. A commercial freight forwarder luckily had found space for the shipment aboard one of the few ships bound for Palestine, and Schalit had just picked up the bill of lading.

It was No. 56, issued by the American Export Lines for the next sailing, on January 3, of its freighter S.S. *Executor*.

XXII

PIER F

The longshoremen, bundled into heavy jackets and thick gloves, watched the wooden case as it rose toward the cargo deck of the S.S. *Executor*. They cursed the winch operator for his slowness. They cursed the cold, the slippery streets, the stalled subways and Saturday work. It was January 3, 1948, on Pier F in Jersey City.

The wooden case split open as it swayed in the wind. The black box tumbled onto the pier. The longshoremen called the cooper and he discovered that the black box contained tins of TNT.

The police came and customs and the Coast Guard. After consulting with the port captain, they pried open more of the crates on Pier F destined for Palestine. Twenty-six of them contained TNT; some of the others contained "used industrial machinery," but they appeared to be machines used in the manufacture of ammunition. The Coast Guard, the Jersey City police, and customs decided that the case was out of their jurisdiction and notified the FBI. A Jersey City police captain told the reporters that there was enough TNT on Pier F to "blow Jersey City to bits." And then he had corrected himself: "Five Jersey Cities."

A young man watched the excitement and then slipped into the Terminal Restaurant to make a phone call. "Phil?" he said. "I'm coming right back. The stuff is all over the pier."

Phil Alper put down the phone and massaged his forehead. There were, at most, four hours before the FBI—or would it be only the New York police?—came knocking at the door of the 112th Street apartment. By then he would have to be gone and so would every scrap of paper in the place. He looked around at the stacks of papers piled on the makeshift shelves, on the bed, even on the radiator.

As soon as Keller arrived, they began calling trusted friends to come and help. They took turns telephoning and packing, piling papers into cardboard cartons, tying them into bundles, rifling drawers, desks, cupboards for every scrap. As friends arrived, some with cars despite icy roads and the ban on nonessential driving, they trundled the bulky packages out, instructing their friends to take them home and hide them, anywhere, just get them out of sight.

Keller telephoned his wife, who was visiting a girl friend, and told her to wait for him there; he would see her later. As he worked, Alper's eyes lit on something else. My God, he thought, Ekdahl's machine gun. One of the prototypes still remained in the apartment. With a dexterity he didn't know he possessed, Alper dismantled it, put the parts in a suitcase and gave it to Keller. Friends came and went. The stacks of papers diminished. It was getting late; Alper decided to leave. Everything was out of the apartment but a pile of large rolled blueprints, the drawings for the tooling for Ekdahl's gun.

Max Brown, the Canadian machinist who had worked on the gun in Industrial Research Laboratories in Toronto and then come to New York, was in the apartment now, struggling to reroll the blueprints more tightly, one inside the other. They seemed to have a life of their own. Slippery and coiled like springs, they would unwind with a buzz and clatter to the floor.

Someone rang the doorbell. Alper's landlady, the Palestinian Mrs. Pines from whom he sublet his two rooms, moved to answer it. Brown hissed at her. "No one's at home." Whoever it was began pounding on the door. Brown rushed to the entrance hall and violently shook his head at the woman. She smiled, nodded her comprehension and shouted in broken English, "No one is at home."

Desperate now, Brown went to a window and looked out. It opened on a side of the building which overlooked the roof of the next building three stories below. Anything was better than leaving the blueprints here. Max lunged back into the living room, gathered up an armful and flung them out, watching anxiously as they rolled to a stop on the roof below. The knocking on the door had stopped. He waited awhile, then picked up the remaining rolls and tiptoed down the stairs, not daring to use the elevator. He would think of some way to retrieve the other blueprints later.

From the apartment, Alper headed alone to Times Square, that seedy crossroads of the world where he could lose himself in the eddying mass of humanity. From a telephone booth he called Rabinovich at the Hotel Fourteen; Rabinovich told him to keep moving and keep in touch. Alper ate a Nedick's hot dog, watched some sailors play a pinball machine, telephoned Rabinovich, went to the movies, telephoned Rabinovich again and kept on the move. He spent three nights sleeping in as many Times Square hotels, eating in cafeterias, reading the newspapers, which were headlining the discovery of the TNT, and telephoning Rabinovich. On the third day he was told to go to the apartment of Rusty Jarcho, who was one of the three full-time employees of the Sonneborn Institute. After one night at Jarcho's he was ordered to proceed to Washington, where he would meet Elie Schalit. From there they would, if necessary, be evacuated, via Mexico, to Palestine.

Alper and Schalit met in a hotel near Union Station in Washington, where Schalit had been hiding from the police and sweating out the *Executor*'s postponed departure. The sailing had been delayed while a thorough inspection of the ship's cargo was made; everything on board was unloaded and then loaded back on again. No connection had been made between Schalit's shipment and Alper's TNT. The *Executor* had finally sailed at 8:15 P.M. on January 6, carrying in its hold the 132 drums of "refractory clay."

Alper and Schalit silently shook hands on that bit of good news and fell to comparing notes and reading the newspapers, where every development in the investigation of the TNT, every theory, speculation and surmise, was being reported in voluminous detail.

It was now four days since the TNT had fallen onto Pier F, and the police, FBI and news reporters were still baffled.

All that trucker William A. Hoffman could tell them was that he hadn't known he was hauling explosives; that the crates were expertly packed, as usual; and that Alper was a good customer—Hoffman had been hauling two or three convoys a month for him for the past year, all perfectly legitimate as far as he knew.

The seventy-seven suspicious crates had been quickly traced, through the truckman, to the Bronx warehouse. There police had found stencils for the Oved Trading Company and the Mar-Tech Trading Company which matched the markings on the crates. They also had found Phil Alper's name and 112th Street address rubber-stamped on some mail, and a stack of business cards of the Machinery Processing and Converting Company with the address 256 West 38th Street. But checking out these leads they had run into one dead end after another.

New York police, accompanied by a fireman and an official of

U.S. Customs, had made a thorough search of the Bronx warehouse; it contained a strange and confusing inventory.

On the first floor were seven barrels of paraformaldehyde, twenty drums of sulphuric acid, nine large packing cases of machinery including two washing machines, a case of power-panel safety switches, a case of machine gears, two cases of machine motors, one of fluorescent bulbs and one of sewer piping.

On the second floor were a .30-caliber cartridge-loading machine, three boxes of radio transmitting units, two boxes of other radio equipment, seven boxes of machine motors and two cases of metal wardrobe lockers.

On the third floor were a .50-caliber cartridge-loading machine and five hand trucks loaded with heavy metal blocks which appeared to be lead "pigs" but might, police speculated, be another metal which could be melted down into bullets.

A couple of old tables with makeshift drawers and some tool cribs furnished the office; old ropes and dusty cartons littered the floors.

While the policemen were searching, three telephone calls came in for "Phil," with the query, "Anything doing?" Each time the police asked who was calling, the caller hung up.

Two patrolmen and a fireman had been posted on round-the-clock watch, but no one had come to the warehouse.

At Alper's apartment on 112th Street they had found only the cleaning woman, an elderly Negro lady named Edna who had come for her weekly bout with the paper-littered office, letting herself in with her own key. She had no idea where Alper was. In the basement? She chuckled. Did he have a girl friend? Edna raised her eyes to heaven: "Oh no, I never saw him with girls."

On a later visit police had found Pines, who denied knowing anything about Alper or the TNT. Alper sublet two rooms from him, Pines acknowledged, but he seldom saw him; the young engineer hadn't been in the apartment since January 3. Why had one of the stencils found in the Bronx warehouse carried the marking "Pines, Tel Aviv"? Perhaps it was for two washing machines he had purchased to send to his home in Palestine, opined Pines. The police checked. Sure enough, the warehouse contained two Bendix washing machines.

At the 256 West 38th Street address, listed on the business cards of the Machinery Processing and Converting Company, all the FBI could learn was that packages arriving there addressed to the machinery company were sent on to the Bronx warehouse. The agents were right back where they had started from. The Machinery Processing and Converting Company had no office in the building and was not even listed on its directory. A firm that was listed was the New England Plastics and Novelty Company, where the manager admitted that MPCC occasionally used his office as a mail drop; beyond that he knew nothing. His boss, Harry Levine, was in London.

Checking the names stenciled on the crates of TNT, it had developed that the Oved Trading Company was registered to someone with the tongue-twisting name of Awadji Yoselevitch. The Mar-Tech Trading Company was registered to one Nahaman Yordeni. Both men were listed as living at 334 Rugby Road, Brooklyn, but neither was at that address; they had returned to Palestine three months before. The registrations, according to County Court records, had been made by a Jack Horowitz of 4522 Beach 45th Street, Brooklyn. That turned out to be a large private residence presently occupied by eighteen youngsters who, all talking at once, explained that they were members of a cooperative, training to go to Palestine. Yes, Jack Horowitz had been there, they said, but he had left a week ago.

Tracking down the nominal lessee of the warehouse, Jules Chender, police learned from his parents that he was in France. In Paris, Chender voluntarily appeared at the United States Embassy and made a sworn statement denying all knowledge of the TNT.

While the police kept watch over the warehouse, searched for Alper, and tried to turn up a clue which wouldn't evaporate on closer examination, the base of operations for Machinery Processing quietly moved downtown. Jerry Schweitzer, first Slavin's and then Alper's faithful secretary, had received a telephone call at her Bronx home instructing her to stay away from 112th Street; to report for work instead to a fashionable address on East 67th Street, the apartment of attorney Nahum Bernstein. There she was trying to keep track of the shipments that already had gone out, the purchases on their way in, and whatever else was not directly affected by the seizures on the dock and the guard at the warehouse. Her job was complicated by a lack of mail; it was still going to West 38th Street. One day about noon Jerry went downtown and waited across the street from the building; she hoped to intercept one of the secretaries at Harry Levine's New England Plastics and Novelty Company from whom she had picked up mail before. As the lunch-hour rush began, there among the stream of people leaving the building was the girl. Jerry motioned to her discreetly. The girl saw her out of the corner of her eye, turned on her heel and sped off in the opposite direction. Jerry followed her for three blocks, but the girl obviously was trying to elude her. "She was scared to death," Jerry reported with a shrug back at 67th Street.

Bob Keller also had surfaced. After hiding out in obscure hotels for several days, he and his wife had rented an apartment. Nobody seemed to be looking for them; apparently Keller's name had not turned up among the papers at the warehouse. His only real embarrassment had been the machine gun that Alper had stuffed into a suitcase and handed to him. Keller had solved that by asking his wife's girl friend, Ricky Hefterman, to hide it under her bed. Now he was trying to reassemble the office records that had been so hurriedly dispersed from the 112th Street apartment. It was hard to remember what had gone where, and Keller was making long and arduous subway trips to the far reaches of Brooklyn, the Bronx and Queens.

Max Brown had made a cautious trip back to 112th Street late Saturday night to see if he could retrieve the blueprints he had thrown onto the roof of the building next door during the afternoon. Two men were standing in a doorway across the street from Alper's apartment house, so he went away. Next morning he drove by with a friend; the two men—or perhaps another pair—were still there. On Monday Brown and his friend came by again, driving slowly and this time getting up the courage to peer closely at the men. There they were, huddled in a doorway for shelter from the wind blowing off the Hudson River. "They can't be from the FBI," exclaimed Brown. "The FBI would be sitting in a car." Boldly he got out, entered the building next to Alper's, went to the roof, gathered up the blueprints and came down. He was about to stride out the door when he saw his friend talking to the two men. He darted back and was looking about wildly for a new hiding place for the blueprints when he heard the sound of laughter outside. He ventured a peek and was loudly hailed by all three. The two "agents," it turned out, were Shoo-Shoo boys, graduates of Nahum Bernstein's intelligence school, sent by Rabinovich to keep an eye on Alper's callers.

On January 7 the seventy-seven seized crates were moved from their mooring in Raritan Bay to the Naval Munitions Depot at Earle, New Jersey, not far from Asbury Park; on a clear day Zimel Resnick probably could have seen them from the top of his ferris wheel.

The FBI announced that there were no new developments in the case. Everyone else seemed to be losing interest.

The Coast Guard, pointing out that none of *its* regulations had been violated, had withdrawn the Coast Guard vessel that had convoyed the suspect crates to Raritan Bay.

An explosives expert at a government arsenal near New York pooh-poohed press reports that the TNT could have blown up Jersey City or five Jersey Cities. If somehow it had been detonated, an unlikely prospect without blasting caps, it might, he conceded, have blown up the ship, damaged the adjacent pier and broken some windows in the harbor.

A friend of Nahum Bernstein's who paid a discreet call on Mayor William O'Dwyer was told that the New York police had very little interest in the case; after all, the TNT had been found in New Jersey.

By now, only a lone fireman remained on guard at the Bronx warehouse, waiting to serve a summons for unlicensed storage of sulphuric acid. No other violations of New York law had been discovered; it was not illegal to store washing machines or even munitions-making machinery in a warehouse.

In New Jersey law enforcement agencies were having a hard time finding a possible law violation. The only one they could pin down for sure was a violation of U.S. Customs regulations regarding the labeling of cargo.

The more serious charge of violating the United States Middle East arms embargo was a Federal offense and would have to be looked into by the FBI.

Meanwhile there was no one to charge. None of the law enforcement agencies had made an arrest.

The newspapers began referring in their headlines to the "TNT Mystery." By January 8, with no new developments and no arrests, the story had disappeared from the front pages.

That night Alper and Schalit, still waiting in Washington for further orders, were told to leave for Mexico. More explosives had been found.

XXIII

LOWY'S FARM

Huey Pond, a self-employed truck driver from Syracuse, New York, pulled into Asbury Park about 8 P.M. on Wednesday, January 8, with a load he'd picked up that afternoon at the Seneca Ordnance Depot at Romulus, New York. Following instructions, he went to a warehouse at 916 Langford Street to get further directions. He was annoyed to find that the owner of the warehouse, Charles Lowy, an Asbury Park moving man, was not there, only a young night watchman who knew nothing about Pond's instructions. It was cold and late; Pond stamped his half-numb feet, paced up and down outside the darkened building, finally parked his truck across the street and went to a diner for a hot cup of coffee and a bite to eat. Returning to the warehouse, he found the young night watchman still alone, and decided to kill an hour or two at a movie. At midnight he returned to his truck. Two men were waiting for him, but neither of them was Lowy. Lowy was already in jail. The two men were Asbury Park police chief Leroy B. Holloway and a detective. They knew where Pond was supposed to take his cargo and they now led him there—to a farm belonging to Lowy on Martin Road, near Glendola in Wall township. At the farm the policemen inspected the contents of Pond's truck and found 34,020 pounds of M-3 demolition blocks. They were not surprised. Already at the farm were two truckloads of the explosive, which had been delivered that afternoon by the Genesee Trucking Company, for whom Pond was working under contract that day.

Asbury Park's FM radio station WJLK had carried the first report of the sensational find at 5 P.M. and had been broadcasting hourly bulletins. An anonymous telephone tip that there was "unusual activity" at the Lowy farm had led New Jersey State Police to investigate. They had found the first two trucks unloading their cargo of demolition blocks. Tracing back the explosives to the Seneca Ordnance Depot and from there to the WAA's Customer Service Center on Long Island, police had ascertained that two hundred tons of the M-3 demolition blocks had been ordered on December 5 by Foundry Associates, a New York firm. By the time Pond's truck had been taken into custody, sixty tons had been accounted for; another sixty-seven tons had left the Seneca Ordnance Depot in three more trucks that afternoon and were still somewhere on the highways—police had issued an eight-state alarm for them. The remaining seventy-three tons were still at the depot.

Leonard Weisman picked up the telephone in his hotel room in Norfolk, Virginia, asked the operator to connect him with the FBI in New York, and said, "I understand you are looking for me. Well I'm not hiding. I'm right here. When do you want to see me?"

In Norfolk on one of his frequent trips to check on the *Attu*—the modification of the aircraft carrier had been left in his hands since Arazi's departure for Europe and Palestine—Weisman had just heard a radio newscast of the seizure of the demolition blocks at Lowy's farm and the report that he, as president of Foundry Associates, was being sought by the FBI. He arranged a meeting for the next morning, January 9, at his home in Mount Vernon and rushed north by plane to keep the date. Promptly at 11 A.M. two FBI agents appeared at his door.

Weisman readily admitted having bought the explosives through Foundry Associates and having turned them over to "three gentlemen interested in acquiring them. They said it was for their country, Palestine, which was fighting for its freedom in much the same way that America once fought for its freedom." It was an act, he insisted, "in the American tradition and I don't feel I did anything that wasn't strictly American." When the FBI men asked if he realized he'd broken American laws, Weisman replied, "I don't believe I have. I bought something made freely available at a government surplus sale and transferred it to others within the confines of the United States." The FBI agents reminded him it had been transported without a license for carrying explosives. "Not by me," Weisman snapped. But there had been a plan to violate the arms embargo, the agents persisted. "Not that I know of," insisted Weisman. He reminded them that the explosives were of a type used for blasting and other industrial purposes and that they had been found in the United States. "How do you know they were not going to apply to the State Department for an export license?"

Ushering the FBI men out the door, Weisman found a score of newspaper reporters waiting. Explosives for Palestine were back on the front page. The Monmouth County prosecutor J. Victor Carton had made an immediate connection between the demolition blocks found at Lowy's farm and the TNT that had rolled into public view on the Jersey City dock less than a week before. There were, he speculated, countless other caches of dangerous explosives hidden about the country, destined for "Haganah, the Jewish underground."

The three missing trucks, reporters told Weisman, had been picked up at Lake Katrine in upstate New York and a search of Lowy's warehouse had turned up thirty-six cases of Navy surplus combat knives and a hundred cases of first-aid equipment. Zimel Resnick, the Asbury Park amusement park owner, although insisting that he knew nothing about the matter and was only a sympathetic member of ZOA (Zionist Organization of America), had posted $500 bail for each of the six truck drivers; Lowy was still in jail on $15,000 bail, charged with storing explosives without a license.

Weisman chatted expansively with the reporters while his wife brought out a spread of beer and corned beef sandwiches. He declared he was "proud" to have helped the Haganah, adding, "If it had not been for the Marquis de Lafayette helping the United States get arms when we were fighting for our independence, we might not have succeeded. Nor did anyone criticize Eamon de Valera when he came to this country for the very same thing."

There had been no time to check with the Hotel Fourteen before his exuberant press conference, but Weisman felt satisfied that he had done the right thing.

There was no longer any use denying the obvious. The next day, the Jewish Agency for Palestine issued a statement acknowledging that it had "made dollar credits available" for the "legitimate purchase" of the demolition blocks which were awaiting "legitimate shipment." The statement added, "The Jewish Agency has the responsibilities of a state about to be born. It must protect the lives and homes of the 700,000 men, women and children of Palestine." It noted that the United Nations decision to partition Palestine had "made no provision for an international force; it therefore devolved upon the responsible defense forces of the Jewish community of Palestine to rush preparations in a race against time in view of the threatened Arab aggression . . . and the announced early withdrawal of British troops."

The Agency statement made no mention, however, of the TNT,

and Weisman denied any knowledge of it. Despite newspaper speculation, no link between the two explosives had been established. On
January 12 the New York *Times* ran a front page story headlined
"Blast Cargo on Freighter Plagues FBI." There was still no solution
of the mystery of the TNT.

On January 14 Al Schwimmer walked out of his new office at
the Lockheed Air Terminal in Burbank, passed through Gate 117 and
saw a man get out of a parked car and walk purposefully toward
him.

The slim sandy-haired stranger greeted Schwimmer by name and
flipped open a black leather pass case. Schwimmer glanced down and
saw the credentials: FBI. The man was Bernarr M. Ptacek, a special
agent of the FBI's Los Angeles office who had been assigned to check
out some of the loose ends in the agency's investigation of the demolition blocks. He wanted to ask Schwimmer about a $20,000 check
which had been made out to him by Foundry Associates, the same
firm that had ordered the explosives from the WAA.

Schwimmer had prepared himself for just such a confrontation.
He had known that sooner or later someone would be asking questions. He had discussed the prospect with Nahum Bernstein in New
York, and Bernstein had said that there was a great deal he was free to
tell.

Schwimmer told Ptacek that he had been sought out by a Palestinian named Albert Miller who wanted Schwimmer to help him start
an airline that would be ready to serve the new state in Palestine the
moment the British mandate ended. It would operate across the
Atlantic and around Europe, carrying immigrants and cargo.

Schwimmer said that, naturally, he had been interested. Aviation
was his line and he was sympathetic to the Jews of Palestine. He had
come out to Los Angeles to buy long-range aircraft and seen the
Constellations that the Army Air Forces had put up for sale. Miller
had supplied the money to buy and recondition them—a total of
$125,000 so far. Foundry Associates was one of the firms through
which Miller made his payments.

Schwimmer pointed out to Ptacek that he could see the three
Constellations standing on the field. There was nothing secret about
his operation; it was literally conducted out in the open on five acres
of space he had rented from Lockheed.

Ptacek nodded. But he wanted to remind Schwimmer that there
were a lot of Federal laws involved in running an airline, especially

one to the Middle East. There was an embargo on the export of fighter aircraft to the Middle East.

Yes, Schwimmer broke in, but the Constellations were hardly fighters. He knew how many laws and regulations were involved: he was spending every evening on the paperwork. He intended to take all the steps, meet all the CAB requirements and get State Department permission to operate overseas. As a matter of fact, as soon as he could, Schwimmer was going to Washington to start the application papers through government channels.

He figured the three Constellations would be ready to start operating from the airport at Millville, New Jersey, on February 15.

"I'd like to know about it," Ptacek said.

"Sure," Schwimmer replied. The two men walked off on their separate ways.

XXIV

ON BALANCE, NOT BAD

I n Palestine events in the United States were being followed with
gloomy foreboding. The loss of the TNT and the demolition
blocks was a bitter blow; even more ominous was the jeopardy in
which their discovery put the entire American operation. In danger
too was the shipment of small arms, still en route from Italy. Their
careful packing by the DPs at Magenta in the "American manner"
might now be a liability; no doubt British customs agents in Palestine
had been alerted to look out for "used industrial machinery" that
might be something else. Elie Schalit's smokeless powder also was still
on the high seas, with a gauntlet of Arab ports to run before it arrived in Tel Aviv. Meanwhile, Jewish defenses were almost as meager
as they had been two months before. In the entire Negev there were
only two thousand rifles.

At the Hotel Fourteen panic was superseded by hard-headed
analysis. There was speculation that the discovery of the demolition
blocks at Lowy's farm had not been as coincidental as the police had
made it out—the result of a chance telephone tip. It seemed possible
that the FBI's investigation of the TNT had turned up the lead to the
demolition blocks. As usual, the two operations had been kept separate. But in the urgency of the past weeks the careful egg-box
compartmentalization of the underground had broken down, lines
had been crossed, caution had given way to expediency. Perhaps a
tapped telephone line, an intercepted letter or some other source
which the FBI did not want to reveal, had given them away. If so,
how much more did the FBI know? How many more leads had it
turned up?

The underground's lawyers decided on a familiar strategy. One
that had worked before when Max Brown was caught with Ekdahl's
gun at the Canadian border and when Reuben Gross's short wave

radio station had been discovered. They would try to cut short the FBI's probings by handing it a solution to the mystery of the TNT. They would try to calm everyone's apprehensions by admitting openly what they had done and why. They would take their losses and thereby try to minimize them; the TNT would be forfeited but they might yet save the airplanes, the *Attu* and the multitude of other projects under way.

In Laredo, Texas, on the Mexican border, Alper and Schalit were basking in the sun and waiting for further instructions. They had flown from Washington to Dallas and then driven down to Laredo. Schalit was all for going straight on to Mexico. He couldn't stand inaction or isolation. He wanted to wade across the Rio Grande. Alper was rather enjoying the sunny respite after New York's cold, and was not keen on the plan to evacuate them to Palestine. In any case, he objected to chilly swims. "If I go to Mexico, it will be in an airplane," he told Schalit. To prove how easy it would be, he got a library card under an assumed name, used it as identification to get a tourist card—Mexico does not require passports or visas for entry—and told Schalit he would meet him in Mexico City.

Before either of them had a chance to put their travel plans into operation, a call came from the Hotel Fourteen. Alper was told to return to New York; Elie was advised to stay out of sight for a while longer, until the *Executor* and the smokeless powder reached Tel Aviv.

On January 15 the newspapers finally could announce a break in the "TNT Mystery." Five men had given themselves up to the FBI. Heading the list and described as the mastermind of the operation was twenty-three-year-old Phil Alper, who by now was wearing a tie. The others were two of the youngsters who had helped crate the TNT at the Pipersville camp, a twenty-four-year-old concert pianist whose name had haplessly turned up as a partner in the Machinery Processing and Converting Company, and Big Moe Wolfson, at thirty-four the oldest of the group. Wolfson's bluff personality and towering physique intrigued reporters, who interviewed him extensively on his experiences as a truck driver on a collective farm in Palestine.

It all seemed very far from the past week's headlines about Jewish terrorists and dynamite enough to destroy five Jersey Cities.

Phil Alper found the FBI agents who questioned him less interested in what he had *done* than in where he had *been*. They were exasperated that they had not been able to find him or the still missing Schalit. They also were interested in knowing why a clean-cut fellow like Alper would get mixed up in such goings on. He replied with a, for him, impassioned speech about the situation in the Middle East and the need he felt to help the Jews who had survived Hitler. "They were quite taken aback," Alper would observe later. "They hadn't really grasped before what the motivation was."

Arraigned before Federal Judge William Bondy, the five men were charged with violating Section 80 of Title 18 of the United States Code by "making or causing to be made false export declarations." United States attorney John F. X. McGohey told the judge that the men had come forward voluntarily and recommended minimum bail. Nothing was said about violating the arms embargo; whatever might have been intended, an accident had prevented it and no one seemed inclined to bring the matter up again. The men were freed on bail of $1,000 each to wait action by a Federal grand jury.

Bench warrants were also issued for Elie Schalit, the absent Yoselevitch and Yordeni of the nonexistent Oved and Mar-Tech Trading Companies and two others. Attorneys promised that more of the men would turn themselves in soon.

Slouched in a chair in his study, which had been the virtual headquarters of the underground during the past harrowing weeks, Nahum Bernstein ran down the list.

The TNT: Finished, confiscated by the government.

The M-3 demolition blocks: Finished too; the Army had suddenly decided it needed all its M-3s and, without due process of law, had canceled the sale, reclaiming the seized explosives and the seventy-three tons undelivered at the Seneca Ordnance Depot.

The contents of the other fifty-one crates seized aboard the *Executor:* They were to be sold at auction to satisfy a lien by the American Export Lines for losses it had suffered when the ship failed to sail on time.

The sulphuric acid: Slavin would have to wait; the New York Fire Department had destroyed it as a fire hazard. The rest of the warehouse inventory and the warehouse itself were free and clear.

Schalit's smokeless powder: Still en route to Palestine; until it got there, Schalit would remain in hiding away from official questions.

The airplanes in California: Under suspicion, and the FBI would not forget about them. An elaborate cover would have to be devised to get them to where they were needed.

The *Attu:* Weisman's volubility with the press might have endangered it, but so far no one had shown up to look askance, despite the quite open connection with Foundry Associates and Weisman. Was it possible that, the bigger things were, the less attention they attracted? There was only one way to find out: push the work and their luck a little further.

Alper, Lowy and the others under arrest: Awaiting trial. No one else had been implicated; no "big names" had been revealed.

The Hotel Fourteen: Untouched.

The Sonneborn Institute: Still meeting every Thursday.

Public opinion: It seemed to be with them. Even the Asbury Park *Evening Press*, which had begun by splashing its front pages with scare headlines, had run a long editorial explaining the historical background of the struggle in Palestine and concluding, "Those who would espouse the cause of young and struggling nations must always take chances; if they lose they are law violators; if their cause succeeds, history calls them heroes."

Funds: The TNT's effect on Americans' generosity was being tested. Golda Myerson, the ascetic-looking woman who had grown up in Milwaukee and Denver, emigrated to Palestine, and become one of the Agency's strongest personalities, had just arrived in the United States on an emergency mission to raise money for Arazi's Yakum Purkan operation, the pending Czech arms deal, and other military expenditures. She met with Sonneborn and others in New York; they agreed that her appeal might be hurt by the TNT's backlash, but there was no alternative but to let her plunge in and find out. Montor squeezed her onto the program of a conference of the Council of Jewish Federations in Chicago. Speaking bluntly, looking like an American frontierswoman, Mrs. Myerson told the meeting: "I have come here to try to impress Jews in the United States with this fact, that within a very short period, a couple of weeks, we must have in cash between twenty-five and thirty million dollars. Not that we need this money to use during these weeks, but if we have twenty-five or thirty million dollars in the next two or three weeks we can establish ourselves." She promptly got pledges totaling twenty-five million dollars from community leaders who, in many instances, then borrowed the money on their personal notes against future donations from their local campaigns.*

* In the two and a half months she stayed in the United States, Mrs. Myerson raised fifty million dollars. In 1956, having changed her name to Meir, she became Israel's Foreign Minister and, in 1969, its Prime Minister.

On balance, not bad, Bernstein summarized. They had been hit, they would have to move more cautiously now, but they were not frightened.

Meanwhile, there could be no pause, not even a brief respite while things cooled off. Arab guerrilla forces, trained in Syria, already were slipping across the border into Palestine and had boldly set up headquarters inside the country under their leader, Fawzi el Kaukji, a Lebanese soldier of fortune. British reports to the United Nations tabulated their arrival: 300 trained guerrillas had filtered into the Safed area of Galilee; 700 Syrians, in battle dress with their own mechanized transport, moved in from Transjordan; a week later 950 more uniformed men with 19 vehicles crossed a bridge from Transjordan and dispersed into villages; 700 more men followed later that night.

The situation was so threatening, a United Nations Commission recommended the organization of a Jewish militia. The British replied that they would not permit any recruitment or preparations before their departure on May 15.

The regular Arab armies were being strengthened too. Syria reached an agreement to buy arms from Czechoslovakia; France, eager to regain the Middle East foothold it had lost when the Vichy regime was driven out of Syria, agreed to sell military equipment to Lebanon. British diplomatic sources, questioned in London, confirmed that Britain was supplying arms to Egypt, Iraq and Transjordan. On January 16 the Arabs announced they intended to occupy all of Palestine when the British mandate ended.

The Jewish Agency appealed to the governments of the world to sell it arms. In the United States numerous prominent people, including Mrs. Eleanor Roosevelt, Mayor William O'Dwyer, Congressman Jacob Javits and Senator C. W. Tobey, asked repeatedly for an end to the American arms embargo. But United States policy was ambivalent, supporting partition while defeating its humanitarian objectives by denying the Jews arms; it reflected a political tug of war that pitted an oil lobby and a group of State Department professionals against the avowed policies of President Truman and a generally sympathetic public opinion. The embargo stood.

Bernstein turned his attention to the practical dilemma that the discovery of the TNT posed to the underground. How, with the FBI presumably watching their every move, could they prepare for the looming May 15 deadline?

The size of the undertaking now facing them was indicated by a document that had just reached the Hotel Fourteen. It was a monumental shopping list for an entire army.

Nahum Bernstein had received it from a sandy-haired young man who had replaced Shlomo Rabinovich as Number One Palestinian at the Hotel Fourteen.

PART
FOUR

XXV

TEDDY KOLLEK

Teddy Kollek looked like a Minnesota farmer who had come in out of the cold and stumbled into things. He was, as a matter of fact, a farmer; at that very moment his home, the collective settlement of Ein Gev on the shore of the Sea of Galilee, was encircled by bands of Arab guerrillas. He was also an experienced underground operative. He had been in the United States only a month when the TNT fell and he had spent that time helping to edit a small propaganda newspaper while studying the American scene. "It provided my cover," he recalls. When Rabinovich, in the midst of the TNT crisis, was summoned home to assume a Haganah command, Kollek took over at the Hotel Fourteen. He brought to his new job a ferocious energy and an appealing personality that stimulated everyone. The Americans were delighted with his square-jawed, rugged good looks; he fitted their notion of how a young man from a settlement on the Sea of Galilee should look. At the same time he was hardly a country bumpkin. Born in Vienna, the son of a Rothschild banker, he had worked for Haganah in Istanbul during the war, smuggled refugees out of the Balkans and done a stint with British intelligence.

His English was so fluent he could flavor his conversation with the kind of self-deprecating humor that drew a sympathetic response from Americans. He would introduce himself as "one of those useless persons whom they really do not need back in Palestine." Or he would enliven a lesson in Zionist dogma with "We may be exaggerating a bit, but we try to live up to these exaggerations."

He saw himself as a catalyst, not a commander; his job was to bring specialists together and leave them alone. He was not interested in details. He disliked formal meetings. Long-winded discussions set him to pacing the room, munching an apple—he always had a sack of apples on hand. Yet he was a "born diplomat," one of the Americans who worked with him at the time recalls. "There was nothing formal about him but he'd get your respect. He had the extraordinary ability of being able to work with all types of people and always seemed to find time for you, as busy as he was." His two-room suite of offices on the second floor of the Hotel Fourteen was "always Grand Central Station, full of people."

It was Kollek who kept tabs on everything, kept the lines open, interpreted, filtered, encouraged, discouraged, relayed good news and bad:

• That the *Executor* had arrived and Schalit's smokeless powder had been safely unloaded.

• That the arms shipment from Magenta in Italy had arrived aboard a Danish freighter three days after the *Executor*. That Haganah had taken no chances and off loaded its cargo secretly at night. Their Italian friends were safe.

• That Maurice Companiez, a Los Angeles hardware merchant, posing as a South American banana planter, had bought two surplus LCIs (landing craft, infantry) and was refitting them in a San Diego shipyard under the pacific names of *Dorothy Lee* and *Audrey H.* for "service on the Amazon." *Dorothy Lee* and *Audrey H.* reached their real destination in December 1948 and were used in amphibious exercises.

• That friends in Miami had bought the *Bonnie*, a German E-boat the U.S. Navy had captured during World War II. Towed across the Atlantic and into the Mediterranean in late 1948, the *Bonnie* was to sink in a storm off Sicily.

• That the *Yucatan*, formerly U.S. Navy submarine chaser PC 1265, had been purchased in New Orleans for $50,000 and needed only a crew to sail. Eventually, with a Filipino cook, a Guatemalan radio operator, and an Annapolis graduate as third mate, *Yucatan* would become the *Nogah*, a Jewish man-o'-war.

• That Bernard Fineman, the movie producer, had arranged for the purchase in Los Angeles of fifteen M-4 medium scout tanks, Marine Corps surplus. That other friends had arranged for their transportation by rail to Houston. That a ship from Mexico was ready to pick them up. That Schalit felt, "They're too hot." That the tanks would stay in Texas.

Kollek would say years later: "My part in all this was that I was the traffic cop; I directed all the moving of these people to and fro. They came with their problems to me and I sent them on to someone who could help them." He liked technicians because they addressed themselves directly to the matter at hand; he liked the United States because it had so many technicians.

Naturally, Kollek found in Nahum Bernstein just the kind of expert he needed to get things going again. They examined the list from Palestine and Bernstein began making notes.

On January 27, Harold Jaffer sent a note on a newly printed letterhead to the manager of the Fisk Building, 250 West 57th Street. "Dear Mr. O'Reilly: Would you please put up on the directory in the lobby the following name for Room 1905: Materials for Palestine, Inc. I would appreciate your doing this as soon as possible."

In a loft building on Broadway, just south of the bustling bargain bazaars of Union Square, a new name went onto the directory: Inland Machinery and Metals Company.

On Fifth Avenue, in the building at number 245, the elevator operator was asked to deliver to an office on the fourteenth floor any mail addressed to Radio Communications Engineering Company.

At 119 Greene Street, in the electrical and hardware center of the Lower West Side, a sign painter went to work with brush and black paint on the door of the second-floor loft: Eastern Development Company.

The register of the Hotel Breslin at Broadway and 29th Street showed a new resident in Room 1202: Land and Labor for Palestine.

Mr. O'Reilly, the manager of 250 West 57th Street, was called on by another tenant, the new one in Suites 515 and 516, to post his company's name in the lobby: Service Airways, Inc.

It was an axiom of ex-OSS man Bernstein that each activity of the underground be compartmentalized in a separate cover company. Then, "if your security miscarries, all you reveal is that one activity." Now, in the wake of the TNT disaster, he was pursuing a corollary of that axiom: If one cover—or several—blows, create new ones.

The new companies were spread across New York. No common root connected them. Some sounded frankly philanthropic; others bore titles as vague as that of General Motors. Different law firms did the paperwork, paid the taxes, signed the leases. Bernstein briefed his colleagues, many of them corporation lawyers well versed in setting up dummy companies, holding companies, corporate structures that could best benefit from existing laws.

"The Palestinians," he explained, "are interested only in the end result. They don't know how to operate on the American scene.

They don't know how to accomplish these things, what corporate vehicles can be used." As a general plan, he repeated what he had told Kollek: "We need a broad organization to bring in all kinds of things, and several smaller organizations, operating under cover, to do the special jobs."

At the next regular Thursday luncheon at the Hotel McAlpin on January 27, Sonneborn waited until the waiters had left the room and then rose. He made no mention of the catastrophic events which had taken place only three weeks before but, tacitly acknowledging that they were on everyone's mind, he began:

"There has been a considerable speculation and discussion as to the future of this group." The fifty-seven members present nodded and exchanged nervous glances. The Institute would continue to function, Sonneborn assured them firmly. In fact, its work was entering a new and critical phase. The deadline for British withdrawal from Palestine was less than four months away. Haganah must begin serious mobilization. Almost overnight it must change from an unevenly trained volunteer guard which slept and ate at home and used farm trucks and the regular intercity buses to go into battle into an effective military force which could protect a nation.

In the next few weeks it would be quietly building up its forces, calling up full-time soldiers from its reserve of sixty thousand men and women. They would arrive at secret camps in mufti with perhaps a sleeping bag as equipment (while their families lived on savings or the generosity of relatives). The immigrants from the DP camps who would be drafted—the young and able-bodied—had arrived in Palestine with only the clothing on their backs. The new army would need everything, from walkie-talkies to khaki underwear.

The Institute's job would be to supply it—not with money but with goods. The emphasis would shift from fund-raising to seeking, through its several thousand members in every industry, donations in kind of a vast list of materials which Haganah would need.

The list that Teddy Kollek had shown to Bernstein at the Hotel Fourteen had been duplicated for distribution at the luncheon. Sonneborn passed around double-spaced typewritten carbon copies:

> Two million sand bags, one thousand tons of barbed wire, one hundred thousand square feet of corrugated iron . . .
> Ten thousand coats; ten thousand pairs of boots; ten thousand raincoats; two thousand rubber boots; forty thousand blankets; three thousand tents (for 2, 8, and 16 men); ten thousand

cots; five hundred thousand emergency rations; ten thousand canteens; ten thousand sweaters; thirty thousand pairs of socks . . .

One thousand pairs of binoculars; one thousand compasses; one thousand telephones and five hundred miles of telephone cable; and fifty switchboards . . .

One thousand jeeps; one thousand bicycles; two hundred motorcycles; fifty water trucks; twenty gasoline trucks; two hundred armored trucks; one thousand 2½-ton trucks; one thousand ¾-ton trucks . . .

Three hundred "light projectors" (searchlights); thirty drafting tables; two hundred Hebrew typewriters; ten English typewriters; a print shop; a multigraph machine; two hundred megaphone systems . . .

The list ran for three pages.

If any of the men perusing it were daunted by its size and complexity, they were given no time for doubts. Collections, Sonneborn was explaining sanguinely, would be made through a new nonprofit membership organization which Nahum Bernstein and his legal team had incorporated under the laws of the State of New York: Materials for Palestine, Inc. Sonneborn would head it, as he did the Institute. Adolf Robison, the textile man from New Jersey, would be the vice-president and Sonneborn's deputy. Nahum Bernstein would be the secretary. Materials for Palestine would operate out of the office at 250 West 57th Street; Harold Jaffer that very day had requested that the name of the new organization be added to the building's directory, thus ending the anonymity of Room 1905. Jaffer's name would come off the door; he was getting ready to leave for Palestine. The Institute's other two full-time employees would take over for MFP: Isaac Imber, who had been in the machinery business, would direct the collections in kind; Rusty Jarcho would run the office.

The Institute would continue to meet weekly at the McAlpin— quietly, discreetly—to discuss policy and strategy. But MFP would operate openly. Its solicitations and shipments would be aboveboard and legal; it would handle no contraband, no embargoed materials. It would be sort of overseas quartermaster for the budding Jewish army—an American uncle sending packages on a massive scale.

MFP

M FP became the clearing house for everything," Isaac Imber would reminisce years later. "If you had a yard of bandage or if your wife knitted sweaters or if you were a merchant with eight thousand overcoats, you came to MFP."

Imber kept up a flow of correspondence with Institute members around the country. He would ask them the names of the big surplus dealers in their areas. Then he went to "the fellow who was buying a lot of surplus and he was sure to disclose his sources, not only of the stuff he had in his inventory but what others had too, because the dealers usually knew who had bought what in which auction. The government was throwing out the stuff so fast that one dealer couldn't buy such big lots by himself; they used to pool their purchases.

"That was the first step, to keep tabs on what was available throughout the country.

"The Hotel Fourteen got the requests from Palestine and sent them over to us. We'd tell them where the specific thing was available. They'd send out an expert to see it and ascertain whether it was what they wanted. They had the experts; Sonneborn used to say the less we knew about things and people, the better. If the stuff was good, or if it could be adapted by slight changes, we would tell our friends out there, 'We want it. Ask no questions.' And we usually got it, free. If we had to buy it, we would go to our local big shot and say, 'We'd like to hold a little meeting in your house. We've got to raise ten thousand dollars by tomorrow morning.' He'd call a meeting that night of the men in town he knew were sympathetic enough to contribute money, no questions asked, and we'd have the ten thousand. The stuff would be bought and paid for and we'd move it to the most likely port."

Among Imber's outgoing mail:

"This will introduce Mr. David Harris. I have suggested that you might be able to introduce him to . . . construction men in connection with a project which he will tell you about. I would very much appreciate it if you would make it possible for Mr. Harris to carry on his work by introducing him to those who may be helpful."

"We understand that Mr. L—— has a number of cargo and personnel parachutes which we would like him to contribute to the cause. If you know him, will you undertake to talk with him? If you don't know him, please tell me and we'll try to reach him some other way."

"Mr. Rey Selk should enjoy full cooperation. Any courtesies extended will be most appreciated."

Sam Sloan, a hefty, chortling professional organizer, was hired as the MFP's convention specialist. Sloan was big and fat and round-faced with a gift for story-telling and back-slapping and a laugh that went all the way from midtown Manhattan to Miami Beach. He would belly up to the bar and make friends.

"The conventions were the opening," Sloan recalls. "Once we got into contact with forty or fifty fellows across the country, we could travel. The big heavy stuff was not in New York, because if a dealer took a hundred thousand canteens off the government's hands, he had to put them someplace. He couldn't afford to transport them to New York or some other big city and pay storage. The fellows who had the most stuff were in the small towns, near the depots with hundreds of acres of dumping ground. Especially in the South."

The dealers Sloan made friends with tipped him off about others. "Hey, Sam," a long distance caller would say, "Joe just bought a tremendous lot of shoes. Ask him for a couple of thousand pair before he sorts them out. You want me to call him up and ask for you?"

Another caller would inform Sloan that in the islands of the Pacific, Army and Navy officers were ordering jeeps dumped into the ocean, "just to get them off the books." Sam would follow up.

He got to know the burlap bag dealers who were importing sandbags from Calcutta and wangled 350,000 out of them in one afternoon.

The sandbags went out in MFP's first shipment on the S.S. *Flying Arrow* of the Isbrandtsen Line, which sailed from Pier 14 on the East River of Manhattan on February 26, exactly one month after Sonneborn had announced the beginning of Materials for Palestine.

The ship also carried 10,100 wool blankets, 10,000 helmets, 12 medical field units, 33 cases of surgical dressings, 4 water distillation units and one milling machine.

The sandbags arrived in time to protect the trucks and buses of a big convoy that opened the road to beleaguered Jerusalem. The water distillation units, with a capacity of eighty-three gallons of potable water an hour, went to the exposed frontier settlements in the Negev. The milling machine was for Slavin.

On February 27 the S.S. *Elmer Bloomquist* of the American Pacific Line put out from Los Angeles with the first MFP shipment from the West Coast: 350 16-man tents, 1,701 steel helmets and 2,000 helmet liners. It arrived in Haifa as house-to-house fighting broke out in that half-Jewish, half-Arab city.

As the weeks went by, new lists came in. A "blue list"—it was typed on blue paper—asked for equipment for carpenters, motor transport fitters, armorers, tinsmiths, field butchers and electricians. It also called for 14,000 skirts, 21,000 blouses, 21,000 pairs of panties, 21,000 brassieres and 7,000 ladies' overcoats, and suggested that a WAC officer be consulted in filling the order. "Kindly bear in mind that the above list was compiled by willing males." The men at the McAlpin assumed that Haganah's female contingent now numbered 7,000.

Some of the requests were specific and seemed to border on the eccentric: recordings of Bach and Beethoven (for a Haganah leave center); fifty scarce antique volumes of The Sacred Books (for Ben Gurion); four Waring blenders (to dispose of secret documents).

Whatever the requests, the members of the Sonneborn Institute would look them over, put in calls to friends, pass on tips to convention-hopping Sam Sloan, to Isaac Imber and to new MFP employees hired to man branch offices in principal cities across the United States.

MFP's network of suppliers was increasing. The outbreak of fighting in Palestine galvanized sympathizers all over the country—Jews and Christians alike, including people who never had taken an interest before. Many who had hung back out of timidity, apathy or skepticism now responded to appeals for help.

It was sometimes hard, Nahum Bernstein recalls, to explain to would-be donors that Haganah couldn't use everything, including worn or defective materials, off-sizes, leftovers. "They had the feeling that, after all, it was being given away, we ought to take what we could get."

Sonneborn announced, "We want to be sure that every item we take and on which we will have to pay ocean freight will be of value, therefore we have adopted a policy of passing on each offering. One of our experts will tell us whether the item is required and whether it can be used to advantage."

"In the long run," recalls Bernstein, "we got two categories of people: those who would give us quality merchandise free and those who would have loved to but just couldn't afford it; they would get things for us and sell them to us at cost, but we had to raise funds to pay the purchase price."

MFP was geared to take fast delivery. An Institute member, Harris J. Klein, an attorney specializing in the trucking industry, organized a coast-to-coast network of 150 trucking lines which always managed to find space for MFP cargo without charge and no questions asked. Klein cleared all of the pickups and deliveries by telephone with Rusty Jarcho, who handled the touchy and complex task of routing them. "Rusty did a job," marvels Klein. "I don't think the Palestinians ever could repay him." Seventy-five per cent of the truckline owners were Jewish, but the non-Jewish fraction was no less eager. Klein once received a phone call from a trucker named Brady in the Midwest "to ask if there was trouble; he'd only moved six loads that month—what's the matter?"

The trucks carried the merchandise to MFP warehouses in Los Angeles, San Francisco, Denver, Chicago, New Orleans and New York to await shipment. The main warehouse was at 177 Water Street in Brooklyn, for which Rusty Jarcho, as the tenant of record, paid $4,000 monthly rent. Clothing was stored at 246 South Street in Manhattan; medical supplies at 155 Columbus Avenue in Manhattan, and "gray goods," like steel helmets, in a warehouse in Elizabeth, New Jersey.

In the ensuing months MFP would be "busier than Sears Roebuck," Rusty Jarcho recalls.

From Wisconsin came a truckload of four-inch sandbags; from Ohio, 92,000 parachute flares; from New Jersey, 25,000 steel helmets.

The burlap bag people in Indiana and Brooklyn contributed a second shipment of 250,000 bags. Chicago sent 100 bales of barbed wire and offered 22,000 pounds of camouflage paint. St. Paul, Minnesota, sent two (and offered 600 more) mine detectors. Miami shipped five antiaircraft searchlights and generators. A group in New York organized thirty veterans to buy thirty pairs of surplus binoculars—they were each entitled to one under WAA rules—to donate to MFP.

The San Francisco warehouse reported it had received 14,000 steel helmets, 4,000 yards of mosquito netting, 2,500 haversacks, 3 large boxes of signal equipment and 4 large reels of copper wire.

An energetic group in New Orleans that called itself Genesis, Inc., sent compasses, mess tins, salt tablets, naval equipment and penicillin.

Isaac Imber got a telephone call from a stranger in Rock Hill, North Carolina. "Could the Jewish army use good shockproof, waterproof watches?" Imber said they could. The voice said, "Okay, we will ship them," and hung up. A few days later "watches began to flow into the office, over three hundred of them from almost every community in the South where a Jewish jeweler can be found, and what community is there where you can't find one?"

Philadelphia sent a mobile hospital unit. Detroit sent generators, motors, searchlights and an octane rating machine. Kansas City sent steel helmets, folding canvas cots, trench shovels, bedrolls and nurses' uniforms. A man in Marion, Virginia, wrote expansively that he would like to know "what Haganah still needs and the method of making shipment." Omaha sent GI knives, forks and spoons.

From Pittsburgh came a letter from a local Institute member: "I am enclosing my check, payable to you, for fifty dollars in exchange for a fifty-dollar bill that was given to me today by a Christian woman who wishes the money to be used (in her own words) for the purchase of ammunition. I think she will be satisfied if the money is used for any purpose that leads to the strengthening of the new state."

Sam Sloan wrote to a New York shoe dealer: "May I take this opportunity of thanking you deeply for your very generous contribution of twenty-four pair of #A6 flying boots. Let me assure you that they are being put to immediate use . . ."

The expanding Haganah needed wheels. MFP sent trucks—the Army's famous 4 × 4s and 6 × 6s—jeeps, cars, trailers, ambulances. It had to turn down an offer from Canton, Ohio, of "eighty medium tanks T-23"; these were embargoed military equipment in which MFP did not traffic. But in Jeannette, Pennsylvania, MFP found a man with a yard full of caterpillar tracks. MFP described these as "sand tracks" and shipped two thousand of them to be used in converting ordinary trucks into half-tracks for desert fighting.

It sent out two thousand parachutes listed as "hospital supplies," explaining dubiously that the field hospitals in the Negev, isolated by Arab guerrillas, could only be supplied by parachute drops.

Machine tools came in from Detroit along with the tip for Sam Sloan that the machinery dealers would be having a national convention at French Lick, Indiana.

Birmingham was asked for sheet steel. Augusta, Georgia, sent pistol holsters and compasses. From Baltimore came jeep caps, communications equipment and, "for the navy," one man hopefully wrote, charts, sextants and binoculars.

One of the requests that, in fact, would come to MFP was for "the full requirements" of a navy. A young man told an Institute luncheon about the problem of defending a long Mediterranean coastline. Against the sizable Egyptian Navy and the smaller fleet of Lebanon, the Jews could array only two corvettes and an icebreaker— three of the eighteen ships which the Institute had bought for illegal immigration, now hurriedly converted to naval use.

The young man who used the nom-de-guerre of Shaul Ben Zvi was obviously an American, but it would be some time before his name and role would become known. He was Paul Shulman, an Annapolis graduate who had sailed on the illegal immigrant ships and would become the first chief of staff of the navy.

The new navy would begin life as a replica of the United States Navy, with Shulman in command, Hal Gershenow (who would leave for Palestine later in the year) in charge of ship maintenance and repairs, and a naval academy supplied with five hundred copies of the *Bluejacket Manual*, fifty copies of the *Watch Officer's Guide* and five copies of *U.S. Naval Regulations*.

Sam Sloan procured naval equipment from his contacts in New York, Brooklyn, Norfolk, Baltimore, Boston, Quincy, Massachusetts, Philadelphia and Jacksonville. For the men: 7,000 pairs of fly-front trousers, 6,000 seamen's caps, 5,000 blue raincoats and 1,000 yards of gold braid. For the ships: manila rope, sail twine, wire brushes, wash buckets, deck scrapers, marlinspikes, 150 sets of international signal flags, 40 sextants, maps of the eastern Mediterranean. And, donated by the New York bookshop Argosy, on East 59th Street, a complete naval reference library, including the memoirs of German Grand Admiral von Tirpitz.

Among the lists of naval equipment Rusty Jarcho received a special request from Tel Aviv: "Won't you please try to obtain a telescope for use by one eye for Moshe Dayan? This is similar to the type that is used in the Navy."

XXVII

BLACK GOODS

To Rusty Jarcho: "The following items can be obtained free: 1 machine to make 88-mm. shells; 1 machine to make 105-mm. shells; 1 machine, a mixer, to make the gelatin for the flame throwers. We do not have the formula but it can be easily obtained."

From Isaac Imber: "We are sorry to inform you that we cannot accept your offer of airplane motors nor can we use the formula for an incendiary bomb you mention . . ."

From Sam Sloan: "I am sorry but we are not in the business of purchasing anything at all and in particular we have nothing to do with the items you mention. I almost wish we were, since your qualifications are so good. Should we ever come into contact with those who might need your services, we would be most happy to recommend you."

As Sonneborn had promised, MFP dealt officially only in "white goods"—those materials that were not prohibited by the U.S. arms embargo. Still, no one expected Haganah, no matter how well tailored and shod, to fight without arms. Kollek and Bernstein had devised a means of bringing the vast know-how and resources of MFP to bear on the problem of procuring "black goods" too. Or, as Sam Sloan would put it in later years: "We had two functions, if I may say so.

"MFP and the Americans involved in it had a very proper and legal function assembling clothing, medical supplies, items not directly military. Of course, everything is important to a new army, including shoelaces. Materials for Palestine dealt directly with items that were beyond suspicion. We were like Caesar's wife in our operation.

"But what we advised and told people privately was a separate matter. There were other military needs of Palestine which had to be met in other ways. We helped with them indirectly.

"First of all, people assumed we handled everything and in their anxiety to help they gave us all kinds of tips and propositions and everything else. Where we could not handle certain ones, we passed them on to the appropriate special agency created for that purpose. Conversely, when these special agencies needed certain things, they came to us. We were scouts. We had the contacts. We helped them to get the stuff, for free or by raising money to pay for it."

The secret side of MFP was reflected in a certain ambiguity at meetings of the Sonneborn Institute. The majority of the members knew no more than Sonneborn had told them: "Only donations . . . of a noncontraband nature can be accepted." But the MFP staff members who spoke at the weekly McAlpin luncheons at times seemed to be alluding to things beyond those limits.*

"Some of the members caught on," recalls Rusty Jarcho. "Some thought they were being left out of a secret."

He got a call one day from a member who was stubbornly incomprehensible. "He had decided," recalls Jarcho, "that we had been talking in code. So he had made up his own."

"I've got some poppy seeds," the caller stated enigmatically.

"So?" responded Jarcho cagily.

"Poppy seeds," insisted the caller.

"Well, come on up and talk to me," Jarcho said. He figured, he recalls, that "maybe the fellow needed a kind word or a doctor. It turned out he had bullets he wanted to contribute."

Jarcho told him whom to see.

One of the things Sam Sloan was always on the lookout for was seamless steel tubing. "Hey," he might say, interrupting a pinochle game, "does anybody around here have seamless steel tubing?" And he would give the exact specifications for the types he wanted.

"We were willing to pay for it," Sloan explains, "but we had to find it first. It was a scarce item. The mills were giving it out on very strict allocation, only to regular dealers, and there were plenty of other people ready to pay for it too. I did a lot of bird-dogging to find it and then a lot of lapel-tugging to talk people out of it."

When he found some, Sloan would tell the MFP office back in New York to notify one of the underground's "special agencies," the Inland Machinery and Metals Company.

---

* Irving Norry, a Rochester, N.Y., electrical equipment dealer, and one of the Institute's most zealous members, was arrested in March 1948, charged with buying and storing six thousand dynamite caps without a license. Norry pleaded guilty to the charge, a misdemeanor, and drew a suspended sentence. He said nothing at the time about why he had bought the detonators.

The staff of Inland Machinery consisted of Phil Alper—out on bail—and Bob Keller, who miraculously had escaped involvement with the law since walking off Pier F that January day.

They had a new office that would have outraged Slavin: a suite on the top floor of a building on the corner of Broadway and 11th Street. It was a rickety old building; its floors sloped so that Alper sometimes felt he was on a ship, sailing through the loft district. But he had spent $150 on secondhand desks, chairs and steel filing cabinets. "A real office," he observed with satisfaction. For storage, he and Keller were boldly using the old warehouse at 4366 Park Avenue.

They were still filling orders for Slavin's growing clandestine munitions industry. Max Brown, the Canadian machinist who had been caught at the border with Ekdahl's gun parts, was preparing to go to Palestine to help assemble tooling. Later Ekdahl himself would go to assist with one more modification of the gun. The seamless steel tubing for which Sloan searched so assiduously was for Slavin's mortars.

On his new stationery Alper sent Sloan a list of some of Slavin's other requirements: an agitator with an explosion-proof motor, a rotary pellet press, a dryer and four crystallizers. "They must go in our next shipment," Alper urged. It would have taken an expert eye to recognize the items as chemical equipment used in the Olsen process for manufacturing smokeless powder. Perhaps only Alper guessed that Slavin was planning to make use of the knowledge he had dredged out of Grageroff during those strange sessions in the Chemists' Club library.

Late in February Alper and five others, including Elie Schalit, who had turned himself in as soon as his smokeless powder arrived in Tel Aviv, pleaded guilty before Federal Judge Sylvester J. Ryan to the charge of making false export declarations. They received a suspended sentence. Judge Ryan called them "rash and impulsive," and explained his leniency: "You endeavored to provide means of defense to an otherwise helpless people. I do not regard you men as criminals . . ."

The case against Charles Lowy, the Asbury Park moving man, was not resolved until June, when he was fined $500 for "unlawful and improper storage." Like Judge Ryan, Judge John C. Giordano was sympathetic: "He [Lowy] was doing something for other people in other parts of the world for whom he had a kindly feeling."

When the fifty-one crates that had been seized on the S.S. *Executor* came up for auction, Alper, Danny Fliderblum and a half-dozen friends were on hand. There were things in those crates that they wanted back, including the "Musica" radio transmitters that Fliderblum and his crew had built and painstakingly disguised as receivers in polished mahogany cases and a quantity of scarce brass stripping for Slavin. Both items could be exported legally. The underground was also anxious to make sure that American Export Lines, with which it was still doing business, was compensated for its losses caused by the TNT. The brass was bid for and bought; then the radio transmitters and a half-dozen smaller items. Alper added up the figures as the auctioneer brought down his gavel on each lot. When the total reached $20,000, Alper quietly signaled and the bidding of his group stopped. "We figured," he explained later, "that American Export Lines had lost about twenty thousand dollars because of us. Now we were even."

As usual, the request went to Sam Sloan. Would he ask around among his friends in the office supply field for drawing tables, drafting tables, straight edges, a camera, a typewriter, a blueprint cabinet and steel partitions? As usual, Sam Sloan found the items needed. As usual, all he knew was that they were for another of the "special" companies: Eastern Development, at 119 Greene Street, New York.

The "West Side Project" or "The Bird," as it was variously known, had started in Boston. Unsolicited and at first unknown to the Hotel Fourteen, a group of advanced science and engineering students at several institutions in that New England citadel of higher learning had put their heads together and decided that the ideal weapon for Palestine was a bazooka and that they would figure out how to make one.

A one-man, hand-held rocket launcher, widely used by the American Army in World War II, the bazooka was capable of destroying tanks and pillboxes. For an army without artillery it would be a godsend. A man holding a bazooka could creep forward and do almost as much damage as an antitank gun. Like the sapper planting TNT by hand in enemy strong points, the bazooka-armed foot soldier could serve as a substitute for heavy artillery, something the Palestinians as yet had little prospect of acquiring.

When it learned of "The Bird"—as the bazooka project was called in Boston—the Hotel Fourteen sent Harry Levine to look into it. He reported back that it was promising. The brainy young amateurs had even produced a set of blueprints. But to amount to anything, the project needed resources, refining and, above all, experienced and practical production men to figure out how to put it into effect. It would be like Slavin's machine gun all over again. Tools and dies would have to be designed, manufactured and shipped to Palestine plus the raw materials for producing the weapon itself.

The ideal man to give a paternal assist to such a project, as Levine had to Slavin's, was available and willing: Moses Heyman, an American inventor who had developed artificial mica when the United States needed it most, in 1943. For years Heyman had been interested in the Technion, the Institute of Technology in Haifa; he had organized the engineering and technical committee of the American Technion Society. In 1947, he had discussed the potentialities of the bazooka with Dostrovsky, advising him that "under the circumstances, the development of rockets would be a necessary feature of the entire defense program."

Still needed was a Phil Alper.

Mota Teumim was thin, nervous, thirty-six and studying for his doctorate in aeronautical engineering at Brooklyn Polytechnic Institute when a professor suggested he meet someone at the Hotel Fourteen. He emerged from the conference shaking his head as if he'd spent the afternoon in a wind tunnel. Like Phil Alper more than two years before, his initial impression was that the whole thing was impossible. As a former machinist—he had become an apprentice at the age of twelve—he knew the practical difficulties of producing finely calibrated tools and dies. "It can't be done on a lathe or drill press," he insisted. "You will need anywhere from $150,000 worth of equipment and up." Besides, he protested, he knew almost nothing about bazookas. Someone recommended a book, *Elements of Ammunition*, by Major Theodore C. Ohart, Ordnance Department, Army of the United States, published by John Wylie and Sons in 1946. Gamely Teumim began reading.

He also asked around among his friends for souvenir bazookas. Hundreds had been brought back by GIs in their barracks bags; it was even possible to buy bazookas, their rockets made harmless, in souvenir shops. Soon he had enough of them to study. "I took them apart," he recalls. "I measured them, weighed them, calculated the stresses. I saw how the parts fit and what the possibility was of jamming or any other malfunctioning. I also asked those who had fired them what it felt like, what were the dangers, what the back blast was like. We couldn't even think of using Pentolite, the explosive our Army had used; we had to think of a propellant made of something obtainable in Palestine. We decided to try various perchlorates."

While Teumim studied, Heyman and Sam Sloan assembled a machine shop in 5,000 square feet of space on Greene Street. There was no talk this time of doing the job in Canada. There was no time. The whole operation would be under one roof, close to Hotel Fourteen headquarters, where it could be pushed ahead with all possible speed. With MFP to help, there were none of the fumbling and false starts of Slavin's early days; within weeks the machine shop was equipped.

Teumim had given up a $20,000-a-year job as a chief engineer to go back to school to study for his doctorate; he had been supporting his wife and two children on the $5,000 a year he earned as a senior research associate. Now he gave that up to develop the bazooka at the munificent salary of $300 a month including traveling expenses.

At that he was the highest paid person in the shop. The others got a dollar and a half an hour if they were skilled, a dollar an hour if they were unskilled. Most of them fell into the latter category. Of necessity, because of the nature of the project, the workers were all trusted Zionists. "They were physically fit," Teumim recalls, "mentally alert, dedicated and dynamic. But they had been trained to work in agriculture and they didn't know which end to milk a lathe from. It takes years to train a good machinist. We managed to teach each man to do one specific thing."

One day Teumim got a call to come uptown to a building in the East Sixties. A man, whose name he does not recall, took him into a dimly lit room and proudly showed him a new acquisition, a crate filled with bazooka rockets, "tossed in any old way," Teumim recalls, "some without safety pins, some jammed, others out of function, all scrambled together like cordwood."

Teumim took one look and ordered everyone out of the room and the adjoining room. He cleared a path between the two rooms so that there would be no obstacles to stumble over or jostle against. He quickly wrote out for himself a procedure to follow and put it on a chair where he could see it. Then, gingerly, one at a time, he disarmed each rocket and deposited it, harmless, in the next room.

That evening, having dumped the useless rockets—they were all defective—into New York harbor, Teumim came home looking thinner and paler than ever. His wife took one look at him and decided he had suffered a heart attack. All he could say was, "I'm all right, I'm all right," as he fell into bed.

Danny Fliderblum, the pudgy young electronics whiz kid, also had been fitted out with a special company. Radio Communications

Engineering had an office at 245 Fifth Avenue, letterheads, and all the trappings of an up-and-coming concern engaged in buying and exporting electronic equipment. It even had its own small plant for reconditioning used equipment. It had gotten into this sideline, Fliderblum recalls, because "we were buying SCR 300s—the standard infantry walkie-talkie—and we wanted to make sure they were in working order when they were shipped. This got us into even more details. We were controlling tens of thousands of minute items—not only procuring complete equipment but even looking for the smallest parts. We had elaborate card indexes, and we got to be walking catalogues—you tell us the name of the set and we could break it down. As a matter of fact, we sort of became consultants for some of the suppliers because we were more familiar with the surplus than they were."

A friend of Fliderblum's, David Bennett, was recruited to run a related project: buying radar equipment which one day would be used by the Jewish air force's first radar group (Squadron 505). Bennett also assembled a secret radar station near Poughkeepsie, New York, where young Palestinians were trained. One of the identifying marks on their scopes as they strained to read the blips and waves was the outline of Vassar College nearby.

Another warehouse was needed to discreetly house the "black goods," which could not be sent to MFP's four New York warehouses. Nahum Bernstein thought he knew how to find one and passed on the tip to Teddy Kollek at the Hotel Fourteen. Kollek, who was finding his job—self-styled as "traffic cop"—more than he could handle alone now that the path to Palestine was becoming a superhighway, had acquired several assistants. Zvi Brenner, a thirty-five-year-old Palestinian who had been with Haganah since the early days when he served as second in command to the British officer Orde Wingate, organizer of Haganah's first night squads, was in charge of "black goods." He in turn was assisted by Shapik, reluctantly parted from his look-alike Cadillac-riding colleague, Moosik, who had remained with Elie Schalit.

On Bernstein's instructions, Brenner—craggy-faced and walking with a limp from a wound he had received fighting with the Jewish Brigade in Italy—accompanied by Shapik—dark and unsmiling, as always—went to the offices of Morris Dolgin, an industrial realtor in Brooklyn. So suspicious-looking a pair were they, that Dolgin's employees, on the alert for "Mafia types," as they explained later,

refused to let them in. When, next day, armed with a letter of introduction, Brenner managed to limp into Dolgin's office and tell him he
was from Palestine, Dolgin waved him to a seat, leaned forward and
exclaimed, "Why didn't you say so right away?" He got them space
in a furniture factory, which they quickly outgrew. He then found
them permanent quarters in a three-story building on Metropolitan
Avenue in Brooklyn which formerly had housed a meat-packing and
canning plant.

The building was bought in the name of Irving Strauss, a businessman who had been brought into the underground in typical
Hotel Fourteen fashion. Strauss was a brother-in-law of a brother-in-
law of Al Schwimmer's (he was married to Schwimmer's sister's
husband's sister) and had been persuaded to take a "short" leave from
his electronics business to help Danny Fliderblum organize Radio
Communications Engineering. Now, for Brenner, he formed the
Sherman Metropolitan Corporation to cover the operation of the new
warehouse.

The building had about 40,000 square feet of floor space.
Among the canned products of its former tenant had been fruit pre-
serves from California and Wisconsin; some of the old labels were still
around. Sherman Metropolitan copied them and continued to ship out
the product. With one important difference—the cans now contained
gunpowder, sent by Sam Sterling in Denver and other volunteer
collectors. The warehouse also became the central collection point
for the souvenir guns which Zimel Resnick, the Asbury Park amusement park owner, and others were rounding up from friends and
veterans' organizations, and which Harry Weinsaft, the young Viennese, was lugging in footlockers from the Railway Express depot at
Pennsylvania Station. Brenner was amazed to see the guns arriving by
the hundreds. At his collective farm settlement of Afikim in Palestine
he was accustomed to hiding with utmost secrecy each gun the
settlement managed to acquire. He found it hard to believe that an
American GI's normal collection of souvenirs might include "a
machine gun, a pistol or a mortar."

In a well-secluded part of the warehouse the souvenir weapons
and other "black goods" were packed in the Alper-Schalit manner as
"used industrial machinery."

On the first floor, in the front of the building, in full view of any
curious passersby, another of the former tenant's activities was continued. A motherly looking woman in white uniform and cap supervised the assembly-line production of chicken soup.

XXVIII

HAWAII

A visiting Indianapolis surplus dealer attending one of the regular Thursday meetings of the Institute whispered to Rusty Jarcho that he had "everything you need" in a yard in Hawaii. The visitor was Nathan Liff, a mild little man with graying hair and glasses who headed the Universal Airplane Salvage Company, which bought surplus naval aircraft, dismantled them and melted down their aluminum into ingots. He had a large operation in Hawaii; he wasn't sure, he told Jarcho, what was out there but certainly aircraft engines and parts that might prove useful.

Jarcho passed on the information to Schwimmer, who was definitely interested. He would need spare engines and he was having a hard time getting parts; he had had to buy a fourth Constellation to cannibalize for spare parts to recondition the original three Connies. He was too busy to go to Hawaii himself and so was Rey Selk, but Selk had a cousin—Hank Greenspun, a tough former Army ordnance officer who had been a company commander with Patton's Third Army in World War II and was currently running a radio station in booming Las Vegas, Nevada. Never one to avoid a fight, especially in a good cause, Greenspun agreed to take a "couple of weeks" off and go to Hawaii to look things over.

He quickly reported back that the Universal Airplane Salvage Company at Iroquois Point, the naval air station on Oahu, was indeed a treasure trove. It was enormous, about half a mile long and a quarter of a mile wide. And it was piled high with planes, plane parts, engines, communications equipment and armaments, distributed in vast confusing piles and a labyrinth of crates. A small army of Filipino workmen separated the salvageable aluminum and melted it down in red-hot blast furnaces.

Willie Sosnow, the Brooklyn mechanic, went over to help Greenspun appraise the possibilities. Sosnow ascertained that some of the engines, with slight modification, could be used for the C-46s. Liff told the two men to take whatever they wanted; it was all on the house. They hired some youngsters from a vocational school to help them and began dismantling and crating the valuable engines.

But Greenspun had seen something else in the yard that interested him. Near Universal's garage was a large pile of .30- and .50-caliber aircraft machine guns that had been taken from the noses and turrets of the planes when they were stripped down for salvage. Greenspun casually checked the action of one of the guns and found that "they functioned almost as smoothly as new." On another lower field there was a second huge pile of machine guns at one end of the yard, and separated from it only by an open space was the Navy "dump," where two Marines guarded a third pile of guns, gun mounts and extra barrels. These were brand-new, still packed in cosmoline preservative. They had not yet been declared surplus and still belonged to the Navy.

Greenspun couldn't get the guns out of his mind. "I knew from St. Lo, Avranches, Falaise Gap and the long push to Nancy that the only way to gain and hold ground is with guns."

Explaining that they were pressed for time, Greenspun and Sosnow took to staying on at the yard in the evening to continue their packing. As soon as the last workman had gone, they would dash to the piles of guns, pick out the best, hurriedly brush off the accumulated dust, dismantle them and douse them with hydraulic brake fluid to prevent further rusting—there were cans of the fluid, which had been drained out of the planes, standing all over the field. Then they packed the guns in engine crates, thirty-five to fifty guns to a crate, carefully weighing each crate to make sure it corresponded to the engine weight already stenciled on the outside. So far, so good, but Greenspun knew from his experience in World War II that in the heat of firing, the barrels of the guns would burn out and warp. Spare barrels would be necessary to keep the guns in action. At the Navy dump were hundreds of barrels, factory fresh, neatly packed, two dozen to a case. It was tantalizing. He watched the Marine guards walking sleepily back and forth; he noticed that every two hours there was an eight-minute span when both guards, patrolling in opposite directions, were out of sight. That was long enough. With a fork lift, he sped in and hauled off several cases of barrels.

These too were repacked in the ubiquitous engine crates. One night Greenspun and Sosnow were startled to hear a jeep drive up. In it was an employee of Universal Airplane Salvage, who at sight of them appeared to be as discomfited as they. He mumbled something about coming to get gas. Greenspun muttered something about collecting guns for a Hollywood film spectacle. "We kind of caught each other," Sosnow recalls. But then, encouraged by two five-dollar bills that Greenspun slipped to him, the employee pitched in and helped. He came back again on other evenings and on several of them received additional encouragement to a total of $250.

Greenspun urged him to keep what they were doing quiet. He now implied that the guns were going to Latin America and, in a way, that was the case. The underground planned to ship them to the mainland, then down to Mexico, where they would be picked up, along with the arms being bought in Mexico, when the time came for the airplanes of Yakum Purkan to take off.

At the end of two weeks there were sixteen crates of machine guns and barrels standing beside forty-two that were loaded with airplane engines. All looked identical except for a small cryptic marking that identified, to Greenspun and Sosnow, which ones contained the guns.

On March 11 fifty-eight crates consigned to Schwimmer Aviation Service in Burbank were loaded aboard the S.S. *Lane Victory* of the American President Lines, bound for Wilmington, California.

Hiding fifteen tons of contraband machine guns in Los Angeles until they could be transshipped to Mexico did not prove to be easy. Rey Selk, to whom the job fell, had them moved uneasily from one warehouse to another. He heard the FBI had been asking questions in Hawaii. Soon it was asking questions in Los Angeles too. To cover the trail, Selk had the guns removed from the crates in which they'd arrived.

The telltale crates were burned and the guns completely dismantled. Selk found volunteers through Bernard Fineman, a Hollywood screen producer who ran the West Coast's "Hotel Fourteen" in a penthouse suite in Beverly Hills, to clean and oil the deteriorating arsenal. Repacked in gunnysacks, the dismantled parts were distributed to whoever would agree to store them. Selk and Fineman talked friends, relatives and sympathetic businessmen into lending space for the mysterious packages in warehouses, factories, even private residential garages in some of the city's best suburbs. Hank Greenspun, back in the United States, was given the job of finding a way to move the guns to Mexico.

It soon became an open secret among the dozen or so skippers trying to make a living by chartering yachts out of Newport Beach, south of Los Angeles, that someone was looking for a boat to run guns south of the border. Several had turned it down as too dangerous. Lee Lewis, a romantic young sailing buff who had grown up on the beach in Venice, California, was interested.

Lewis had been an officer in the merchant marine and a navigator with the tuna fleet operating out of San Diego. A few years before he had managed to buy his own boat, the *Idalia*, an elegantly rigged seventy-five-foot sailing vessel, built at the turn of the century in Boston for the commodore of the New York Yacht Club and later owned by California's flamboyant advertising dentist, Dr. Painless Parker. Lewis, living on the boat, had spent two years restoring the ship's stately rosewood circular companionway, its teak paneling, its five commodious cabins and ninety-eight-foot main mast. He and the *Idalia* had just returned from a charter cruise to Acapulco with a party of fishermen. That is where Greenspun wanted Lewis to return, but with a different sort of cargo.

Greenspun and Lewis met at Newport Beach to discuss the proposition. Greenspun told Lewis frankly what it was all about. Lewis was "very willing. I was imbued with the idea of sailing and adventure, and the combination of that with doing something for Palestine appealed to me."

That was about the last point of agreement between the two men—or in their accounts of what happened during the ensuing weeks.

With the FBI closing in—U.S. Customs found and seized the entire Hawaiian shipment of aircraft engines and noted the absence of sixteen crates—Greenspun, Sosnow, and Leo Gardner, the pilot who had come to work for Schwimmer Aviation, with an assorted group of volunteer assistants, hurriedly collected the sacks of machine gun parts, loaded them on a truck and headed for a rendezvous with the *Idalia* in San Pedro, the port of Los Angeles.

Loading began just before midnight from the dock of a deserted lumberyard. The guns had to be moved from the truck onto a Higgins landing craft and ferried to Warren Newmark's Yacht Center at the end of the quay, where the *Idalia* was moored.

"It must have been low tide," recalls Leo Gardner, "because the Higgins was way down from the side of the dock and each sack of guns had to be handed down and handed down and handed down. The guns had been packed five or six to a sack. Well, you can't put half a dozen fifty-caliber machine guns in a sack and lift it."

The amateur stevedores were soon "spent, shaken and exhausted."

The barge made several crossings of the port, dodging a Coast Guard patrol. At Yacht Center, the hundred or so heavy sacks had to be hoisted back up the side of the wooden barge, then lowered down the *Idalia*'s narrow twisting staircase. As the tired men slung them down, the rosewood companionway gave way; the slender carved columns supporting the graceful chained railing broke. Lee Lewis protested. "It was sort of a cry in the dark," he says now. Literally— since the *Idalia*'s electrical system was out and the loading was being done by candlelight. Greenspun remembers hearing Lewis and the "sound of splintering wood," but he was "too busy to answer; I set up planking to serve as a jury-rigged gangway. It was the worst kind of nightmare . . . Most of us were glassy-eyed and puffing for breath." Some of the men gave out. Gardner says his shins are still scarred from the metal that bounced against them as he continued to lug, shove and push the bags of guns.

The *Idalia* sank lower and lower into the sea as fifteen tons of cargo were piled into the thirty-four-ton vessel. The half-submerged portholes began to leak.

Lewis, surveying the wreck of his vessel, announced he wasn't going. The overloaded ship, he assured Greenspun, would never make it. He wanted the guns unloaded, immediately. The two men argued acrimoniously, their charges and countercharges ranging over matters of money, motives, promises and patriotism. Finally Lewis agreed to take the cargo as far as Catalina, where Greenspun said another boat would meet them.

The *Idalia* slipped past the lighthouse at the entrance to San Pedro harbor and into the channel; Lewis, in faded dungarees and a big fur-lined jacket, was at the helm when Greenspun pulled out a Mauser and ordered him to turn over the wheel to Nathan Ratner, one of a three-man crew whom Greenspun had brought along. "There is no boat waiting for us at Catalina," he told Lewis curtly. "The *Idalia* is going all the way to Acapulco."

Lewis says he can "still feel the anger rising in me; if you want to make someone mad, take their boat away from them."

Greenspun, for his part, says he had "never been so angry in my life."

The tense moment passed. Lewis went off to get some sleep, thinking, When I am rested, I will know what to do. He woke late the next day to find "the boat making poor speed, the crew bickering, Hank giving orders and everybody mad." The provisions for the ship had been left behind at the dock; the only food on board was marshmallow cookies, canned sardines and stale bread. There was no compass and the crew wasn't sure how to let out more sail. To pick up speed, Lewis helped with the sails and went back to work at the helm.

He had a scheme: "I decided that sooner or later the others would fall asleep and I would again be master of my own vessel. By dusk we'd be in a position where I could head the boat into the Coronado channel near San Diego. I remembered very clearly that there was a big bell buoy in the middle of the channel. I thought my best bet would be to jump off the boat and swim to the buoy, where a fishing boat would pick me up in the morning. Before going overboard I would lash the wheel and head the boat toward Coronado, where it would crash on the rocks. The first part worked out fine, just as I planned. I was about to slip over the side when I found I couldn't do it.

"That was the turning point of the whole trip. Greenspun probably doesn't realize it; probably never knew it. The overwhelming factor was that I couldn't abandon my ship and destroy it. The second factor was I felt those guns ought to get to Palestine."

Leo Gardner, after seeing the boat sail, flew down to San Diego in a single-engine Beechcraft and cruised around until he sighted the *Idalia* off the coast of La Jolla. He then landed in San Diego and chartered a speedboat to try to take the forgotten provisions out to the yacht. Heading out at night, he ran into a flotilla of U.S. Navy ships on night maneuvers. Since they were blacked out, Gardner blacked out too. Dodging among gigantic shadows—"You could tell how close you were by the rock of the little boat in the wake of the ships"—he was unable to find the *Idalia* again.

By the time the *Idalia* reached Ensenada, a Mexican city south of San Diego, the next day, Greenspun, crew and captive skipper had "established a certain rapport." They refueled in Ensenada, bought provisions and Lewis made a quick trip to San Diego.

Lewis's recollection is that he met Larry Ives, the ex-Marine major who had been negotiating for arms in Mexico, at the U.S. Grant Hotel to discuss getting another boat to continue the journey. Ives instead persuaded him to go on in the *Idalia* with a promise of $6,500 for the journey.

After Ensenada the trip went smoothly. Contrary to Lewis's pessimistic predictions, the *Idalia* didn't sink. The sailing was good. The five young men slept on deck—the cabins were full of guns—

and discussed life, love and the importance of getting the guns to Palestine.

"One minute Lewis was ready to go all the way with us," recalls Greenspun. "He was even going to Palestine to fight. Then he'd turn cool."

Lewis, looking back on it, says, "What put me off was that there was no trust. Greenspun was pugnacious from the beginning. But he did accomplish the job he set out to do."

The *Idalia* reached Acapulco ahead of schedule, eleven days after leaving Ensenada. It dropped anchor in front of the yacht club, in the same spot it had occupied a few weeks before when Lewis had been down there with his charter of vacationing fishermen. Lewis went ashore to stay with a friend—and report on his recent voyage to the American consul and, ultimately, the FBI. Greenspun went to Mexico City to arrange for the transfer of the guns. The two men would meet again two years later—in a Federal court.

XXIX

SCHALIT'S RETURN

Not all of the shipping problems were on the West Coast. An urgent telegram reached New York from Tel Aviv:

ALL BOATS CALLING EGYPTIAN PORTS WITH CARGO FOR JEWISH FIRMS PALESTINE ARE DETAINED AND FORCED EITHER GIVE UP PALESTINE BOUND CARGO FOR CONFISCATION OR UNDERTAKE NOT PROCEED DESTINATION PALESTINE STOP SEVERAL IMPORTANT CONSIGNMENTS THUS CONFISCATED OR RETURNED PORTS DEPARTURE STOP . . . PLEASE TAKE APPROPRIATE STEPS . . . SHERTOK

Not only were possible war materials being seized (200 of Danny Fliderblum's walkie-talkies), but Egyptian authorities in Port Said had confiscated 9,036 tons of flour, 5,000 tons of maize and canned goods and 5,000 bales of fodder from two ships bound for Palestine from Australia.

Elie Schalit had been "fighting to keep the shipping lanes open"; to persuade ships carrying important Palestine-bound consignments to bypass Arab ports; to cajole reluctant ship owners into going there at all.

At a stormy session at American Export Lines, one of the companies with which Schalit had been doing a large volume of business, an executive put the matter bluntly: "Look, Elie, let's get away from fantasies. Seven Arab states against a possible Jewish state. Do you think you have a Chinaman's chance? We've got to take a realistic point of view."

American Export, like a number of other lines, would later suspend its Palestine service temporarily.

It was not an unforeseen development. In March Schalit and another Palestinian, Raphael Recanati, formed what would become the American-Israeli Shipping Company (financed by Schalit's old employer the Palestine Economic Corporation and by the American-Palestine Trading Corporation). AIS chartered Greek, Panamanian, even Lebanese ships—its first ship was chartered from a prominent Portuguese Jew, José Ben Saud, who operated out of the Azores—to carry goods directly to Palestine. This insured their getting there and guaranteed better security all the way, from their loading at two piers, one that had been leased at Pots Cove at the foot of 9th Street in Astoria, the other being Pier 37 in Manhattan, both on the East River, to the ports of Tel Aviv and Haifa.

Only "white goods" were shipped by AIS, normal commercial cargo and such "gray" military equipment as did not come under the U.S. embargo. Schalit steadfastly refused to touch any "black goods." He felt, since the TNT incident, that he was too hot himself; and he didn't want to endanger the free flow of shipping with anything that might cause trouble. A variety of other people and other means were tried for getting black goods through, with varying success.

Finally Teddy Kollek summoned Schalit to a meeting at the Hotel Fourteen. It was held in Kollek's sleeping quarters on the top floor. Zvi Brenner was present. The meeting went on all night. Kollek wanted Schalit to take on the shipment of black goods again. Schalit demurred. Kollek and Brenner insisted. In the end Schalit agreed, but laid down two conditions. He would ship only cargo he considered "cool" enough to handle—a stipulation that kept him at loggerheads with some of the excited provisioners he met at the Hotel Fourteen, who, in his view, "bought a great deal that just couldn't be shipped"— and once something was turned over to him, he would assume complete control. He didn't trust the "security" at the Hotel Fourteen, where, he felt, Arazi and now Greenspun had set much too flamboyant a tone.

To help him in his moonlighting—because he would still carry on in full daylight at AIS—he assembled assistants with the necessary esoteric specialties. As usual the ebullient Schalit found one of them right next door. Like the overworked warehouse foreman Jules Chender, who had finally escaped from his drafty chores in the Bronx to Paris, David Mersten, a twenty-three-year-old bachelor, was a neighbor of Schalit's in the building at 325 Central Park West. An alumnus of City College and of U.S. Army counterintelligence, Mersten was charged with, among other things, taking photographs of shipments from International Harvester, General Motors, Ford and other manufacturers of bulky merchandise to the Ideal Stencil

Company on Cortlandt Street, where stencils exactly duplicating their markings were made. Mersten worked out of an office at 10 Beaver Street, where, he recalls, the telephone was kept in a locked desk drawer, its hidden cord drawn up through the bottom of the desk, and used only in case of emergency. Most calls were made through the pay telephone downstairs, which they could be sure was not tapped. He also traveled a great deal, checking on shipments coming in from all over the country—for Schalit's system of concealment began at the source.

Three of his young men roamed the United States in a Nash, towing a large trailer equipped with a portable gasoline generator, power saws, staplers, a banding machine, paint and stencils. They bought lumber or whatever other supplies they needed along the way. They slept in the car—it had reclining seats. Wherever a black shipment was to go out, they pulled up and did an instant crating and camouflaging job. Sometimes they caught up with the shipment again, somewhere else, to give it still another new look and destination and further confuse its trail.

When a shipment arrived in the East, carefully camouflaged with a boldly stenciled destination that had no connection with the place it was really bound for, it was sent to a regular commercial warehouse in Perth Amboy or Bayonne, New Jersey. If it was particularly hot, it might be sent to cool off for a spell in even more discreet storage. A large radar trailer might spend a few weeks in an open lot in the Red Hook section of Brooklyn; small planes, bought as scrap, would be stashed in an empty seventeen-acre sand pit in Woodbury, Long Island, owned by Institute member Moses Heyman, the inventor of artificial mica. When they were ready to move out, the shipments would be labeled and addressed to accord with the shipping papers Schalit had procured.

Every truck convoy taking merchandise to a ship had special "dispersal instructions" in case anything went wrong.

At the pier Schalit had his own cooper on the job with extra steel strapping, planking and nails; if a crate dropped or broke, the cooper could patch it up before prying eyes could get a good look or curious onlookers ask questions. There would be no more surprise discoveries of TNT.

Even as the merchandise was being loaded, extra precautions were taken. The FBI arrived once just after a shipment of airplane parts had disappeared under a load of alfalfa. Another time, when the loading of one of the ships was being closely watched, crates of

Danny Fliderblum's communications equipment were taken by small boats around to the far side of the ship to be put aboard, out of sight of observers on the dock.

Only when it was safely aboard—usually on one of the chartered ships of AIS—did the black merchandise achieve the respectability of free association with the white; by then only a few coded notations on the crates and in the messages that went back and forth between New York and Tel Aviv differentiated it from thousands of mundane items that flowed across the ocean to help found the new state.

But all of these would be triumphs of the future. In January and February of 1948, as MFP, Inland Machinery and the other special companies, the trucking networks, warehouses and shipping lines were being organized, the Jews of Palestine had little more than a paper army—a table of organization and a gigantic shopping list.

XXX

LAND AND LABOR

I n 1793, in the first case of its kind, Gideon Henfield, an American who had volunteered to sail aboard a French privateer in that country's sea war against Great Britain, was prosecuted for violation of the "law of nations" considered to be a part of American common law. He was acquitted.

The following year a neutrality act for the first time made it a felony for anyone to "enlist or hire himself, or hire or retain another person to enlist or enter himself or to go beyond the limits or jurisdiction of the United States with intent to be enlisted in the service of a foreign prince or state." Federal law later spelled out the punishment if convicted: a maximum of a $1,000 fine or three years in prison, or both. But the law did not dissuade interested parties from seeking recruits among Americans—or Americans from responding, whether out of good will, conviction, self-interest, perversity, ancestral ties, yearning for adventure or hard cash. Sometimes they were answering the quiet undercover call of an American governmental agency.

Americans fought in the nineteenth-century revolts of the South American colonies against Spain, with the armed forces of Great Britain in the Crimean War, in the Lafayette Escadrille of World War I, in the Spanish Civil War of 1936–39. With tacit governmental approval, the American Eagle Squadron served with the Royal Air Force in the Battle of Britain and General Claire L. Chennault's famous Flying Tigers were quietly recruited in 1940 by the "Central Aircraft Manufacturing Company" and sent under assumed names to Burma for training to fight with the Chinese against Japan.

The key words in the neutrality law were "hire" and "retain." As President Roosevelt said in 1940, in commenting on an American aviator's attempt to enlist with the Finnish armed forces in their fight against the Soviet Union, "If the American were merely seeking information as to whether or how he might enlist, there was nothing wrong. If the Legation were inviting or inducing the enlistment, it would be another matter."

To Nahum Bernstein and the other lawyers, as they studied the legal precedents of recruiting volunteers in the United States, small and nebulous details like that now became vital. There was also the most intangible factor of all: The government might indict, as it had done in other cases and in other wars, but if public opinion differed from the strict interpretation of U.S. neutrality, no jury would convict.

Francisco Miranda had been acquitted of the charge of organizing a military expedition in the United States to help the South American colonies against Spain. The neutrality laws had been held inapplicable to the Santo Domingo rebellion on the technical ground that an insurrectionary group was not "a foreign prince or state." The Americans who had responded to British recruiters during the Crimean War had been held innocent, despite a seemingly airtight case—they had not actually enlisted within the territorial limits of the United States. No one had even tried to prosecute the hundreds of Americans who jumped the gun on World War II to serve with foreign armed forces; no jury would have convicted.

Just where the line might be drawn in respect to Palestine was less obvious. But, however thin and shaky, the line would now have to be walked.

Veterans' groups and individuals were offering their services to every organization concerned with Palestine. They besieged the speakers at the meetings held by Americans for Haganah, tugged at the coattails of members of the Sonneborn Institute, filled the mailboxes of the well-known Zionist organizations. And now Tel Aviv had asked for men and women.

A new Palestinian had arrived at the Hotel Fourteen to work under Teddy Kollek. With a stout "Righto," Major Wellesley Aron filled MFP requests for a rousing speech at a parlor meeting. Every inch the British officer, his credentials were tip-top. He had commanded the first Palestinian unit in the British Army. His Britishness astounded some of his audiences in Far Rockaway or Boyle Heights, but there was nothing of the Colonel Blimp about him; he knew what he wanted and he kept a sharp eye out for it: specialists to man the sophisticated equipment that an army would need if it was to fight, in only four months' time, against six invading Arab states.

Teddy Kollek authorized the formation of a new organization: Land and Labor for Palestine, Inc. Ostensibly it was to carry on a job that had been done for years by other organizations: recruit men and women to work on the land and thereby fulfill the Zionist ideal. Many of these organizations had training camps where, during the summer holidays, youths learned the rudiments of agriculture. Land and Labor would have a camp too. For its more urban activities, it took offices in the Hotel Breslin, Broadway and 29th Street, starting in a single room, 1202, and branching out in quick time with offices in Chicago, Boston, Philadelphia, Baltimore, Pittsburgh, Cleveland, Detroit and Miami. Often its branch offices shared space and manpower with Materials for Palestine; MFP helped in many ways to make the new organization welcome. It gave L and L's "regional directors" letters of introduction to members of the Sonneborn Institute, who made sure they were invited to address meetings of key organizations in their areas, or to meet small informal groups in private homes.

But the biggest help that MFP was able to give L and L was access, through a friend, to the chaplaincy records of World War II. Thus L and L started out its double life knowing the name, rank, branch of service and a fairly recent home address of every Jewish veteran of the United States and Canadian armed forces.

It could do little more than invite the men (and women) to a talk on the situation in Palestine by Major Aron or another staff member. Any man who expressed interest would get a carefully worded letter—first on rubber-stamped copy paper, then, as confidence and resources grew, on a variety of local office letterheads:

"We have been informed that you are interested in lending assistance to Palestine. We should like to discuss this matter with you. Please telephone this office for an appointment."

From the Hotel Breslin office in New York, Major Aron and his staff (six by March) sent out a stream of instructions, carefully numbering the most important of them, and advising, "Each copy of the instructions has been numbered for certain reasons. Your copy is Number ——. It will be clear to you that the attached document is NOT FOR FILING and should be kept in close and secure possession of the person responsible for this matter in question."

Whether addressing a group or only one man, the speakers were told what to say:

> The struggle in Palestine needs manpower.
> Struggle doesn't necessarily mean fighting. Labor, to provide food and other necessities, is not less important.
> The aims and objectives of Land and Labor for Palestine are to encourage and assist individuals interested in strengthening

and developing the Jewish Homeland by providing technical and agricultural skills. Land and Labor for Palestine is the official body deputed to advise individuals as to the needs of Palestine and the procedure recommended. . . .

The need is for people of integrity with an urgent desire to assist, to the utmost of their capacity, for the duration of the present emergency in Palestine.

Volunteers are needed who can adjust themselves to a new environment, rugged living conditions, and who are ready to do any kind of hard labor. . . .

The minimum stay required is two years, or the emergency to be determined by the Palestinian authorities. . . .

Members of any reserve organization are not thereby prevented from offering their services. . . .

Speakers were also told how to say it:

The technique of speaking shall be a cold, factual presentation of the subject matter. It is essential that the speaker should not discuss anything that would lend itself to misinterpretation or distortion as to the aims and nature of work of Land and Labor for Palestine.

It should be made clear to the audiences that Land and Labor for Palestine is operating as a perfectly legal organization. At the same time, it must be emphasized that careless talk, based upon misunderstanding of highly emotional individuals, may result in misinterpretation, also rumors, and thereby endanger our project.

A speaker, upon completion of each mission, shall report in a manner substantially as follows:
a. Date
b. Place
c. Organization
d. Number of persons addressed
e. Remarks, viz: age level, response, and recommendation

The number of persons at any meeting thus addressed shall be small and those present vouched for.

Another of Aron's memoranda emphasized that news of Land and Labor was not to be spread by "printed matter or press releases, but by chain reaction." And the application blanks that were distributed to audiences were to be counted before and after, and all blank applications collected as well as those that had been filled out.

Some of Land and Labor's regional offices were advised by civilian panels. Again the nationwide contacts of the Institute were called upon. To some of the volunteer panelists, the work of interviewing applicants was old stuff—they had served on World War II Selective Service boards. After the first screening of names, the survivors were asked to fill out a "personnel placement questionnaire" in four parts, which asked his family background, his life history, his occupation or skills and the jobs he had held, including any military experience.

An applicant was never told in any of the preliminary interviews whether he had been accepted or rejected. There was no way for outsiders to determine just what Land and Labor was looking for, only the carefully weighed words of its speakers and interviewers.

Sample questions to be asked by interviewers:

> Why are you anxious to offer your services on behalf of Palestine?
> Do you expect to make any financial gain in this project?
> Are you prepared to do any kind of job that may be required of you, even though it may involve hard, dirty work?
> Would you be ready to perform a task that is not the sort of work that you have been doing?
> Are you prepared to accept primitive living conditions?
> Will you accept orders and instructions without question?

In some cities the medical examination included a session with a psychiatrist.

The applicant, once accepted, would request a passport at the State Department passport office closest to his home. He might get help in filling out the State Department form from a regional volunteer who had been especially briefed in this specialty:

> The applicant will give his destination as either Scandinavia, Holland, Belgium, France, or Switzerland. In order to be able to give advice as to what ships sail to these countries, where those ships travel, from where they leave, etc., the local passport person should familiarize himself with the sailings of various lines, information which can be procured at any travel bureau.
> When giving advice, he [the local passport person] should keep in mind the following:
> Don't give too many the same story.
> Don't send too many down to the Passport Office on any given day.

To the passport application's question about the "Purpose of the Trip" different answers were recommended as the situation changed. At first applicants had simply stated they intended to go to Palestine. When the State Department began rejecting passports for Palestine-bound travelers, the applicants were told "the purpose of the trip should be given as: to visit relatives (if the applicant has any in Western Europe), to tour, vacation, or trip; if [he is] a soldier who served in the ETO, the applicant can say: to visit a friend, or his girl; he must NEVER say for a job or education unless the applicant has actual proof that a job really awaits him. As the summer months roll around, hundreds will be preparing to go for their vacations abroad."

When it was noted that many applications by military-age young men wanting to travel in Europe—especially if they had names regarded as Jewish—were being rejected by the State Department, L and L advised its applicants to say they were going on business.

Through MFP it asked business firms around the country to lend a hand—or, more specifically, a letterhead. Forty firms agreed to give applicants letters backing up their assertions that they had business abroad. Aron's office saw to it that no firm "hired" more than one overseas representative; the State Department and the FBI might be interested in a sudden spurt of foreign trade.

Once he had his passport, the applicant waited for word to proceed to New York.

The New York office kept tabs on every man that the regional offices were processing. It was interested in the men secretly classified as "specialists." A specialist was a commissioned officer or a noncom with combat experience or other qualifications that were particularly needed in Palestine. (A "regular" was an enlisted man who had not seen combat.) Most of the specialists, except those who had served in the United States Army Air Forces or the Royal Canadian Air Force, were invited to meet the Panel.

No one talked much about the Panel. Its ostensible purpose was set forth in another memo: "In view of the age limits involved [only those between eighteen and thirty-five were being considered], it was obvious that the greater part of the male applicants would have had more or less military experience. In determining their general suitability for life in Palestine, it was desirable that the statements of the applicants and such documents as they had be reviewed by men of military experience in order that the reliability of the statements made and the significance of the documents presented be evaluated."

The Panel usually met at night, often in the offices of a textile firm on Fourth Avenue (now Park Avenue South) in Manhattan. Its most active member had been one of the most aggressive tank commanders in General Patton's Third Army; another had served on General Eisenhower's staff. The questions they asked the future farmers could have been inspired by the dictum that "good soldiers make good farmers." But no one who met with the Panel came away with the impression he had been competing for a 4-H Club prize.*

The applicants—they were never called "volunteers" in writing—came to New York shortly before their ship was due to sail. They picked up their tickets at a travel agency in the Hotel Breslin, but only the "group leaders"—particularly trusted volunteers—went upstairs to the offices of L and L. Tickets in hand, the men were sent by train to L and L's training camp in the sylvan surroundings of Peekskill, New York, across the Hudson River from West Point. The camp was called in all L and L communications the "Seminar." Its director was a Palestinian, Zvi Caspi, who gave lectures on the history of Palestine, talked about life in settlements, and started each day with a brief session of close-order drill commands, shouted in Hebrew to accustom the applicants to the sound of the Homeland's language and improve their muscle tone.

Most of the applicants brought along their old uniforms, but others, falling into the unmartial spirit inspired by Major Aron's instructions, arrived in civilian clothes without even a change. It fell to the ubiquitous Sam Sloan to supply the Seminar.

> Dear Mr. Sloan:
> I shall arrive in New York on Friday afternoon to see off a group of eight boys who will be going overseas. I shall appreciate your preparing for these eight boys the same type of equipment

---

* On the Arab side, all non-Palestinian Arabs who entered Palestine to fight against the Jews were, of course, foreign volunteers—until the invasion of May 15, 1948. Some nationals of European countries also served with the Arabs. In January, the London office of the Palestine Arab political mission announced it had applications from over four thousand Britons—"men with experience in every branch of the British armed forces and from every walk of life"—and, while it would not encourage these men, the office said, it pointed out: "Britons who apply here for visas to enter Arab countries and state their open intention to volunteer would most probably not receive visas. But there is no reason why they cannot enter Arab states for any other bona fide purposes." In January, three former Indian Army officers flew from London to Paris with the announced intention of joining the Arabs.

as for the previous bunch: viz: for each fellow—2 khaki trousers; 2 khaki shirts; 1 coverall; 1 pair boots; 2 towels; 1 blanket; 1 mess kit and 1 duffle bag. I have managed to obtain sizes for six of the boys. The other sizes I will supply in New York.

Even the Seminar's cots, mattresses, towels and kitchenware came from the growing stockpile of surplus goods MFP was getting from its friends in the Institute and their friends. At MFP's warehouse at 177 Water Street in Brooklyn, Rusty Jarcho strung up a curtain across one corner of the main room. On one side of the curtain volunteer women sat mending uniforms, cutting off insignia and sewing on buttons. On the other side the volunteers tried everything on. It was the only underground haberdashery in town.

The applicants were interviewed one more time at the Seminar by someone from the New York office of L and L. He asked them to fill out still another of Major Aron's forms, Form B. It asked the usual vital statistics and then got down to business—it wanted the applicant's military qualifications in detail.

Every Form B was carried back to New York and retyped in five copies. One copy was sent to Tel Aviv. Another went to the Paris office of Haganah, the first overseas stop for most of the volunteers. A third was handed to the group leader just before the ship sailed. Two copies went to the Hotel Fourteen, into the old safe in Ruby Barnett's office on the mezzanine. Barnett, eying the growing pile of papers in his safe, would shake his head and mutter, "Go ahead, fill it up, I got nothing else to put in." But no one had time to listen to the financial problems of the underground's reluctant host.

Hundreds of men were passing through New York on their way to Palestine. Many came from Canada, where they had been recruited by Ben Dunkelman, the former major in the Queen's Own Rifles of Canada who had won the DSO during World War II. It was decided to form an all-Canadian unit and Dunkelman went over himself to head it up. It would never come into being—things were not that well-organized—but Dunkelman would command a brigade that captured Nazareth. Altogether, more than 1,500 men and women would go to Palestine from the United States and Canada to fight with the various units of the Jewish army.

They usually left New York by ship, often one of the converted Victory ships, the *Marine Carp* or the *Marine Tiger*, which provided cheap dormitory-style passage across the Atlantic. In Le Havre they were met by a young Palestinian recognized by the book he was carrying: *A Farewell to Arms*. He shepherded them onto a train to Paris and into the building at 187 Avenue de la Grande Armée, French headquarters of Haganah, to be checked in by Ruth Berman, a former officer in the ATS, the British equivalent of the WAC, who earlier had put in a tour of duty at the Hotel Fourteen. Another Palestinian guide took them to the Gare de Lyon and put them aboard the train to Marseilles, where a bus met them and took them to the Grande Arenas displaced persons camp outside the city. They would wait there, with the DPs, for space on one of the illegal immigrant ships still plying the Mediterranean. If they had not yet decided why they had come, they would learn there.

In Tel Aviv Harold Jaffer, who had been the Institute's first employee, was in charge of the reception center for the "Anglo Saxon volunteers"—Mahal, the Palestinians called it. One of the things he told the new arrivals was that their families could reach them by writing, care of Harold Jaffer, to 250 West 57th Street, New York.

There was one category of applicants that Land and Labor treated with special concern—although preliminary interviewers were cautioned in another one of Major Aron's memoranda not to betray their interest—men with aviation experience. They went through the same preliminary routine as everyone else, but interviewers were instructed to take special pains to document their experience and ascertain whether it was sufficient for what L and L had in mind. The qualifications were simple to establish:

"Pilots. Ex-military (check Log Book and AAF Form 5). Commercial (at least 1,000 hours total time, of which at least 100 twin-engined with valid CAA license. See Log Book).

"Navigators. Ex-military (at least 500 hours; should include celestial navigation. Check Form 5).

"Flight radio operators. Minimum 500 hours. (Check Form 5. Should hold appropriate FCC license.)"

There was one more qualification: the man must be available within three weeks from the date of acceptance.

When he was checked out and his references established, the interviewer took the man aside for a chat. If things worked out, the interviewer told him, he would be paid a small salary plus expenses. If he had dependents, they might receive a small allotment.

Then he was handed a ticket, by rail or air, given enough money for a few days' expenses, and sent to New York with a telephone number—and instructions to ask for "Sam."

The telephone number was for Land and Labor. Sam would ask him where he was staying and make a careful note of the telephone number, then he would ask if the applicant would be in that evening. Sam was quite specific about the time: "Someone will call you."

The someone was "Steve." His voice was reedy and rapid-fire with an unmistakable Brooklyn accent. He sounded as if he had a cigar clamped between his teeth, but he was surprisingly jovial and relaxed. He would make a date to meet the man at his hotel room. He arrived promptly, short, wiry and a fast talker. He knew airplanes and in his slangy, slurred Brooklynese he managed to ask a lot of questions. He sized people up in a hurry and, as he looked them over, he spun out an airy barely coherent offer.

He had jobs . . . an airplane . . . cargo . . . Palestine. The salaries were poor . . . long hours . . . might be dangerous. He sounded like the Mad Hatter describing a flying Wonderland and accompanied his spiel with winks, leers and a good deal of staring at the applicant through the smoke of his cigar. He seldom finished a sentence; nothing he said could be used as evidence against him in a court of law. But the implication was clear to anyone sufficiently interested to discern it.

Those who did—and passed Steve's scrutiny—were invited to drop into the offices of Service Airways.

PART
FIVE

XXXI

SERVICE AIRWAYS

Service Airways was the newest of the underground's "special agencies," the cover company for the ambitious plan to airlift supplies into Palestine and create a fighting air force. Under its protective umbrella of legitimacy a multitude of activities would be carried on. Planes would be leased, bought and deployed; pilots and crews would be hired, air routes would be established. As usual, Nahum Bernstein had devised the legal structure.

Only a month before, Service Airways had been a dream unrealized, gathering dust in a thin folder of papers in the Forest Hills apartment of Irvin "Swifty" Schindler, a tall curly-haired Floridian who had flown for the Air Transport Command during the war. In 1944, looking ahead to a future in civilian aviation, Schindler had incorporated Service Airways, Inc., with his wife, Edyth, who also had a pilot's license. They had bought a four-passenger Beechcraft and run charter flights out of a little airport in Andover, New Jersey, between Swifty's regular trips. It wasn't a paying proposition and they had given it up, sold their plane. But Schindler had kept up his company's registration, always hoping to do something with it again. Meanwhile, he was working discontentedly as co-pilot for a non-scheduled airline with no hope of promotion—the chief pilot had said he'd be goddamned if he'd have a Jew as a captain.

During a London layover Schindler shared his disgruntlement and boredom with a navigator for the airline, an Air Force veteran from Brooklyn, Irwin "Steve" Schwartz. Over a midday breakfast of salami and eggs at Bloom's, a well-known East End kosher restaurant, Steve confided that he was so disgusted he was ready to give up aviation; he had applied to sail as a radio operator on one of the ships taking illegal immigrants to Palestine. He was only waiting for the word to go—"the sooner the better." Schindler nodded; he knew how Steve felt. "Let me know," Schindler said, "if you ever hear anything about airplanes."

Soon afterward Schindler got a call from a "friend of Steve's" who plied him with questions over lunch in an Automat. During his next New York layover he was invited by another "friend of Steve's" to meet him in an office at 250 West 57th Street. Their discussion was friendly and wide-ranging but inconclusive. Back from another trip, Schindler's wife gave him a message from still another "friend of Steve's," a lawyer named Nahum Bernstein.

Bernstein wanted to know if it was true that Schindler had his own incorporated and registered airline. Yes, acknowledged Schindler. "Is it clean?" Bernstein asked, looking over his glasses at the young flier.

"It certainly is," said Schindler. The short life of Service Airways, Inc., had been an exemplary one.

In that case, said Bernstein, fixing Schindler with his eyes, he had a business proposition to make. How would Schindler like to be president of a revived Service Airways, fleshed out with three Constellations, no less, and several smaller cargo airplanes? All Schindler would have to do was find some business for the airline—say, cargo-carrying jobs between Latin America and Europe that would keep them busy until they were ready for bigger things.

Schindler didn't have to think twice. It sounded like the opportunity he had been waiting for with a chance to do something idealistic and adventurous thrown in. The remarks of his boss rankled and the memories of more exciting days with the ATC were fresh.

Within days Service Airways had smartly outfitted offices in Suites 515 and 516 at 250 West 57th Street and $50,000 in a bank account at the Chase National Bank.

Steve Schwartz—still in aviation, after all, thanks to his fortuitous conversation in London with Schindler—became its vice-president and Bernstein sent over some papers that made Rey Selk, of Schwimmer Aviation, Burbank, California, another vice-president.

Schindler quickly came up with just the kind of Latin American proposition Bernstein had in mind.

Martin B. Bellefond, a big good-looking ex-Air Force major, had had better luck than Schindler with the independent company he started after the war. World Airways, which he had begun with one surplus C-47 bought for $15,000—$750 cash—operating out of a tent pitched at Teterboro airport next to a pay telephone booth so that

Bellefond could get calls and, when he had a nickel, return them, had grown into one of the biggest non-skeds flying Puerto Ricans to New York.

But the CAA was cracking down on this profitable operation and Bellefond was looking for a new base.

One day, pondering his problems as he walked around the Battery in lower Manhattan, he stopped to watch some ships coming into the harbor. He noticed that several of them flew the Panamanian flag. "Why," he said to his wife that evening, "can't airplanes fly the Panamanian flag too?"

His wife recalled that one of her friends, when she was a college student at Radcliffe, had been a young Harvard student named Gilberto Arias, whose uncle had been president of Panama. Bellefond, who could now afford a telephone, put in a long distance call to Arias that evening. He posed the same question to him that he had to his wife. Arias, by now a prominent Panamanian attorney, thought the idea feasible. He invited Bellefond to come down and talk it over.

Panama had its own domestic airline, a couple of DC-3s. But it had an airport that could hold a hundred or more: Tocumen, built just after the war at a cost of $8 million on the Pacific side of the isthmus, a considerable distance from Panama City.

A country that linked two oceans and two continents, and whose flag appeared on so many ships at sea, had seen itself as a major link in the skies as well. But it hadn't worked out that way and the airport was something of a white elephant.

Bellefond hired the well-connected Arias as his attorney and, with his help, obtained a franchise for Líneas Aéreas de Panama, Sociedad Anónima, or, for short, LAPSA, which was to be the flag line of Panama.

Under terms of its charter, LAPSA would get not only Panamanian registration for its planes but the right to "rent and lease vessels, airplanes of any nature and description . . . maintain, operate and repair workshops and ports, buildings, hotels, hangars, runways, airfields . . . manufacture, make, buy, sell, have the right to operate, rent, lease, attend, repair, design . . ." The possibilities were endless. In addition the Panamanian government would instruct its embassies and consulates overseas to request landing rights for LAPSA's planes all around the world. "It was a hell of an opportunity," Bellefond recalls.

There was just one hitch. While he had been negotiating the Panama franchise, things had reached a point of crisis with World

Airways, and the other stockholders had "booted me out. There I was with a franchise and no airline."

It was about then that he ran into Schindler, president of the reborn Service Airways, who had once worked for Bellefond at World Airways. It didn't take the two men long to discover that their interests might coincide.

On January 26, a Constellation, with a temporary NL registration, took off from the Lockheed Air Terminal at Burbank, climbed above the smog of the San Fernando Valley and headed out over the Mojave Desert toward New York. Sam Lewis, the veteran Connie pilot, was at the controls; Leo Gardner was co-pilot; Al Schwimmer was at his old post as flight engineer. It was the first of the three Connies to be airborne; this was its first long flight. It was a triumphant moment, but Schwimmer was worried.

He wondered what Arazi, just back from Palestine, would have to tell him. He knew what he must tell Arazi and Bernstein: The FBI was still on his tail. Ptacek, the FBI agent who had come to see him after the TNT discovery, had been seen around the terminal chatting with Schwimmer's mechanics. Schwimmer and Selk were convinced that some of their employees had been induced to spy on them. There were problems with the airplanes too. The CAA was insisting that Schwimmer install a fuel-injection system which could add as much as $80,000 to the cost of each plane; without it, the CAA would not approve the Connies for service in the United States. The delivery of the additional C-46s by the WAA was unaccountably delayed.

The Connie landed at Millville, New Jersey, a former Army Air Force base converted to a rental operation. Schwimmer had chosen it as his eastern base because it was out of the public eye, but it meant a two-hour drive to New York.

At the Hotel Fourteen Bernstein greeted Schwimmer with news of Service Airways and Arazi regaled him with the plans for airlift Yakum Purkan, "deliverance from the skies"—which had been evolved during his stay in Palestine. Schwimmer told of the problems besetting him in Burbank. Ancient Aramaic prayers were all very well; the logistics of an airlift were something else. They would need pilots, bases, maintenance crews, spare parts for repairs, loading equipment, landing rights. And, to begin with, airplanes that were ready to fly, with legal registrations and licenses and clearances.

By far the most promising way out of all their difficulties seemed to be that presented by the chance meeting of Schindler and Bellefond. A Panamanian franchise could solve most of their problems.

Outside the United States there would be no insistence on equipping the Connies with expensive fuel-injection systems instead of carburetors; Schwimmer would be out from under the welter of CAA regulations in one swoop. And, presumably, once he began operating in Panama, he would be away from the jurisdiction of the FBI as well.

As for Yakum Purkan, a Panamanian company operating out of Panama would not be subject to the restrictions of the U.S. embargo of arms. And the need for maintenance and bases would be taken care of by the terms of LAPSA's charter, which gave it broad rights to build and operate every kind of facility.

Bellefond made a quick trip to Panama to sew up the charter and spell out its terms. He rented a building for offices and living quarters for air crews. On February 15 LAPSA and Service Airways signed a contract and Bellefond moved into 250 West 57th Street. The name of Líneas Aéreas de Panama, Sociedad Anónima appeared separately on the building directory, but upstairs on the fifth floor it was sharing office space with Service Airways.

Schwimmer returned to Burbank by commercial plane, leaving the Constellation at Millville, and started making plans to move his whole operation to Panama—planes, parts, pilots, ground crews, everything that was portable. He told his employees about the plans and invited them to go along. He explained to William Zadra, one of his mechanics, that the move was necessary because of the CAA's insistence on the costly fuel-injection systems. In his friendly undramatic way, he called aside Neil Bolander, another mechanic, and said he expected to turn up a good deal of business in Latin America carrying passengers and cargo to Europe and refugees out of Europe.

Schwimmer dropped in to see Harold Brown, his insurance man, and asked him to change the insurance policies on the airplanes from Schwimmer Aviation to Líneas Aéreas de Panama.

The WAA notified him that, at last, four more of his C-46s were available at its surplus depot in Ontario, California. They had been inexplicably delayed for weeks and it was now almost too late to complete the necessary modifications before the move to Panama. Schwimmer rushed mechanic Robert W. Frieburg down to Ontario to prepare the planes for the flight to Burbank. "I looked each of them over," he reported, "gave it a good inspection, gassed and oiled it, ran the engines, made a good preflight." As each plane was ready, Frieburg telephoned Burbank and pilots Sam Lewis and Leo Gardner hurried down to fly it back.

Meanwhile the mechanics and workmen at Burbank—who by

now numbered close to two hundred—were working furiously to complete the work Schwimmer had ordered on the planes: modifications which would not only make them airworthy but strip them of all their military trappings and convert them to civilian aircraft that could be exported under U.S. law. Out of the two remaining Connies went the bucket seats and in went regular passenger seats, five abreast; carpets were laid on the floors and separate lavatories installed labeled "Men" and "Women." Even food service equipment was put in.

The C-46s—eventually Schwimmer got ten of them—which had been built for airborne infantry, were divested of everything that might be of military use. Rey Selk made sure the mechanics removed the gun racks and parachute static lines. Military radios were taken out and commercial sets installed. When a mechanic noticed that the planes had been delivered by the WAA with their secret IFF signal systems intact (Identification Friend or Foe emits a signal on a radar screen which notifies friendly antiaircraft batteries not to open fire), Selk ordered them removed and dismantled. Some of the C-46s had artillery loading ramps folded inside their cabins; when opened and fitted into notches in the doorway they became gangplanks for the speedy loading and unloading of jeeps and artillery. Again Selk ordered that they be removed and dismantled.

Ptacek, the FBI agent who had visited Schwimmer, was still seen around the terminal; he made no secret of his presence or of his curiosity. But then Schwimmer was making no secret of what he was doing either.

As soon as a plane was ready, it was sent on to Millville, New Jersey, for some final work and a checkout. On February 28 the first C-46 left Burbank, followed by a second on March 8 and a third the following week. There they would await the others for a mass flight to Panama.

XXXII

THE SHEPHERD

FOR NORMAN AWAITING NEWS FROM YOU CONCERNING THE CHRYSLERS AND NASHES IF AVAILABLE CHANCE AND DATE THEIR TRANSFER.

"Norman" was in reality Hyman Sheckman who arrived in New York from Palestine at the end of February, looking, with his trench-coat and old B-4 bag, like any other Air Corps veteran come to the big city. He was, however, a shepherd come for his flock.

It was his mission, having been a navigator in the United States Army Air Forces, to guide Operation Yakum Purkan to the Promised Land and to that end he had brought from Tel Aviv, secreted among the shirts and socks in his B-4 bag, a roll of microfilm. Teddy Kollek had it developed and blown up into large prints which revealed secret codes and aerial photos of the landing fields the Palestinians were building in vegetable fields and orange groves along the coast.

Most of the landing strips were 150 feet wide and from 2,100 to 3,300 feet long, Sheckman explained, big enough for the C-46s. "We can enlarge them for the Connies when they're ready." There were also RAF airstrips which the British were evacuating as they gradually withdrew their forces; Haganah hoped to control several of these and was prepared to defend the perimeter of any of the strips long enough for a plane to come in, unload and take off again.

Among Sheckman's coded documents were detailed instructions to guide such landings. Two hours before an airplane was due, a secret ground transmitter would start sending a signal, repeating it for five-minute periods at five-minute intervals: V VV VVV DIX DIX DIX . . .

The approaching plane would respond with its own call signal and be acknowledged from the ground with still another prearranged signal. This elaborate dialogue was designed to prevent the Arabs from diverting the plane to an enemy airfield.

Then the ground station would tap out, in code, the number of the airstrip (each one had a number) that had been chosen for that particular landing, the direction of landing, the weather and any changes in standard procedure:

"Shortcake" meant Go ahead and land.

"Toppers": The airplane was over the field.

"Avenue": A request to turn on the strip lights, powered by portable generators, which would illuminate the airstrip with different colored lights showing the point of touchdown.

"Merry-go-round": The aircraft was joining the traffic pattern.

"Sunbeam": It had seen the light signals from the ground.

"Spinner": An emergency on the ground; have pistols handy for a fight, keep the plane's engines running after landing and immediately after unloading taxi to the end of the runway for a fast takeoff.

Sheckman had also brought along a shopping list for an air force—for the fighting wing of the aerial salvation the Palestinians now envisioned. Yakum Purkan would deliver the matériel; the air force would provide their protection. The list started from scratch, as everything had to, and ran eight pages long, from bomb racks to training films for the future pilots of the future air force. And a projector to show the training films. On its eighth and final page it got around to airplanes.

The code in which the underground would communicate with Tel Aviv assigned the names of American automobiles to the various types of planes. Schwimmer's big Constellations not surprisingly were "Cadillacs"; the C-46 transports were "Dodges." And the two planes that Tel Aviv most wanted for its fledgling air force were "Chryslers"—the deadly P-51 fighter, and "Nashes"—the versatile B-25 medium bomber.

Arazi and Schwimmer hoped to get both "Chryslers" and "Nashes" in Mexico. The planes were available in the United States—Schwimmer had cast a covetous eye on several P-51s during a brief stopover at a WAA depot in Walnut Ridge, Arkansas, with Willie Sosnow—but they could not be exported because of the United States embargo on arms to the Middle East. Arazi was awaiting word from "Mr. Brown," the airplane dealer he had met a few weeks before who claimed to have excellent contacts in Mexico.

Other Haganah agents were looking into the possibilities in other parts of the world. Boris Senior, a former South African pilot, had been sent home to look for aircraft; Harry "Freddy" Fredkens, an ex-RAF pilot, had been dispatched to England.

Schwimmer and his "boys"—Selk, Sosnow, Schwartz, anyone who could be spared for a few days—were scouring the United States for aircraft that could get past the United States embargo. They had bought a couple of BT-13 Vultee trainers in Boston and they were looking into the possibility of buying B-17s. Ironically, the B-17, the enormous Flying Fortress which had bombed Germany's cities during World War II, seemed to be as available as the large economy size in a supermarket.* The United States had built 9,000 of them at a cost of $204,370 each and was selling them as surplus for a tenth of that. Converted to civilian use, they were being used to carry passengers, haul prime beef, deliver fresh flowers. A man in Ohio had even turned one into a tourist attraction; he put up a sign, "See the Flying Fortress," and charged people a quarter to walk through.

Traveling about the country under a series of aliases—Ervin L. Johnson, Alvin J. Allen—Schwimmer learned from an airplane dealer in Florida that two B-17s were available from Miami entrepreneur Charles Winters, who had had less luck with a plan to fly cargo around the Caribbean. "Business is lousy," Winters confessed to Schwimmer and he was interested in selling out. The planes, Schwimmer ascertained, were in good condition, already converted to civilian cargo use and, most important of all, had bona-fide American registrations. He asked Winters if he would "consider guiding them to somewhere in Europe." Winters said he would think it over.

HAVE LIMITED NUMBER DRIVERS . . . GETTING MORE BUT DELAYED OBTAINING PASSPORTS . . . NORMAN

"Drivers" of course were pilots and it was Steve Schwartz's job to find them; in a more conventional enterprise than Service Airways he might have been known as the vice-president in charge of personnel. His problem was lack of personnel. Referrals from Land and Labor were not coming through fast enough. Schwartz tried asking friends. Stabbing his cigar at whomever he met, he would demand, "Who do you know? Whatever became of . . . ?" And then he'd get on the phone. When even the friend-of-a-friend approach proved too slow, Schwartz evolved a new system. Carrying a sack of some $200 in nickels, he would lead a recruiting platoon of six or seven men

---

* Excerpt from a letter that came to Materials for Palestine: "Dear Sir: The reason for my writing you is to acquaint you with the material that can be offered. I am enclosing specifications on one type of airplane suitable for operations in your area. These units are the well-known U.S. Army unit, 'B-17.' These are a four-engine job and capable of carrying a 7-ton pay load. . . ."

to one of the hotels in the Times Square area. They would mount guard over the row of telephone booths until they had discouraged other callers, then, with privacy assured, take over the booths. Schwartz would hand out lists of names that he had obtained from Land and Labor and from the United States Army Air Force's register of reservists.

"There wasn't much time to do it scientifically," he explains. "We just picked out all the names that looked Jewish and called them." Talking enigmatically about "jobs in aviation" and "Palestine," they jotted down names and numbers and made appointments with the men who sounded interested. The calls were made in the morning; afternoons were reserved for interviewing. In the evenings Schwartz and Sheckman held navigation classes for newcomers in the office of Service Airways.

By one means and another Schwartz got results. The roster of Service Airways' "drivers" reflected the diverse routes by which they reached its fifth floor offices on West 57th Street.

Norman Moonitz, a muscular, towering New York City fireman, on a day off from Hook and Ladder 168 in Brooklyn, was delivering a parcel of souvenir guns to Materials for Palestine and casually mentioned to one of the men in the office that he had been a flier during the war. The man, remembering Steve's cigar, told Moonitz to stop in at Service Airways on the fifth floor before he left the building.

Art Yadven, who had been a Navy pilot and had been flying commercially since, heard from a friend about a vacancy with "an airline." Oddly, the friend would discuss the details only outside a certain building on West 57th Street. Yadven listened, thought it over for a moment. "I'd never been occupationally Jewish, but why not? I hadn't been in a good war for a couple of years." He nodded and the friend wheeled him into the building and up to Service Airways.

Phil Marmelstein, a former Navy pilot who loved airplanes so much he was studying aircraft mechanics in order to stay in the field, was having breakfast in his home in Philadelphia when his telephone rang. "I have an interesting job in aviation for you," the caller said. "Are you interested?" Marmelstein definitely was. He went to New York, met Steve, agreed to be ready to leave as soon as he was called. He switched from mechanics to a refresher course in instrument flying.

Lou Lenart, a former Marine Corps fighter pilot, went to a meeting in Los Angeles to hear Major Wellesley Aron speak on the situation in Palestine. The Hungarian-born Lenart had been strongly affected by the Nazi massacres in Europe. "We had won as Americans, and lost as Jews," he'd decided. He went up to Aron after the speech and offered his services. Aron suggested he write a letter—then took a look at the burning-eyed crewcut youth who stood next to him with his fists clenched and said, "Why don't you drop off a résumé of your background at my hotel?" Lenart got it to him the same night.

Trygve Maseng, a former Air Force captain who was studying "creative writing" at Columbia University, had reached an intellectual impasse. "I had come to the realization that you didn't learn to write at a university." A friend to whom he confided his discouragement put him in touch with "some people who are recruiting fliers for a worthy cause." This interested Maseng, an idealistic Protestant of Scandinavian descent. As he would explain his motivation later, "I was too late for the Spanish Civil War." Maseng became Service Airways' first check pilot. "They had me out at Teterboro airport checking out the pilots they were getting. I ran through about a dozen of them. Some couldn't fly. One turned out to have had four hours on a Piper Cub. Some could fly but they were unstable screwballs. We got all kinds."

Harold Livingston wanted to be a writer too when he got out of the Air Force. His mother loaned him $1,500 to invest in a small advertising agency. He bought a brown snap-brim hat and settled down to commuting from his parents' home in Haverhill, Massachusetts, to his office in downtown Boston. He was rushing to catch the Boston and Maine commuters' special when he spied in the morning mail a blue envelope from a man he'd met while working briefly for TWA in Cairo after the war. He snatched it up and got a moment to read it on the train as it carried him, with frequent stops, to another day of writing copy for shoe accounts. All the letter said was "Contact Service Airways in New York." Livingston flew down the same afternoon. At Service Airways he met Steve Schwartz, whom he'd known slightly in Cairo. They went out for dinner and had a long frank talk about Palestine and the plan to use Service Airways to fly in materiel to help the Jews. Livingston listened to the names of faraway places, the dangers that might be involved and he knew he could never go back to writing about shoes.

Larry Raab, a slim baby-faced lad with soft brown eyes and long curling eyelashes, had such a look of untroubled innocence it was hard to believe he had been a bomber pilot during the war and was twenty years old. It took several trips to the Philadelphia office of Land and Labor to convince anyone he was serious and obtain the magic password—the address of Service Airways in New York.

Very few of the volunteers were Zionists. One of these rare birds was Gideon Lichtman, whose father had bought an orange grove in Palestine "but he never made it over there." In World War II Lichtman had been a fighter pilot with the Third Air Commando Group in the Southwest Pacific flying P-51 Mustangs. He was anxious to put his skill to use in the defense of the Jews of Palestine. At a meeting of a Zionist organization he was told to write Land and Labor. He wrote and got back "a sort of half-assed questionnaire. I filled it out. Then I got a message to meet some guy in the street, 57th Street. He would be wearing a red scarf. I met him and we went to some hotel and talked. Okay. He told me to come again and meet another guy. We went to another hotel and talked. Okay. Finally they introduced me to this guy Steve Schwartz." Most fighter pilots are fidgety and Lichtman's patience was wearing thin. He exploded when Schwartz told him he wasn't sure whether they'd be flying fighters or C-46s. "Let's stop the bullshit. Where's the action?" Lichtman stormed.

A quieter but equally ardent Zionist was William Gerson, a former transport pilot, who joined up even though he had a wife and children and a newly established business in Los Angeles.

Steve Schwartz rounded up some more volunteers in a feat of rustling out on West 55th Street. He had heard, through the Hotel Fourteen, of a meeting of volunteer pilots who had been recruited by the New York arm of Irgun Zvai Leumi, the right-wing extremist organization. They had been brought in by Ben Hecht's prose and the busty chorus girls of the American League for a Free Palestine and they were waiting for Irgun to buy Catalina PBY flying boats in which they were to fly armed guerrillas to Palestine. Schwartz led a raiding party composed of just about all the hands down on the 57th Street ranch, at that time less than half a dozen. On the pretense of reaching some accommodation—they had the airplanes, Irgun had the crews—they went to the meeting at the Hotel Wellington. The negotiations became recriminations, the voices grew louder and, in the excitement, someone stole the Irgun membership list.

Out of that foray came Al Raisin, a former B-17 pilot who left his family's wholesale dairy business to join up, and Ray Kurtz, the second New York City fireman to take leave from the Civil Service to join Service Airways. Kurtz, who had been a policeman in Brooklyn before transferring to a hose company, was even bigger than the other fireman, Moonitz, and more frightening when aroused. Beetle-browed, ham-handed—or, preferably, pastrami-fisted—he had, like Raisin, been a B-17 pilot during the war.

Probably the oddest concatenation of circumstances brought in one of Service Airways' most valuable men. At thirty-one, Hal Auerbach was older than the average volunteer. He had been a Navy lieutenant commander during the war and he was making a satisfactory career in flying as a flight inspector with the Civil Aeronautics Administration in Oakland, California. Auerbach was also a bachelor, a handsome one. A matchmaking friend suggested that on his next flight to Bakersfield he look up an attractive well-to-do woman there named Elynor Rudnick, who shared his interest in flying. In fact she owned her own airport and ran a flying school.* Auerbach flew in, met Miss Rudnick, found her "very sweet, with a good business sense," and fell madly in love. But not with Miss Rudnick. She told him of an airline that was being organized to fly to Palestine which had bought three Constellations. "The chance to get my hands on a Constellation" was all Auerbach could think of as he set off for Los Angeles, where Schwimmer, delighted to get someone so experienced and mature, promptly hired him as director of operations for Service Airways.

One evening all of the airmen who so far had joined up were told to come to the offices of Service Airways for a briefing. Leo Gardner was there from California. Also on hand were ex-fireman Norman Moonitz, appropriately garbed in black jacket, black boots, a neck scarf and sunglasses pushed up on his forehead, and a half-dozen others. The shades of the office were pulled down and a gray-haired compactly built man with a slight limp strode in, leaned against one of the desks and began describing in a low, dramatic, lightly accented voice the plan for Yakum Purkan which would begin with the move to Panama. It was Yehuda Arazi, playing to the hilt his best role: the taut, mysterious hero of the underground. The young men were mesmerized. Arazi finished his briefing, fixed them with his intense

* Miss Rudnick's flying school was later used to train Palestinian pilots.

blue eyes and then suddenly said, "You are all now members of Haganah."

"There was a deathly silence," recalls Gardner. "We didn't know which way to jump, some taking it in their stride, some with a certain misgiving, apprehensively. There were mixed sentiments. But it was seriously listened to. He described the problems, briefed us as much as he felt he could at the time. Certain things were reserved to those in the know, so to speak, and there was a bit of subterfuge because you can't always get people to do something if you tell them the dire consequences to begin with; like a patient with a doctor, they'd jump off the operating table. The one truth was right: This air operation was most urgently needed."

TEL AVIV . . . CADILLACS WILL LEAVE FROM LATIN DETROIT
. . . NORMAN

Not surprisingly in an underground which called its airplanes by the names of cars, America was known as "Detroit" and Latin America emerged with a code name that sounded like a character out of *Guys and Dolls:* "Latin Detroit."

One day the Constellation that had brought Schwimmer east in January and had been laid up ever since in Millville for further work on its fuel system was taken out; the Panamanian registration RX 121 was painted on its wings and tail and the name LAPSA along its fuselage. Off went the American NL registration and the Connie stood reborn as a flagship of an international airline.

On March 13 it took off for Panama, stopping in Newark to clear customs, where Sam Lewis, the pilot, signed the outward manifest, giving the owner of the plane as Líneas Aéreas de Panama. The RX 121 made a direct 1,800-mile flight to Jamaica, where it stopped for gas; three hours later it arrived in Tocumen, Panama.

Martin Bellefond, who had gone on ahead, was at the airport. So were Panamanian officials, wreathed in smiles as they saw the big Constellation with its distinctive triple tail and graceful swallow-shaped body come in down the long runway. Bellefond's Panamanian attorney and benefactor, Gilberto Arias, was on hand. His family owned the English-language newspaper, the Panama City *Star,* and its reporters were present to interview Bellefond and report on the new company. Arias had some other surprises: printed letterheads, LAPSA identification cards and a contract for a gala inaugural flight. An election campaign was in progress in Mexico, and Arias' uncle,

Dr. Arnulfo Arias, one of the candidates, had chartered the big airplane, which now glorified Panama, for a campaign trip to the city of David, a town on the Pacific side of the isthmus. Part of the cost would be paid for by the local Pepsi-Cola bottler, who was taking the opportunity to make a big shipment by air. The $1,100 that LAPSA received for the flight came in handy; it paid the hotel bills and immediate expenses of the crew and mechanics who had come down with the plane.

Yakum Purkan now had its Panamanian base, a European way station at the Ambrosini airfield in Italy that Arazi had found, Schwimmer's planes that were nearing completion in Burbank and Millville, the crews that Steve Schwartz was recruiting, the landing fields that were being secretly prepared in Palestine.

But what was it going to deliver?

Haganah scouts in Western Europe were meeting with little success. Careful soundings had been made in Eastern Europe and the tacit approval of the Soviet Union obtained through delicate discussions in New York between Andrei Gromyko and the Agency's representative at the United Nations, Moshe Shertok. But even with this green light, Czechoslovakia had been the only one of the satellite countries willing to sell the Palestinians arms—the 4,300 rifles and 200 machine guns that Dr. Felix had contracted to buy in December. Getting the arms out of landlocked Czechoslovakia had presented almost insuperable difficulties. Poland would not permit them to pass through her territory to the Baltic Sea; Rumania refused to give them passage to the Black Sea. Finally the use of a Yugoslav port on the Adriatic Sea was arranged and the guns had gone out on the S.S. *Nora*, hidden under a load of potatoes, in mid-March.

Encouraged by his success, Dr. Felix had suggested to Tel Aviv that he try to buy airplanes in Czechoslovakia too. He had visited an aircraft plant, made friends with the manager and felt he could go back. The manager had some World War II German fighter planes, Messerschmitt Bf 109s, he wanted to get rid of.

The reply was negative. Tel Aviv wanted the P-51s that Arazi was negotiating to buy in Mexico. Nothing available in Czechoslovakia could compare to the speedy American fighter. Furthermore, the Palestinian leaders did not want to become too dependent on Czech help for either arms or planes. Apart from the touchy political position it put them in internationally, they were old-line socialists, many of them from Russia, and they distrusted both Communist ideology and its traditional anti-Zionism.

Their greatest hope, still, was the American operation based at the Hotel Fourteen and they waited daily for news that something was on the way.

XXXIII

WHEN? AND HOW?

W hy aren't you starting with Yakum Purkan? We are prepared and waiting . . ."

This time it was not a cable but a letter, dated March 14, which a courier from Palestine brought to the Hotel Fourteen for "Norman" —Hyman Sheckman—from his superior in Tel Aviv, "Roni"—Aharon Remez—a veteran of the RAF and the son of one of Ben Gurion's closest associates in the shadow government that would take over the new state on May 15—now only two months away.

> Much rain has fallen recently [read the letter], making the use of the two runways which had been enlarged fairly problematical, but in the meanwhile, we have started lengthening the Tel Aviv runway . . .
>
> Freddy [Harry Fredkens, who had been sent to England to buy airplanes] was here on a short visit, returned to Europe and is now in the Belgian Congo. Boris [Boris Senior, who had been sent to South Africa on the same mission] is in South Africa, investigating the possibilities . . .
>
> What has been bought [in the Americas] and what can be bought of the B-25 bombers and P-51 fighters? What are the possibilities of bringing each type over here? What would be the possible dates? Have you investigated the possibility of bringing them over by the CVE [the aircraft carrier *Attu*] . . . When might it be done?

The efforts of the underground had, of necessity, a streak of wild improvisation. Tel Aviv tried to maintain a rough order of priorities and a line of command. But there was no time for careful planning; there were no certainties on which to base calculated schedules; there was not sufficient communication among the scattered purchasing agents in Europe, Africa and the Americas for coherent coordination. Each small group was engaged in its own frantic scramble to get something, anything, as quickly as possible. Planes were bought which could not be cleared for export. Pilots were hired for whom there were no planes which they were qualified to fly. Schemes were hatched which foundered on chance mishaps. Procedures were laid out only to be obliterated by the stampede of changing necessities.

Remez and Sheckman, veterans respectively of the British and American air forces and admiring of their orderly professionalism, had worked together on the careful codes, aerial maps and lists which Sheckman had brought to the United States, secreted among his luggage in best James Bond fashion.

But the truth was he was not an actor in a neatly plotted cinematic whodunit. There was no Organization with an omniscient Chief, sagely pulling strings and, in the end, tying them in a neat knot which he had envisaged all along. The script for this thriller was being written as it went along and to none of the anxious questions in Remez's letter could Sheckman give a reply.

They all hinged, in a way, on the negotiations taking place in Mexico, negotiations that seemed to be dragging on interminably. Larry Ives, the ex-Marine arms dealer, was down there with the $70,000 that Arazi had given him. He had sent back encouraging reports of guns, artillery, armor, everything that was needed. "Mr. Brown" reported the Mexicans were ready to sell some B-25 bombers and some fighter planes but not the coveted P-51s. They were offering slower, shorter-ranged P-47s.

Arazi and Kollek were impatient and uneasy. The Mexicans seemed ready to dicker and dawdle for weeks; the Palestinians were counting the days. To try to pin things down, they sent a series of emissaries to Mexico and asked a Mexico City banker, Elias Sourasky, who had helped Elie Schalit buy the smokeless powder, to intercede.

As time grew shorter and the May 15 deadline loomed, the frenetic activities of Schwimmer's "boys" took on a quality of desperation which bordered at times on the chaotic. Rey Selk would be asked to suddenly drop whatever he was doing in Burbank and fly up to Seattle to take a look at some P-51s reportedly available there. Schwimmer would dash to Tulsa to check on another B-17. A school district in northern California was reported ready to sell the C-46 which it had been given by the WAA "for educational purposes." An attempt was made to buy a plane "for a movie being made at Metro-Goldwyn-Mayer."

Steve Schwartz, in New York, would receive a call from Teddy

Kollek to "drop everything and do this or do that. People would come in and offer us B-29s in boxes, atom bombs, all kinds of things and you had to take care of them. I would go out and see the boxes or whatever it was." Almost every day that he was in New York, Schwartz dropped into the Hotel Fourteen. "Kollek would be talking on two phones at once," he recalls. "I'd wait around. He'd give me cables asking always for the same thing: more planes, more men. I'd ask him for more money. It was a routine."

FOR NORMAN . . . INFORM IMMEDIATELY IF YOU HAVE AR-
RANGED BASES AND CONTACTS IN ILLINOIS . . .

It was decided to fly one of the C-46s to "Illinois"—the code name for Italy—to look over the Ambrosini airfield at Castiglione del Lago, near Perugia, which Arazi had found.

With Leo Gardner as captain and Steve Schwartz as navigator, N 7960 of Service Airways left Teterboro airport in New Jersey. Ernie Stehlik, the expert Constellation mechanic who had been work-ing for Schwimmer in Los Angeles, went along as flight engineer and as Schwimmer's alter ego to see if the Ambrosini company, which had made airplanes during the war but now manufactured accordions, still had facilities to service the planes.

They hopped across the North Atlantic, stopping to refuel at Goose Bay, Labrador, at Bluie West One in Greenland, again in Prestwick, Scotland, and landed in Geneva for lunch. They had filed a flight plan for Rome, since they did not want their true destination known, but instead flew directly from Geneva to Castiglione del Lago.

The field was something of a surprise. It was a dirt strip, in bad repair. Stehlik, an old-timer who had worked for TWA all over the world, muttered, "You ain't gonna bring no Connies in here, or any more C-46s. You were just lucky. This field is no good for planes, loaded or unloaded."

Shaken by the flight and the rude landing, Steve Schwartz tele-phoned Danny Agronsky, Arazi's erstwhile assistant in New York who was now in charge of operations in Rome. Steve excitedly described their arrival, then fell silent while he listened to Agronsky. Cupping his hand over the phone he souted to Gardner, "Leo, they're out looking for us."

Neither Schwartz nor Gardner had thought to notify Rome to "close" the flight plan they had filed; when their plane failed to arrive as scheduled, it was reported missing, probably over the Alps. Search planes already had been sent out to look for it, Agronsky had told Steve; the Italian authorities had been alerted.

So had the American Embassy in Rome, which now knew that Service Airways had a plane wandering around Europe. Embassy officials were concerned; it was a time of smuggling and contraband, of political plots and intrigue.

In New York Swifty Schindler received a sudden spurt of messages and visitors at the office of Service Airways. First came an enigmatic cable from Agronsky: "PLEASE AWAIT FULL REPORT . . . PRIOR SENDING SECOND C-46 STOP FIELD SURFACE BAD STOP ATTEMPT-ING OTHER ARRANGEMENT STOP." Next the Associated Press called to ask about the "missing" airplane. Schindler, mystified, said he knew nothing about it and started making some calls himself. He finally reached Agronsky in Rome, who explained the situation and assured him the plane was safe in Perugia.

His next visitors were two men from the U.S. Treasury Depart-ment. They wondered, ah, just what service Service Airways was providing. "I produced the documents in connection with our con-tract with Ambrosini," Schindler recalls. "They seemed to accept it. About three days later they were back with the economics of the operation all figured out and it didn't really make sense. Why were we flying the airplanes all the way over to Ambrosini's at Castiglione del Lago?"

Was Schindler going to set up a European operation? the T-men wanted to know. "Oh, yes," he assured them, there was a lot of business in Europe; Service Airways would be using Ambrosini as a base.

They were polite, interested: almost as interested as if they were going to invest money in the project. They even had a report from the American Embassy in Rome detailing Ambrosini's facilities—or lack of them.

"In view of the fact," one of the T-men began, "that Ambrosini is not a very well-equipped field, the aviation attaché of the Rome embassy felt . . ."

Schindler listened and interrupted: "Well, his analysis just doesn't agree with mine."

The T-men left and Schindler wondered if Service Airways' Italian cover had gone out the door with them.*

---

* While in Italy, Steve Schwartz took part in the land and air search for the *Lino*, a small ship headed for Beirut from a Yugoslav port with six thousand rifles, ammunition, and explosives the Arabs had purchased in Czechoslovakia. He may have been first to positively identify the *Lino* at anchor in Bari harbor,

There was no time to worry about it. Finding another base in Italy would be up to Danny Agronsky. The job of Service Airways was to ready the crews and planes in the United States for the move to Panama. From there they could pick up the smaller Mexican arms as soon as they were available. And the *Attu* lay waiting to take the bigger, heavier stuff, including fighter planes, by sea.

Or did it?

On March 19 ten of the contractors who had been working on the modification of the escort aircraft carrier filed liens in the United States District Court in Norfolk to satisfy claims against the Pratt Steamship Lines, in whose name the *Attu* had been bought by Arazi and Pratt's owner, Leonard Weisman, the opportunistic trader who had so expansively offered to help at meetings of the Sonneborn Institute. The liens totaled $48,595.02.

Arazi had not seen Weisman since the sensational discovery of the M-3 demolition blocks which Weisman had helped him buy. Neither had anyone else in the underground.

There was an element of prudence in the oversight. So far it appeared that the FBI had not linked the *Attu* with the underground despite Weisman's connection with both and his exposure as the purchaser of the demolition blocks. Any contact with him might provide additional leads for the FBI's dossiers. At the Hotel Fourteen it was assumed—when anyone took a moment to think about it—that Weisman was carrying on with whatever work on the *Attu* was necessary.

But Weisman was resentful; he felt deserted. He was convinced the FBI was watching him and he was fearful of the consequences to his other businesses. A catastrophe with the enormous aircraft carrier, as he had told his wife at the outset, could ruin him. He stopped all work on the ship and stopped paying the bills as well. He already had put in more than $50,000 of his own money, he later would claim.

With the filing of the lien, the whole problem was dumped on the startled Hotel Fourteen. Nahum Bernstein always had been skeptical of Arazi's "grandiose" purchase. So had some of the powers in Tel Aviv when Arazi told them about it during his visit there. But Arazi had returned to the United States with his dream still intact: an aircraft carrier loaded with weapons arriving off the new state on May 15. Skeptics had scoffed at his plans before; he had pulled off

where a Haganah sabotage team subsequently fixed a mine to her hull and sank her. When the Arabs salvaged the arms and put them aboard another ship, the *Argiro*, a Haganah "fishing boat" seized the *Argiro* at sea, later transferring the arms to the two corvettes the Sonneborn Institute had bought in Canada.

countless feats which had seemed impossible to everyone but himself. Now, with the lien on the *Attu* and the delays and disappointments in Mexico, the dream was receding like a desert mirage—and his personal reputation with it.

Bernstein summoned a meeting at his law office on Pine Street. Weisman, meeting his old hero Arazi for the first time in three months, hardly recognized him. "His spirits were low; he felt that through a combination of circumstances one of his most brilliant schemes had collapsed." The ebullient, indomitable supersmuggler of only a few weeks ago hardly spoke while the argument waxed around him.

Weisman bore the brunt. He was accused of having sold Arazi a hare-brained scheme in order to get the ship, ultimately, for his own Pratt Steamship Lines. Arazi, whose greatest gift had been his ability to infect other people with his own enthusiasm and determination, protested, but he could not defend himself. In the welter of nit-picking and legal language, how do you defend a dream? No one was enchanted any more. The argument finally came down to a $50,000 dilemma.

If they did not pay the lien, they would lose the ship. If they paid up, it might bring the FBI down on their heads. Even if they escaped FBI notice, there were other uncertainties. How many more thousands of dollars was the remodeling of the ship going to cost? And would they ever be able to get it out of the United States?

They decided to send an attorney, David Michaels, to Norfolk to see what settlement he could negotiate with the claimants. He and attorney W. E. Kyle, whom Weisman had retained to represent the Pratt Steamship Lines, offered them eighty-eight cents on the dollar.

At noon on April 3 Michaels handed the United States marshal an agreement signed by the ten libelants dissolving the attachment and a certified check for $2,070.57 covering court expenses.

Michaels completed one more piece of business while he was in Norfolk; he arranged to have the *Attu* moved from her Army base pier, where the rental was $150 a day, to an anchorage off Sewells Point, where she rocked gently in the Atlantic swells as if ready to sail at a moment's notice.

In Tel Aviv no one any longer was counting on it. As the mission of the *Attu* faltered and the negotiations with Mexico dragged on, an important decision was made. After a meeting in Dostrovsky's bedroom with the chief of staff (who was suffering from a recurrence of ulcers); Yigael Yadin, Haganah's young director of operations; and

Golda Myerson, just back from the United States, Ben Gurion sent Shaul Avigor, one of his most trusted troubleshooters and a member of Haganah's high command, to Europe to step up efforts to find arms and airplanes there. Dr. Felix in Prague was instructed to explore every possibility offered by the Czechs. Less than six weeks remained before the Palestinian Jews would have to stand alone to defend their new state. They still had no fighter planes, no tanks, no artillery, not enough small arms. They could not afford to put all of their eggs in Arazi's leaking basket.

CALCULATED RISK

<hr>

I n Washington, on March 26, at three minutes before noon, President Truman issued Proclamation 2776, which greatly expanded the list of "arms, ammunition and implements of war" that would require State Department licensing before they could be exported. The principal four amendments concerned aircraft: "All commercial type aircraft and all aircraft components, parts and accessories; fire control and range finding equipment; certain military electronic devices including radar . . ." For more than a year permission from the State Department had been required for the export of military aircraft.

Now the export of even commercial planes would come under the scrutiny of the Department's Munitions Control Board, even for export to friendly neutral countries in the Western Hemisphere, like Panama.

The Proclamation, the President said, would go into effect on April 15.

Nahum Bernstein telephoned Schwimmer: They had exactly twenty days to get the planes out of the country.

In Palestine March 26 was a day of crises for other reasons.

A large convoy had been ambushed and destroyed by the Arabs near Jerusalem; most of the armored cars that had maintained a frail supply line between Tel Aviv and the inland city had been destroyed in the action. Jerusalem was completely cut off.

On the same day, Haganah had been forced, finally, to abandon attempts to supply the Negev settlements by land. The narrow tortuous inland road had proved too vulnerable to ambush and the coastal road, which ran through densely populated Arab towns and villages, was too heavily mined. Only two Piper Cubs now maintained contact with the isolated settlements in the southern desert.

Ben Gurion and the Haganah high command decided on an all-out effort to save Jerusalem. They ordered the concentration of a force of 1,500 men, an enormous number for Haganah, which had never operated with a body of more than 500 men before. There was the usual shortage of arms. Brigade commanders throughout the country were told to requisition arms from the settlements and get them, somehow, to Tel Aviv. The Negev settlements and those near Jerusalem were, of course, cut off. The settlements in the north, in the Galilee area, although severely beset themselves, rallied loyally and attempted to send guns and ammunition to the force forming in the south. Most of the arms were held up by a British curfew on the Haifa–Tel Aviv road; only a small part got through to Tel Aviv. It seemed the operation would have to be postponed or canceled.

Ben Gurion sent an urgent message to Prague. The first Czech shipment of rifles and machine guns was on the high seas, bound for Palestine. Dr. Felix had just negotiated a second purchase of 10,000 more guns and ammunition. Ben Gurion ordered him to get hold of a plane—any plane that could make the trip and would take the risk—load it with as many of the guns as it could carry and dispatch it to Tel Aviv. Preparations to receive the shipment were turned over to Aharon Remez, the young ex-RAF man who had been planning the Palestine end of Yakum Purkan and recently had sent such plaintive messages to "Norman" in New York.

Felix shunted the plane problem over to the underground's office in Paris, where Freddy Fredkens just happened to know of a possibility. He had been looking for back-up transport aircraft ever since the falling TNT in Jersey City had endangered the Schwimmer operation by putting it under FBI surveillance. In Geneva, he had met a tall, composed American, Gerald Rowland, who represented a small American airline which owned one four-engine C-54 that flew in and out of Paris. Rowland, a former Air Forces major and navigator, had been scouting business around Europe. On that first meeting, he had told Fredkens: "We'll carry anything you want." "Two dollars a mile with the minimum on costs; we were talking three or four dollars a mile," Rowland recalls. His airline's interest in "Palestine—in a Jewish nation—was less than nil," Rowland recalls. As for his personal interest, Rowland was a reticent man, an army officer and the son of an army officer, but his closest friend in the service, and partner afterward, was another navigator, Seymour Lerner.

Fredkens now told Rowland that the charter would originate in Czechoslovakia. Rowland felt "reluctant to go behind the Iron Curtain —but I knew the area from flying UNRRA supplies into Eastern Europe." The deal was set.

About midnight on March 31 the American C-54, with Rowland and Lerner in its crew, signaled its approach to Beth Darass, an airfield south of Tel Aviv, deep in Arab territory, which only recently had been evacuated by the British. A Haganah battalion had moved quietly into the deserted field at 8 P.M.; a portable generator now lit up a flarepath. As soon as the big four-engine transport touched down, Haganah men hastily unloaded its cargo: two hundred rifles, forty machine guns and a large supply of ammunition. Mechanics were on hand to service and refuel the plane, which had arrived with only half an hour's fuel left in its tanks. One hour and twenty minutes after its arrival it was gone, on its way back to Europe. Gone too were the generator, the flarepath, the fuel truck and the convoy that carried away the soldiers and arms. The next morning a British search party, called out by neighboring Arabs who reported activity at the field, could find no trace that anyone had been there.

Within twenty-four hours, the first Czech arms were in action. A few days later, the S.S. *Nora* arrived in Tel Aviv from Yugoslavia carrying the first purchase of 4,300 Czech rifles and 200 machine guns, hidden under a load of potatoes. These too were thrown into the effort to open the road to Jerusalem. In the ensuing three weeks, three large convoys loaded with supplies were pushed through to Jerusalem; the road was secured, the city saved. It was Haganah's first large-scale military operation and it had been a success. Deliverance had indeed come from the skies. It could be done, with planes free to fly and arms available for them to bring in.

Rey Selk was working literally night and day to get the C-46s in Burbank ready for the flight to Panama. With Schwimmer out scouting for more planes and commuting frequently to New York, the Burbank operation had been left largely in Selk's hands. Daytimes he spent in the bustling workshop at Lockheed Terminal; evenings he put in long hours filling out the scores of forms required for CAA registrations and permits. He preferred doing the paperwork in his room at the Traveler's Lodge motel on San Fernando Way near the airport. It was quieter than Schwimmer Aviation's offices at the terminal, and more secure. Selk had stopped keeping important papers in the office after discovering that some of them were missing. One of his head mechanics, William Zadra, whom Schwimmer had brought over from TWA, where he was so highly thought of he had been assigned during the war to the crew that maintained President Roosevelt's plane, offered to come by in the evenings to help Selk with the tedious paperwork. But Selk refused. There was something about Zadra. He was a zealous worker, seemingly everywhere at once and a model of efficiency; he trusted nothing to memory but jotted every one of Selk's instructions down in a notebook that he carried about with him and hauled out of his pocket to consult whenever a question came up. The notebook annoyed Selk but he had to admit that "it helped; we were moving so fast we needed someone who could keep things in order." One evening, returning to the motel after dinner, he worked for a while but was so tired he lay down on his bed for a nap before returning to his papers.

He was awakened hours later by Zadra and his landlady, standing over him fanning his face. All the windows in the apartment were open. Selk stirred and found he had a splitting headache. Zadra told him what had happened. The mechanic had stopped by, found the door locked, knocked, gone away, returned and knocked again. Since there were lights on in the room, Zadra felt sure Selk was there. Worried about why he didn't answer, Zadra had called the landlady to open the door. They had found Selk unconscious; a defective heater had been leaking gas.

Selk thanked Zadra for saving his life and bid him good night. When his head had cleared, he got up and went to his desk to check his papers. Everything was just as he had left it. But the wastebasket caught his eye; some papers that he had crumpled up and thrown away earlier that evening were gone.

Selk was still nursing his suspicions when an aircraft broker named Laurence M. Krug waylaid him outside the air terminal building, handed him his business card and said he would like to sell Schwimmer Aviation some P-51s. Selk didn't know what to make of the offer. Were all of their secrets known? Or was this only a coincidence? And a fortunate one? Krug went on talking. For a commission, he said, he could find any kind of plane Selk wanted; he had heard they were looking for P-51s. What else were they interested in?

Selk warily broke off the stranger's monologue: "I'll call you in a few days and discuss it with you." "Okay." Krug shrugged and crossed the street to the parking lot where his wife was waiting for him in their car. After Selk no longer was in sight, they were joined by Special Agent Ptacek of the FBI, who talked with them for a few minutes, then drove off in another car which had pulled up beside theirs.

Schwimmer nodded impassively as he listened, during his next visit to Burbank, to Selk's account of Zadra's visit and Krug's offer. He wasn't surprised and, as usual, he did not appear to be perturbed. "We can't keep on hiding from the United States government forever," he told Selk. "We're not professionals in this game. There is only one thing that we can traffic in and that is this: We can work very quickly. We can outpace them. The Federal machine is very big and ponderous and we can always keep a day ahead of them."

By now Schwimmer was counting the days. It was early April and President Truman's proclamation limiting the export of commercial aircraft would go into effect on April 15.

Bernstein and Schwimmer met in New York to review the situation.

The three Constellations were spread across the Americas. The RX 121 was already in Panama, enjoying a brief life of glory as flagship of the new Panamanian airline. But the RX 123, which had moved from Burbank to Millville, New Jersey, resplendent with carpeted aisles and "his" and "hers" lavatories, and the RX 124, still in Burbank undergoing alterations, were mired in red tape, blocked from leaving the United States by a long-standing presidential proclamation requiring State Department permission for the export of any plane weighing more than 35,000 pounds. The RX 121 had gotten past this requirement by flying out under Panamanian registration as a plane which already belonged to a Panamanian company, LAPSA. It was unlikely this stratagem would work a second time, especially in view of the close watch the FBI was keeping on the activities of Schwimmer Aviation. Bernstein advised Schwimmer they would have to go through regular formalities of requesting an export license to Panama for the two remaining Connies from the Munitions Control Board of the State Department.

The ten C-46s were another matter. They still could be exported legally, without State Department approval, provided they got out before the April 15 deadline set by Truman's proclamation.

The C-46 that Leo Gardner and Steve Schwartz had flown to Italy was waiting uneasily in Perugia, its unfulfilled flight plan having brought it to the attention of the American Embassy in Rome and to the Italian authorities. Four of the planes were assembled in Millville, New Jersey, at the big former Army air base, which was now a rental field extending hospitality to paying guests of every description;

Schwimmer Aviation shared warehouse space with a fruit-packing company. The remaining five C-46s were still in Burbank.

The nine planes in the United States should be moved out to Panama as soon as possible, Bernstein advised. Schwimmer warned that they were not really ready to fly. "They are in pretty good shape but they still need work." He also was worried about the crews. About twenty men had been recruited, nine of them pilots, but none of them had had any experience on the C-46 and few of them had done any transoceanic flying. They were living convivially at a hotel in Vineland, New Jersey, checking out on the C-46.

They needed more flying time on the plane and more experience working together, but there was no arguing with the calendar. Schwimmer and Bernstein agreed that any early departure was "a calculated risk we just have to take."

XXXV

LATIN DETROIT

The order to go was brought to Millville by Hal Auerbach, the thirty-one-year-old former Navy pilot who had gone to meet a young lady and fallen in love with a Constellation instead. He had resigned his CAA job in Oakland, California, and come east as director of operations for Service Airways. Under Auerbach's direction, the men in Millville began getting ready to leave.

It was a do-it-yourself operation.

"We began equipping ourselves with maps, survival equipment, life rafts, emergency rations, clothing and cigarettes," Auerbach recalls. One of the men had heard that soap was good for trading in Europe so they stocked up on soap. Some of the others got the names of friendly surplus stores from Materials for Palestine and picked up whatever they felt they might need "on credit." Each man packed his personal gear in a parachute bag; these and other supplies were stored in the warehouse that Service Airways shared with the food company. Auerbach, stumbling over cases of jams and jellies as he looked for his life rafts and flight boots, despaired of maintaining any sort of security. He posted round-the-clock watches over the airplanes and cautioned the men not to talk about their plans.

On April 7, a Wednesday, Swifty Schindler came out with a list of crews and new Panamanian registration numbers for the planes. Auerbach would lead the flight in the RX 135 with Livingston, the Boston advertising man, as his wireless operator; RX 136 would be flown by Moonitz, the first fireman from New York; RX 137 would be Swifty Schindler's plane; RX 138 would be piloted by Larry Raab, the baby-faced Air Force veteran from Philadelphia.

The men spent the next day loading the aircraft. In went two dismantled BT-13 Vultee trainers which Moonitz and Raab had flown down from Boston, the R-2800 engines, spare wheels, toolkits, parts for the Connies, paint and lubricating oil. Auerbach realized they did not have enough maps and sent Raab to Washington to get some more at the Hydrographic Office of the Navy.

The flight plan called for the planes to fly to the Durham-Raleigh area using the lights of Philadelphia, Baltimore, Washington and Richmond as landmarks and then, near Charleston, to slip out over the Atlantic and head for Jamaica with the lights of the American coastline to their right as a guide. In Kingston they would refuel for the direct 550-mile flight to Panama.

Mechanics painted the new registration numbers on the planes and the Panamanian flag. One by one the men slipped off to call their families. The mood of joking horseplay had given way to tense anticipation. They would leave the following day.

The next morning, April 9, at his motel Auerbach got the call that he had been dreading. "The FBI," reported the man who was standing watch over the planes at Millville, had "moved in." A big black government car was parked on the apron of the field as if prepared to intercept the C-46s if they tried to taxi away.

Auerbach and several of the other men jumped into a car and drove quickly from Vineland to Millville. Sure enough, there was the official-looking black car parked on the edge of the field. Auerbach walked up to it and introduced himself to the men inside. They were not, it turned out, from the FBI. They were customs agents. The airplanes, they said, did not have proper clearance and would not be permitted to take off. They were there to make sure the planes did not leave the field.

Auerbach tried to reach Schwimmer and Bernstein; neither was available. They were in Washington trying to get export permits for the Constellations. He called Bellefond, who rushed out with LAPSA's Panamanian charter. There were anxious conferences on the field and at the motel in Vineland. Nothing would budge the customs agents. Late in the day Auerbach got through to Bernstein; they made a date to meet at the district customs office in Philadelphia when it opened its doors the next morning.

The black car, with the customs agents sitting inside, stayed parked on the Millville apron all night. So did another car, occupied by four of Auerbach's men. A sentry stayed on duty in the cockpit of one of the planes. They stared at one another, a silent hostile tableau on the dark cold airstrip.

Bernstein confronted the district chief of customs in Philadelphia on April 10. The previous day in Washington with Schwimmer had

been discouraging. Their application to export the Connies to Panama
had been denied. They had made a new application, this time to
export three Constellations to South Africa in the name of Transcaribbean Air Cargo Lines, Inc. Now it was the C-46s that were held
up, with only five days to go before they too would come under the
jurisdiction of the State Department's Munitions Control Board.

"By what authority are you holding these planes?" Bernstein
demanded.

The customs chief quoted a Federal law that empowered him to
detain any plane suspected of carrying contraband cargo pending
investigation.

"You know there is no contraband aboard," Bernstein snapped
back. "You are using a legal technicality to hold them up until April
15, until the President's proclamation goes into effect and we can't
take them out. It is arbitrary use of authority and we will not accept
it."

Bernstein felt sure of his legal ground. He could go to court and
ask for an injunction, but that might take days. He looked at the
customs chief. "I am going to instruct Mr. Auerbach to hire fifty or
even one hundred people from the Millville area to come to the field,
empty every plane, lay everything out on the field. You can go and
look at it. And then we'll put everything back. There is no contraband on those planes."

The chief was unmoved; Bernstein concluded that "he had
orders to stop us." There was no use appealing to law or logic.
Speaking very deliberately and gathering up his papers to leave, he
played his last card. Once again he would make use of the peculiar
ambiguity in United States policy toward Palestine, of the tug of war
going on within the government between those who supported the
founding of the new Jewish state and those who were still trying to
thwart it, of the gap that yawned between a generally sympathetic
public opinion and an intransigent group of State Department professionals.

"I am going to advise my client to take off," Bernstein told the
customs chief. "You have no legal grounds for stopping these planes.
If you want to stop them, you will have to do it by force. You will
have to shoot at them. This will lead to a Congressional investigation
and you, as a government official, will have to explain on what basis
you used force and violence to stop these planes."

The four C-46s took off at 7 P.M. that night, their customs
clearance duly signed and approved. As planned, Hal Auerbach led in

the RX 135. He had been so preoccupied the past several days with the hurried loading and clearance of the planes, he hadn't considered, until that moment, how little he knew about flying a C-46. I've never flown a landplane of this size in my life, he now thought. It was little comfort to recall that the other pilots were even less experienced in this sort of flying. They had planned to fly in a loose formation, keeping one another in sight, but they soon became separated.

Auerbach set his engines at "twenty-thirty"—2,000 RPMs and 30 inches of pressure—as he was accustomed to doing in a Navy PBY, and hoped for the best. The lights of the cities and towns along the Atlantic coast slipped by below. Over Florida he realized that the RX 135 "was using a tremendous amount of fuel because we weren't cruising at its best angle of attack." It would be best to refuel before heading out over water, but if he put down, there might be questions, a delay. It was Sunday morning, April 11; it would be Monday, April 12, he calculated, before anyone could reach customs in Philadelphia to check his clearance. There, they might find a new technicality to delay him three more days until the April 15 deadline. He checked his fuel again.

There was no choice.

At 3:30 A.M. he landed at West Palm Beach, taxied up to the control tower and apprehensively asked for gas. In a few minutes a fuel truck rolled up and filled the tanks; Auerbach paid for 500 gallons in cash. A sleepy attendant laconically asked where he was headed; Auerbach replied that he was cleared for Panama and, without waiting for further conversation, started up his engines.

One of the engines was coughing badly. Under normal circumstances he would have had it checked, but nothing could stop him now. He gave it some pressure and the coughing cleared up; the plane soared out over the dark sea.

It was midday as the RX 135 came in low over the Panama coast, low enough to sight thatched huts along the beach. At 1 P.M. Auerbach landed at Tocumen airfield. All four planes had gotten in safely. At the Tivoli Hotel the men slapped one another on the back and exchanged notes. Only one of the pilots, Swifty Schindler, had landed at Kingston as scheduled. Moonitz had refueled at Nassau and Raab had gone down at Camaguey, Cuba, with only forty gallons of gas left in his tanks. But they had all made it. Planes and crews were safely in Panama. Exultantly they congratulated one another.

Auerbach gave the men one day off to catch up on their sleep; then he organized instruction in instrument flying, navigation, radio, parts and equipment. He was determined that they would be better prepared for the next flight.

Classes had been in session for only a day when Auerbach got a telephone call from Los Angeles. He and Bill Gerson, the quiet Los Angeles businessman who had been Schindler's co-pilot, were to leave immediately for California. The five C-46s remaining in Burbank had to get out of the country before the April 15 deadline too; Auerbach and Gerson were to pilot two of them.

They arrived in Burbank to find the planes loaded and ready to go. They were crammed with spare parts, tools, everything that could be squeezed aboard. Gerson's plane carried the communications equipment for all of the planes; it would be installed in Panama. Schwimmer Aviation was moving, bag and baggage.

"Where is the weight and balance on these things?" Auerbach asked. He was told there was no time to worry about such niceties. It was the kind of thing he would have worried about a great deal during his days in the Navy or with the CAA, but "by then, I was haphazard in my own acceptance of the emergency, of flying here and flying there without thorough preparation. The stuff was in and the only question was, were you going to fly it or weren't you?"

The planes took off on April 14, clearing American customs at Mines Field in Los Angeles, and putting down only 150 miles away in Tijuana, the Mexican border town south of San Diego, to clear Mexican customs. From Tijuana they went in three short hops to Mexico City. On the way down Auerbach noticed smoke in the cockpit. "Luckily the co-pilot knew which hydraulic pump to shut off; I wouldn't have known; I wasn't that knowledgeable or that able in the C-46." At Mazatlán the planes, each of them from 5 to 10,000 pounds overweight, barely cleared the 3,300-foot runway. The pilots were uneasy as their overloaded planes wobbled like overweight acrobats in and out of the unfamiliar provincial Mexican fields. They put down in Mexico City with a sense of relief which quickly gave way to euphoria. Amid the exotic sights and smells of the Latin capital they felt strangely elated, disoriented, suspended from life's usual judgments and inhibitions. They were on foreign soil; there was mysterious talk of big deals for arms and fighter planes; they heard that Al Schwimmer had been there. There were also girls and bars and the heady excitement of being embarked on the Great Adventure, twentieth-century knights errant of the skies.

The mood of derring-do held as the five planes warmed up their engines at the Mexico City municipal airport a week later to take off for a non-stop flight to Panama. Sam Lewis, who would lead the flight as he had the flight down from Burbank, taxied out first. He had gone the full length of the 7,300-foot runway before his heavy plane lifted into the air. The second plane too barely cleared the field. Bill Gerson was third in line with Auerbach and the fifth plane waiting to follow. There was a puff of dust from the wheels of Gerson's plane as it reached the end of the runway and ran off into the dirt. It jumped into the air, hovered for about ninety seconds at an altitude of one hundred feet, then the left wing dipped and the plane plunged to the ground.

Auerbach cut his engines and jumped from his plane. Everyone was running, panting for breath, down the long runway. They arrived at the same moment as the field's crash truck. Pieces of Gerson's plane were scattered over an area of fifty yards; there were several small fires. Gerson and his mechanic, Glen King, had been thrown from the plane. King was dead. Gerson was crumpled up but moaning. Auerbach and the others eased him onto a canvas, picked up the four corners and carried him to the ambulance. Auerbach went along on the ride to the American hospital, whispering words of encouragement. He soon noticed, "I was talking to myself, he was unconscious." At 7 P.M. he was dead.

Each of the pilots took whatever money he had—they carried about $500 apiece for emergency expenses—put it into Gerson's wallet and sent it to his widow in Los Angeles. It seemed especially ironic that Gerson, the only man among them who had a family, had been killed. He had always been the quietest of the group; he was not along for the adventure but only because of his dedication to Zionism.

The next day the remaining planes were unloaded, several thousand pounds of their cargo was put in a bonded warehouse, the gas load was lightened and they flew on to Tocumen in Panama.

DR. JOSÉ ARAZI

O n April 16, in Washington, the second application that Schwimmer and Bernstein had filed for permission to export the Connies—this time to South Africa in the name of Transcaribbean Air Cargo Lines—was denied. The State Department not only was not prepared to let the two Connies in Millville and Burbank leave the United States, it wanted the one already in Panama to come back.

Nor was the *Attu* destined to reach foreign shores. Ten days after the liens, amounting to almost $50,000, had been paid and the aircraft carrier towed to its Sewells Point mooring, it was attached again, this time by Leonard Weisman's lawyer in Norfolk, W. E. Kyle, who said he had not been paid his fee and expenses for the first attachment proceedings. His bill came to $1,250. Again the lien was paid; Al Robison, the Hotel Fourteen's all-purpose expediter, went down to Norfolk to look over the situation. He reported back that he saw no possibility of getting the *Attu* out of the United States. It was turned over to a member of the Sonneborn Institute with a scrap metal business in Baltimore; he agreed to hold the ship for ninety days on the off chance that a way still could be found to use it. He kept it for ninety days and beyond, but the *Attu* was never reclaimed. In the end it was broken up for scrap and the Institute recouped about $50,000 of its huge investment in Arazi's dream.

By the time the *Attu* was headed for the scrap pile, Arazi was far from the scene of its ignominy. Years of underground dealings had taught him to recognize the signs of approaching disaster. He liked to tell how he once returned to his hideout in Nazi-occupied Bucharest and noticed three nondescript men in civilian clothing loitering near the building. There was nothing noteworthy about them except that all three were wearing sturdy well-soled shoes that only policemen could afford in wartime Rumania. Arazi darted into a labyrinth of alleyways and basements, which he had studied carefully in advance, and escaped.

This time too he had planned his escape route well ahead of time. Shortly after arriving in the United States, Arazi had made a short mysterious trip to see General Anastasia Somoza, the dictator of the Central American republic of Nicaragua, and come back with one more alias, Dr. José Arazi, emblazoned on a Nicaraguan diplomatic passport. Arazi's dealings with Somoza dated back to 1939, when his arms purchases for Haganah in Poland were made in the name of Nicaragua. Now he was ready to use the special ambassadorial status that Somoza had conferred on him to rescue both his cause and his reputation as the miracle man of the underground.

To friends in Rome, he sent an urgent cable: "HASINI IS AT THE AMBASSADOR HOTEL IN ROME UNTIL THE THIRD OF APRIL. PERSUADE HIM TO WAIT FOR ME THERE ON THE FOURTH."

"Hasini" was Arazi's code name for the Polish Count Stefan Czarnecki, with whom he had made the scouting trip to Europe in December. They had discovered that arms were available from manufacturers and dealers in a number of Western European countries provided a suitable "cover" could be provided which would obscure the fact that they were really going to Palestine.

What better cover than a Central American military dictator?

Arazi flew off to join Czarnecki in Rome. Irving Strauss, the brother-in-law of a brother-in-law of Al Schwimmer, who had been coralled into helping the underground "for a month," was dispatched to Nicaragua to dicker with General Somoza.

Once again Strauss explained to his business partners that he would be busy on other matters and took off for Managua, the capital of Nicaragua. Using the contacts Arazi already had established, he quickly gained an audience with Somoza in his palatial hilltop residence whose fortresslike appearance was not entirely accidental—the country's armory was conveniently located in its basement.

Strauss was shown into an anteroom. He sat down next to a diminutive Nicaraguan soldier who had been waiting for three days to ask Somoza for money for his father's funeral. Armed bodyguards kept both men under suspicious surveillance.

Somoza was just waking up from a siesta—he took at least two a day, Strauss was to learn—when Strauss was ushered into his presence. He found the dictator still a little sleepy, his jowly face flushed, his stocky body slumped into a chair—but genial. Strauss was surprised by the lack of ceremony as Somoza waved him to a chair.

Taking his cue from the general, Strauss came right to the point and explained frankly what he wanted: Somoza's signature on receipts which would be presented to him from time to time attesting to the arrival in Nicaragua of European armaments which, in fact, would have headed east to Palestine. Somoza would be well paid for this service, in cash, by deposits made to his private account in the Bank of London and South America, Ltd., at 84 William Street in New York City.

Somoza nodded. As a military man he understood the problem; he even took a professional interest in the plans; but what really interested him, Strauss observed, was the money. "He was strictly a businessman."

Somoza invited Strauss to come along on his daily tour of his cattle farms and other properties—he was the biggest cattle merchant in Nicaragua and also had substantial sugar interests. An even more profitable sideline was his virtual monopoly of the black market in his country's currency.

They drove in the general's Cadillac, which was big, black and equipped with bullet-proof windows. Tommy-gun-bearing bodyguards rode fore and aft. Somoza proudly showed Strauss his prize bulls, which were used for stud, his cows, which, he assured Strauss, were prolific milkers, and his process for making cheese. On the way back to town they made a stop at a modest frame house across from the airport, which Strauss—who waited in the car while Somoza spent half an hour inside—later learned belonged to Somoza's mistress.

In the next several months Strauss would make eight trips to Nicaragua, carrying papers for Somoza to sign. More than $200,000 would go into Somoza's private bank account in New York. Strauss also gave the dictator several personal gifts: a billiard table, on which they later played billiards together, and a large diamond. Strauss brought the diamond to Somoza along with a catalogue of settings, explaining that he would take the diamond back to New York to be mounted in the style the general preferred. Somoza brushed the catalogue aside. "Forget it," he said and dropped the loose diamond into his coat pocket.

Somoza, Strauss learned, could be generous with gifts too. He granted the young soldier's request for money to bury his father. And on the birthday of General Rafael Trujillo, his fellow dictator on neighboring Santo Domingo, he sent him a sentimental offering of fifty .50-caliber submachine guns.

He never gave anything to Strauss, but he scrupulously kept his agreement to sign the arms receipts, even when, later, there was considerable American and French pressure to renege. His natural sympathies were with the little countries against the big countries; it was nice when those sympathies coincided so well with his pecuniary interests.

Arazi's first purchase in Europe, using his Nicaraguan "cover" and Count Czarnecki's contacts in Switzerland, was five 20-mm. Hispano Suiza antiaircraft guns. They arrived in Palestine aboard the S.S. *Resurrection* on April 23. Haganah had just won a sharp battle for Haifa, the northern coastal city which the British had suddenly evacuated two days before, leaving the Jewish and Arab inhabitants to fight it out. It was struggling to keep open the recently won supply corridor to Jerusalem and to secure the city and surrounding settlements. It was planning a series of operations in the Galilee to establish contact with isolated settlements and occupy strategic towns and villages in preparation against a possible invasion from Syria and Lebanon in the north. The arrival of Arazi's 20-mm. Hispano Suizas —the first big guns of any kind to reach Haganah—aroused "great hopes and expectations." True, they were antiaircraft guns, but until something better came along, they would be Haganah's "artillery." There were only five, but they could be spread out and moved fast. In the next few critical weeks they would be hauled about the country, doing duty one day atop a factory near Haifa, another day in a battle in the suburbs of Jaffa, the Arab sister-city of Tel Aviv, still later in the defense of northern settlements facing Syria.

By the time the Hispano Suizas got to Palestine, Arazi was in Marseilles, supervising the loading of a large shipment of French arms aboard the S.S. *Santa Ciara*.

The old master had done it again.

XXXVII

CZECHOSLOVAKIA

I n Prague, Dr. Felix had been carefully keeping open the Czech offer of planes and assiduously renewing old friendships among the new Communist bureaucracy. Some were Jews and had been Zionists at Charles University but after the Munich appeasement and the Nazi occupation, they "got tired of waiting and moved left." Dr. Felix recalls that "they would jeer at me as a 'dirty reactionary.' In no way did they show themselves prepared to help. Yet they did. Sometimes you can learn to live with a tiger. We played intellectual games together. I would quote to them certain lines in Marxism-Leninism that 'proved' our victory was inevitable. They made all kinds of difficulties. But in the end they helped."

The most influential Communist official among Felix's prewar acquaintances was Bedrich Reicin, who had returned from Russia with the Czech Brigade of the Red Army to become deputy to the Minister of Defense and head of military intelligence in the new regime. With his access to the dossiers of all officials in Czechoslovakia, past and present, Reicin was considered by American diplomats to be "the most powerful man in Czechoslovakia." A hulking giant of a man, Reicin was the son of a provincial rabbi, but he had never been sympathetic to Zionism. He and Felix spent long evenings in hair-splitting arguments. "None of these men thought there was any safety in Zionism," recalls Felix. Reicin never softened in his attitude, but "the mere fact that I was seen going very often into Reicin's office gave me standing." Another important Communist official with whom Felix dealt was Dr. Otto Fischl, deputy to the Minister of Finance, who would sometimes threaten him at the climax of a particularly bitter argument: "Beware, you have offended the Communist Party." But Felix knew that Fischl had a soft spot for the memory of a dead brother who had been a Zionist.

When in mid-April an order finally came from Ben Gurion to buy the German fighter planes he had been offered, Dr. Felix was ready. He went to the factory manager with whom he had become friendly and told him he wanted ten of the Me-109s. The Czech snorted, "Ten are nothing. After a few days, you will have only three or four." The manager had twenty-five planes to sell; he advised Felix to take them all. Felix queried Tel Aviv. The reply came back that ten would be enough. "Only Ben Gurion was convinced there would be an invasion and a real war," Felix recalls. "The others always hoped for a miracle."

Felix bought the ten planes for $44,000 each, including some spare parts and armaments—cannon, machine guns, bombs and ammunition. He also, on his own, took an option on the other fifteen planes. The contract was signed on April 23. Dr. Felix hoped to fly the planes out as soon as they had been reassembled, with refueling stops in Italy and Greece.*

Right after seeing off the last C-46s from Burbank, Al Schwimmer made a quick trip to Mexico City and at last succeeded in pinning down the ephemeral offer of aircraft. He flew to Rome, met Arazi and together they went to see Shaul Avigor, the emissary Ben Gurion had sent to Europe to direct arms procurement when hopes for the *Attu* and the Mexican arms had waned.

Triumphantly Schwimmer told Avigor that Mexico was pre-

* During the infamous Czech treason trials of 1952 Reicin and Fischl would learn there was no safety for them in Communism either. Both men were charged with conspiring with Rudolf Slansky, secretary of the Czech Communist Party, and Bedrich Geminder, director of the Party's international department, to work "in accordance with the plans and directives of the Western imperialists for the severance of Czechoslovakia from her alliance with the USSR." On November 21 the court was told, "The conspirators were interested in connections with hostile Zionist organizations. In the second half of 1948, Slansky sent Bedrich Geminder a representative of the Israeli Embassy in Prague, Doctor Felix, with whom Geminder discussed various campaigns by the Embassy in Czechoslovakia . . . Slansky ordered Geminder to support these campaigns. Bedrich Reicin was entrusted with the organizational aspect, Otto Fischl with the economic and financial side." As a matter of fact, Felix's work in Prague began in late 1947, not the "second half of 1948"—before there was an Israeli Embassy. He never met either Slansky or Geminder. Slansky, Reicin, Geminder and Fischl were executed December 3, 1952.

Dr. Felix holds the rare distinction of being condemned as a Western agent by the Communists, who saw Zionism as an instrument of Western imperialism, and later as a Communist agent by some Western sources anxious to link Israel with Communism.

pared to sell them planes. Not the P-51 fighters they had been hoping for, but serviceable P-47s.

Avigor listened and shook his head. It was too late, he told Schwimmer, they had just concluded the agreement with Czechoslovakia to buy fighter planes—Avia 111s, as the Czechs now called the wartime German Messerschmitt Bf 109, which had been manufactured in Czech factories during the German occupation.

Schwimmer argued against them. The Me-109, by any name, was a tricky plane, difficult to fly and unreliable. None of the fighter pilots he was recruiting had ever flown it; they were Americans, trained on American planes. Nor would his mechanics know how to service the German plane. Avigor understood, but there was nothing to be done. All of the money available for fighter planes was committed to Czechoslovakia. Nor was Avigor interested, for the moment, in Mexican arms. Again the underground's limited funds had been committed to the purchases which Dr. Felix, Arazi and others had been able to make in Europe.

Avigor's announcement was a stunning blow to Schwimmer. It upset all of the calculations for a Panama-based airlift which would ferry arms and men from the Americas to Italy and from there to Palestine. He thought of the struggle to get the planes out of the United States, to legitimize them with LAPSA's Panamanian charter. There would be no point in keeping them in Panama now.

And what was he going to tell the fighter pilots, navigators and ground crews which Service Airways had been recruiting—that they would go into action in German airplanes, bought from a Communist country?

He remonstrated, but Avigor was adamant. The deal with Czechoslovakia had been made, it had been a bird in the hand and there was no money left for Mexican plumage, however attractive.

Elsewhere in the world Haganah agents looking for aircraft had met with less success than Dr. Felix. In South Africa the former South African pilot Boris Senior had located fifty surplus American-built P-40 fighters for sale as scrap and had even organized a syndicate of sympathetic businessmen to buy them. The project had foundered on the usual obstacle: without proper certification there was no way to get them out of the country and across the continent of Africa. In England the ex-RAF pilot Freddy Fredkens had bought three light bombers, Ansons, under cover of a nonexistent Singapore airline. The planes had gotten as far as the island of Rhodes in the presumably friendly country of Greece when the Greek government suddenly yanked in the welcome mat and seized them.

So much for the Ansons. And so much for the hopes of Dr. Felix that the Czech Me-109s could get to Palestine under their own power by refueling in Italy and Greece.

XXXVIII

MRS. SILVERMAN'S AIRPLANES

W hen all the experts had tried and failed, it fell to Mrs. Sol
Silverman of Roanoke, Virginia, to come up with a winning
suggestion. Mrs. Silverman had never heard of the Hotel Fourteen,
Materials for Palestine, or the Sonneborn Institute. She knew nothing
about strategy or modern warfare. But she had a brother, a former
lieutenant colonel, retired from the United States Army Air Forces,
who had settled in Paris as a dealer in secondhand aircraft. At a fund-
raising meeting in Roanoke, Mrs. Silverman mentioned her brother
to the speaker, who passed on his name, David Miller, and address,
28 Rue de Franqueville, to the Hotel Fourteen, where they reached
"Norman" Hyman Sheckman, who dutifully sent them on in a coded
message to Paris.

Freddy Fredkens, returning to the Continent from his disap-
pointment in Greece, dropped in to see Miller, posing as the representative of a Belgian company that planned to operate a freight airline to Spain.

Miller, gravely accepting Fredkens' description of himself and
his mission at face value, said he knew of just the right airplane: the
Norseman, a big powerful single-engine cargo plane that the Americans had manufactured and used extensively during World War II.
The American occupation forces in Germany had just put up twenty
for sale. They had cost the Army $35,000 each and Fredkens could
buy them for less than half that. Most important of all to Fredkens,
they would be delivered with American registrations. In the year
1948 that meant they could go anywhere. All that was needed were
the pilots to fly them and a base where they could be reconditioned.
Miller obligingly suggested the latter—Toussus-le-Noble, a small private field southwest of Paris. Fredkens exultantly notified Haganah to
send on the pilots.

France was a logical base for the Norsemen. Haganah long had enjoyed an amiably ambiguous relationship with French officialdom. French Jews had played an important part in the French wartime underground—about one-fifth of the Maquis were Jews—and popular French enthusiasm for the Jewish cause was strong. After V-E Day the French government, moved by mingled portions of sympathy for the survivors of Hitler and guilt for the Vichy government's anti-Jewish measures, had admitted thousands of DPs from Germany and Eastern Europe. It had allowed areas near Marseilles to be turned into a giant staging ground for illegal immigration to Palestine and had ignored Haganah's collection of small arms from former French Maquis and American GIs waiting in Marseilles to ship out to the Pacific theater.

There had been occasional sudden shifts in French policy—an arrest here, a crackdown there—as one unstable French government succeeded another and momentarily paid heed to protests from the British. They permitted the office of the Jewish Agency on Boulevard de la Grande Armée, near Neuilly in Paris, to run an overt clearing and reception station for "volunteers" while the extremist Irgun group maintained a similar propaganda and recruiting office at 18 Avenue de Messine. Haganah and the French Secret Service exchanged information about British secret service agents operating in Paris. Haganah even maintained a rogues' gallery of British agents, a wall chart of candid photos, at its Shoo-Shoo headquarters in the Hotel Lutetia on the Left Bank.

Haganah even had its unofficial emissary to the French government, a prominent Paris attorney named André Blumel who had been close to General Charles de Gaulle in the French wartime resistance and a key official in the Interior Ministry of de Gaulle's postwar government.

Blumel interceded with French officialdom when there were problems, defended Haganah agents when they were arrested. He had even gotten clearance from the Interior Ministry for a short wave radio station in a villa in the St. Germain-en-Laye suburb of Paris which kept Tel Aviv informed of the movements of illegal immigrant ships.

When Shaul Avigor arrived in Paris, Blumel assured the cautious Palestinian he could stop moving from hotel to hotel and took him to the building on the Rue des Saussaies occupied by the DST, Direction de la Surveillance du Territoire, France's counterespionage service, to meet its director, Roger Wybot. The two men left with Wybot's tacit agreement that the underground could operate its arms procurement program as it pleased so long as it kept the DST and the Interior Ministry informed of what it was doing and so long as it kept its activities inconspicuous. It had carte blanche unless it became an embarrassment.*

Mrs. Silverman's airplanes were the biggest thing the underground had tried to hide in France. However, the twenty planes would not all be in the country at the same time. They would be flown from Germany, two or three at a time, then taken north to Amsterdam, where KLM, the Dutch airline, would make several modifications, including the installation of long-range fuel tanks connected by special feed lines to the normal tanks. This would boost the planes' flying time from eight to fourteen hours, long enough for them to fly non-stop from Italy to Palestine. The whole operation would be quiet and discreet. The planes would have American registration; Miller, the American airplane broker, would be the nominal owner; and the pilots ostensibly would be working for him.

The first Norseman was ferried into Toussus-le-Noble from the U.S. airbase of Oberpfaffenhofen near Munich by Phil Marmelstein, the Philadelphian who had been so anxious to get back into aviation that he had been studying aircraft mechanics. He had flown from New York to Rome with three other pilot recruits, spent a couple of weeks marking time in Rome, then been told by Danny Agronsky to move on to Paris.

Other men began arriving: an American named Bob Fine; a Persian Jew, Abe Nathan, who had flown in the Indian Air Force; an English navigator named Lew Nagley who had been a prisoner of war in Germany; a French Algerian named Maurice Ben Simon, who had flown French Air Force transports between France and Indochina; a Russian calling himself "Richard Brown," who said he had deserted from the Red Army Air Force;† a millionaire Dutchman named Willem Van Leer, who made a scouting trip down through Greece and Cyprus to feel out safe landing spots in case a plane was forced to stop for repairs or refueling.

* The working agreement between Haganah and the French would be considerably expanded in scope and warmth during the next nineteen years. Israeli and French intelligence agencies worked closely together, to the mutual benefit of both, until de Gaulle's break with Israel during the Six Day War of June 1967.
† Twenty-three Jews and twelve non-Jews in the Red Army are known to have deserted from the Soviet occupation zone of Germany immediately after VE-Day and made their way to Palestine.

Ernie Stehlik, the old-time Constellation specialist from TWA, showed up one day. He had been in Europe ever since the first C-46 had landed in Castiglione del Lago and found the field unsafe. Leo Gardner and Steve Schwartz had returned to the United States, but Stehlik had stayed on in Europe, performing the same job for the underground he had had at TWA: roving mechanic-at-large. He flew with Marmelstein to Amsterdam, gave some advice on the Norsemen, then disappeared.

The Dutch mechanics and administrators at Schiphol airport outside Amsterdam were especially cooperative and helpful. "They all knew we were going to Palestine," recalls Marmelstein, "and they went out of their way to help."

The Netherlands had suffered a bitter occupation under the Germans and had been outraged by the deportations of Dutch Jews; public opinion was firmly behind the attempt to establish a Jewish state. Dutch pilots at the field discussed weather and routes with Marmelstein. When he decided to do some practice night flying in anticipation of the long haul across the Mediterranean, the control tower personnel put him through several landings without making the usual extra charge for night work.

By the end of April the first three Norsemen were ready to go. They flew to Rome, where Italian mechanics gave them a final checkout. On May 2 they were loaded up and took off for Palestine, where the British had turned over to the Jewish authorities some of the airfields close to Tel Aviv which were to be part of the Jewish state. Coleman Goldstein, a friend of Marmelstein's from Philadelphia, led the flight.

For the first four hours it was tough going against strong head winds. As usual, the planes were overloaded; there had been no room for life rafts; Goldstein's plane carried a stack of guns behind the radio equipment; the only map was a Mercator projection, unsuitable for air navigation. Goldstein wondered whether "we would run out of water or gas first"; the gas held out and the planes arrived—the first to reach Palestine to back up the tiny fleet of Austers and Piper Cubs. The flight had taken eleven and a half exhausting hours.

At 4 A.M. the next morning Goldstein was awakened. His plane had been stripped and reloaded. A young Palestinian explained what he was to do. Four settlements, known as the Etzion bloc, had been surrounded and cut off by the Arabs. Situated in the Hebron Hills, where King David and other kings of Judah once had reigned, the Etzion bloc was of both sentimental and strategic importance; it guarded the southern approach to Jerusalem. Two relief convoys trying to reach it had been beaten off; one of them, composed of thirty-five university students, had been wiped out to the last man. Piper Cubs had been flying in food and medical supplies to an improvised airstrip. Goldstein's first mission in Palestine—less than twelve hours after his arrival—would be to drop a life-saving load of supplies and arms to the beleaguered settlements.

That night, May 3, another plane that had made its way across the Mediterranean from Italy landed at Ekron airfield. It was the C-46 that had been marooned for so long in Perugia. Agronsky finally had wangled permission for it to leave. Arnold Ilowite, an American pilot who had been recruited by Service Airways, was at the controls. Like the Norseman, the C-46 was pressed into service immediately. The day after its arrival Ilowite flew it north to drop supplies to an isolated settlement in Galilee.

The other eight C-46s were still in Panama, where their crews, mechanics, and baffled Panamanian sponsors were waiting and wondering what would come next.

XXXIX

CATANIA

The mood of the men matched the gray rain that had been falling in Panama for days. The crash in Mexico City, the deaths of Gerson and King, had ended "the whole delusion of immortality," Auerbach recalls. "You had abandoned the normal safeguards, just shoving off and going to Panama without much thought or preparation. That ended with the crash."

The men were bored and demoralized. Ray Kurtz, the second fireman from New York, who had teamed up with first fireman Moonitz, the two burly men forming an inseparable pair, wrote his wife, Ruthie, whom he had left working at her family's bakery back in Brooklyn: "There is absolutely nothing to do here but gamble and fool around with prostitutes. The whores get twenty dollars per, the classy ones. The others get three dollars to fifteen dollars . . . most of them are as ugly as sin."

Some of the men had sought out the Jewish synagogue, where they were made welcome by the local Jewish community, especially the families with marriageable daughters. Schindler put a stop to this and cryptically warned the rabbi: "Avoid these boys. We may be doing things that will have unpleasant repercussions."

One of the men complained that the humid Panama climate was bad for his asthma and left. Schindler fired another who was loud in his denunciation of the whole operation. But Schindler himself was "really disturbed by the information I had from the crews arriving from California and Mexico. They told me about the condition of the airplanes, the overloading; they came to me to do something about it."

Schindler telephoned Schwimmer in New York and told him there was an "open rebellion," the operation was falling apart. He protested about the overweight planes and the sloppy loading. It had

been foolish, he said, to put all of the radio equipment in one plane—
the plane that crashed. It would all have to be replaced. "A great deal
that is being done is being done loosely," he went on. "I want to tell
you, I think you killed those guys. Not consciously, but because of all
this sloppiness."

Schwimmer listened at the other end, exhausted after the rush to
get the airplanes out of New Jersey and California, disappointed by
his fruitless trips to Mexico and Italy. He let Schindler talk and then
replied tersely. Schindler was through as the boss in Panama;
Schwimmer himself would come down and settle things.

He arrived two days later with Sheckman. In the Packard
Building, a modest two-story stucco structure where LAPSA had its
offices and, upstairs, living quarters for the men, the two men quietly
addressed the flight crews. Sheckman said something about "this is
war." But it was Schwimmer who laid it on the line. "This is the best
we can do; if you are in this for a soft airline job, you'd better get out
now."

No one had heard Schwimmer speak so vehemently before. He
had been the detached technical expert, dispassionate, uninvolved in
the emotional eddies that stirred other men. A childhood friend
would recall that Schwimmer had always been called Adolph, never
Al, in his youth and was the kind of a stolid loner "you never thought
much about, he was just there." Now he revealed the underlying
determination and peculiar qualities of leadership which evoked men's
loyalties.

Schindler got Schwimmer aside. "He thought I was going to
quit," Schindler recalls, "but I surprised him. I resigned as president
of Service Airways but told him I was perfectly satisfied to continue
as one of the pilots. I wanted to go with the planes." None of the
other men quit either.

It rained and rained. A group of mechanics who had come down
from Burbank worked on the planes. First fireman Moonitz flew to
Mexico City to pick up replacements for the communications equipment that had gone down in the crash—it had been smuggled into
Mexico from Los Angeles by Leo Gardner and Hank Greenspun.

Schwimmer stayed on in Panama. He made salary arrangements
with each of the men; they were paid and made deposits at the Chase
National Bank in Balboa, the Canal Zone. On May 2 the rain stopped
and the sun came out. Since it was a hot sticky Sunday, the boys went
swimming. In the evening they gathered at the Packard Building to
meet five new arrivals, including Tryg Maseng, the Norwegian-

American who had quit Columbia University to live his experiences before he wrote about them. The newcomers brought to twenty-five the number of pilots, navigators and radio operators now in Panama. Schwimmer introduced Rey Selk who had come down from Burbank to supervise loading operations, and promised all of the men raises in salaries in a month. Second fireman Kurtz jubilantly wrote to Ruthie, "I've been getting $500 a month and I'll be getting $600 next month, twice as much as I got at the Fire Department."

Sheckman, after the showdown meeting in the Packard Building, had taken the first commercial flight out of Panama, via Puerto Rico, for Europe. He wasn't ready yet to give up the plan for Yakum Purkan that he had brought to America, so carefully coded and mapped, in his B-4 bag. He wanted to see Avigor. Even if the Mexican planes were out, there were still the armaments and ammunition. "The Mexicans are ready," he insisted to Avigor in Geneva. "And the C-46s are still in Panama. It would be a simple matter . . ."

Avigor, a grave, sad-faced man with a wrestler's build and a scholar's manner, shook his head. It was May 2. Only thirteen days before the British would leave Palestine.

Only Czechoslovakia had been ready to sell. The money had been committed, the contracts signed.

"There is nothing to do," Scheckman told Agronsky in Rome. The planes would leave Panama empty. And then what?

That is what Agronsky had been worrying about. With the field Arazi had found at Castiglione del Lago unusable, the planes had no place to go. And it wasn't only the C-46s in Panama that were on his mind. Italy was supposed to be the staging area for the entire nascent Jewish air force, which was being bought and recruited all over the world. The Italians had been more than hospitable, allowing a steady flow of illegal emigrants to embark for Palestine from Italian ports. But as a poor country, engaged in her own economic and political battles, and as a defeated country, trying to ingratiate herself with her victors, she could not go too far in defying British and American policy. Diplomatic pressure had increased in the past weeks.

The truth was, until it could move on to Palestine, the "air force" was homeless. Agronsky didn't tell this to the pilots who were coming into Rome from the United States, Canada, England, South Africa. He put them up in hotels around the railway station. Most of them were ex-fighter pilots, high strung as jockeys, and when they asked him, as they often did, what kind of airplanes they would be flying, he didn't dare tell them. The purchase of the Me-109s was top secret; they were still being reassembled in Czechoslovakia and a way was being sought to bring them out. Meanwhile Agronsky tried to keep the men occupied or on the move. A pilot recruited in Ottawa would be shuttled to Geneva, to Paris, to Rome.

Gideon Lichtman, the boy from Newark who had been so impatient with the Land and Labor questionnaire, arrived via Zurich, still impatient. He was "wearing a sky-blue zoot suit," he recalls, "and everyone spotted me for an American right away. Naturally, I met a girl, but one of the Shoo-Shoo boys at the hotel told me she was working for the Arabs. I said to myself, 'a piece of ass is a piece of ass,' but when I went up to her room, the closet door was slightly ajar and I got out of there real fast. It was a tense time."

He teamed up with George "Buzz" Buerling, a twenty-six-year-old Canadian flying ace who had rigged up a screen in his hotel room to practice "angle offs"—the technique of split-second air-to-air firing when both planes are in motion. With a stick he shifted the silhouette of an aircraft behind the screen and calculated how much of a lead would be required to shoot it down. He kept in condition by running ten miles every day and ate only foods he considered good for his extraordinary eyesight. In combat he was always the first to spot the make of enemy planes and the formation they were flying. Buerling had shot down twenty-nine German planes in fourteen days during World War II.

"We were both very restless," Lichtman recalls. "We wanted to get flying already and nobody seemed to know when, what, where we would be flying."

All Agronsky—the harried host to some fifty restless crewmen—knew was that the base couldn't be in Rome. Through his contacts, an airfield at Urbe, on the outskirts of the city, had been made available for the odd airplane that came through. A Rapide bought in Britain; a once-a-week DC-3 owned by Universal, a brand-new South African airline that conveniently originated most of its trips in Palestine; a Norseman or two with their American registrations. At Urbe too was the Alicia flying school, which was owned by Count Gino di Rovere, a former Italian combat pilot who had been a British prisoner during the war. The count was hardly the Haganah type. He wore his long black hair slicked back, a double-breasted camel's hair coat; he owned a villa in Bordighera and one of the few running sports cars in postwar Italy. Yet he was a Haganah sympathizer and on its payroll; the ten students in his flying school were young DPs.

They had been selected from among the husky youths who had helped pack and load the secret arms shipments from Magenta—their reward for the back-breaking work was flying lessons. They flew a sixty-five-horsepower Lombardy primary trainer under the eye of di Rovere and his fellow ex-Fascist instructors, while ORT (Organization for Rehabilitation and Training), a welfare organization, paid the bills.*

Agronsky had found a possible alternative to Castiglione del Lago in a neglected bombed-out World War II air base at Catania on the island of Sicily. He and Sheckman flew down to take a look at it. The location was perfect, Agronsky explained. It was out of the way, remote from the Roman bureaucracy and the diplomatic pressures of the capital, cut off from the mainland by antipathies as well as the Straits of Messina.

There was one potential problem. An airplane was expected to travel according to a flight plan filed in advance. It was a safety precaution—if the plane did not arrive at its stated destination, someone would go out looking for it. For an operation like Agronsky's such solicitude could be troublesome, as he had discovered when the C-46 failed to land in Rome. He solved the problem with the help of Haganah in Paris.

The airport commander on the French island of Corsica had agreed that if any LAPSA planes left Sicily with a flight plan filed for Corsica, he would confirm their arrival even if he never saw them.

The airport manager in Catania was delighted to see the two emissaries from LAPSA. His patched-up runway had scarcely been used since the war and he welcomed the prospect of turning it into the European terminus of the new Panamanian airline. If he was surprised that Sicily should be so honored, he didn't show it. The local hotel keepers and the gasoline supplier were excited too. Perhaps on the wings of LAPSA prosperity would reach Catania.

The first planes would be arriving very soon, Agronsky assured them.

---

* One of the Alicia flying school's graduates, Morty Fein, would become Mordecai Hod, commander of the Israeli Air Force in the Six Day War.

TIMETABLE

From Panama second fireman Kurtz sent his wife a postcard that showed the RX 121 Constellation with its LAPSA markings and Panamanian flag parked at Tocumen airport. "This is a picture of one of the company planes," he wrote. "It is the only one I could find, so please show it to my mother."

Gilberto Arias, LAPSA's Panamanian attorney and benefactor, wondered why Bellefond and Schindler were not out drumming up business for the new airline. Watching the build-up of idle planes and pilots, he "began to suspect that the venture was not a bona fide business operation . . . The large number of aircraft as well as the number of personnel . . . was evidently out of proportion to any possible commercial cargo transportation. In addition, the fact that the pilots remained in Panama for a substantial period of time without work was a cost unbearable for any business enterprise." Despite his suspicions, Arias continued to help LAPSA. Even when, months later, he learned exactly what Schindler and the others were up to, he stuck by them. "I felt an identity of cause with them," he recalls, "and it would have been very difficult to avoid being influenced by the integrity of the group as well as the Jewish cause still so fresh in our memories . . ."

Even though there was no visible commercial use for their skills, the men in Panama were now working hard to improve them. Training on the C-46s, which had been interrupted by Auerbach's absence, had resumed. Some of the volunteers hadn't flown since the war; some were obviously incompetent, but there had been no time to weed them out and it was too late now. Sam Lewis, who had been most disturbed by the crash in Mexico—as chief pilot, he felt responsible for the men—pushed to bring them up to standard.

On May 4 the mechanics began installing long-range fuel tanks and loaded in survival equipment—life rafts and parachutes. Lewis made tentative plane assignments and told the men that five of the C-46s would go out soon with Auerbach leading the flight. Lewis would stay behind with the Constellation, which needed a new engine, and the three C-46s, which still needed work.

The planes would go by stages via South America and Africa to Italy and from there into Palestine. By the time they arrived, the beleaguered Jewish colony would be an independent state, very possibly defending itself against invasion by several Arab armies. The C-46s and the Norsemen would constitute the "air force." Hopefully—but Lewis did not mention this—joined by the fighters from Czechoslovakia.

Obviously the flight must be made as secretly as possible. The fiction that they were a Panama-based commercial operation was to be maintained all the way, for there would be danger at every stop of Arab sabotage and of diplomatic pressure from England and the United States to detain the planes.

On May 8 Kurtz wrote his wife, "Taking a little trip. Don't write me at this address until further notice." At 7 A.M., with only a week to go until the May 15 deadline, the five planes took off from Tocumen and headed for Paramaribo in Dutch Guiana.

Tryg Maseng was uneasy about the navigator in his plane: "He had a second mate's ticket in the merchant marine but had never looked at the ground from the air. We hit the hump of Brazil and just kept on going. After an hour or so I got suspicious at not seeing any land at all. I asked where we were. He looks at his map and looks down and says, 'I see a river.'" Maseng managed to get two radio bearings and homed into the airport. He hoped his late arrival would not attract attention. As he taxied to a stop, he saw a group of men who looked like Indians rushing toward the plane. He tried to catch what they were saying—it was in a language strange to him. Finally they got close enough for him to make it out. Waving their arms and smiling, they were shouting, "Shalom, shalom."

"Some secret operation!" Maseng exploded.

Panama's mood of gloom was broken. The two firemen, Moonitz and Kurtz, clowned as men waited, tired and hungry after their eleven-hour flight, for transportation into town. "Moonitz was bigger than life," recalls Maseng, "like William Bendix only bigger." Kurtz twitted Livingston, the diminutive Boston advertising man, about his penchant for tall women and speculated about the physical proportions of the women in Paramaribo. A bus took them to the Palace Hotel, where they spent the next day—it was Mother's Day, one of them recalled—waiting for some repairs to be made to the planes. On Monday two of the planes took off for Natal; the other three were laid up until Tuesday, when they too took off. Auerbach reflected that he was leading a flight of straggling sick airplanes over the Amazon jungle "as casually as men in sports planes out for an afternoon's flying." There were high cumulus clouds but to go over them would mean climbing to 25,000 feet, and the planes were not equipped with oxygen; instead Auerbach flew under them, skipping along at treetop height and trying not to look down at "that foreboding jungle."

The five planes were reunited in Natal on May 11. A newspaper there ran a story saying they were bound for Palestine. The harsh fighting in the Holy Land was front page news; someone had put two and two together.

Auerbach laboriously wrote out a denial, had it translated into Portuguese and took it into the newspaper office. The improvised press release told about LAPSA and its plans for a worldwide operation, but it was obviously ridiculous. The five shabby airplanes that had arrived at Natal could never be passed off as the vanguard of an international airline.

The men waited uneasily while their planes were being serviced; the flight had been rough and some of the planes were in bad condition. "Everybody expects to make it himself and the other guy not to," one of the men wrote in his diary. His next entry, on May 12, noted, "Boots at five dollars. Food awful. Auerbach sick. Spanish and Portuguese interpreters. Moonitz and Kurtz buy marmosets. Flight test 130 and 136 [two of the planes]."

In Palestine on May 12 the British suddenly announced they would quit the country a day early, at midnight of May 14 instead of on May 15 as they had been saying since December. The announcement had hardly been made when the Transjordan "Arab Legion," which was in Palestine by British sanction as a "police force," commanded by British officers and deploying British artillery and armored cars, launched an attack against the four Jewish settlements of the Etzion bloc which guarded the southern approach to Jerusalem. Ben Gurion called it an "invasion" and the Jews wondered if the other neighboring countries that had been threatening to invade would advance their timetables too.

"If we are left with only the arms we now have, then our position can be counted on as very dangerous," Ben Gurion told a worried meeting of the newly formed "National Administration," the cabinet, in fact, of a provisional government, although it was not called that.

Haganah's military position had improved during the past six weeks, since it had taken the offensive with the successful drive to open the Jerusalem road. It had opened a road to the Negev and secured the main arteries north into eastern and western Galilee. It had occupied a number of important cities, including Haifa, and some one hundred strategic villages throughout the country. It had defeated the irregular military forces of the Palestinian Arabs in several battles and mobilized over 30,000 full-time soldiers.

Its victories had not only saved the future Jewish state from fatal massacre but had been largely responsible for warding off an eleventh-hour diplomatic offensive against it at the United Nations.

There, the American delegation, at the instigation of a die-hard group in the State Department, still hoping to thwart by political maneuver President Truman's policy of support for partition and a Jewish state, had proposed an "indefinite" trusteeship for Palestine—ostensibly to stop the fighting. The proposal was welcomed only by England. Other countries, looking squarely at military realities—as Aubrey Eban had predicted they would at the meeting of the Sonneborn Institute in New York six months before—concluded that the partition that the UN had voted in November was taking form, in fact, in the field, and refused to nullify it.

"What the world needs now," declared the delegate from New Zealand, "is resolution, not resolutions." Nevertheless, discussions and proposals—including a Security Council resolution creating a truce commission and a vain last-minute appeal from the United States to Great Britain to remain in Palestine two extra weeks—went on for more than a month while time ran out.

The British—after refusing admission to a UN Palestine commission charged with acting as liaison in the orderly transfer of powers to the respective Jewish and Arab administrations—continued evacuation, leaving behind them civil as well as military chaos. By May 1 most of the agencies of the Mandate government had ceased operations completely. Except where scattered local authorities, Jewish or Arab, maintained continuity, taxes were no longer collected, municipal services were disrupted, police were disbanded, courts did not function, trains ceased to run, Palestine no longer belonged to the International Postal Union.

Discussions of the "Palestine problem" were still going on at the

United Nations when Ben Gurion met with his shadow cabinet, the National Administration, on May 12 to consider Haganah's military position in the light of the Arab Legion invasion and Britain's final withdrawal, two days hence.

Haganah had done well in the opening skirmishes with Arab irregulars, but casualties had been high—over 750 killed in six weeks, a large loss in an army with few seasoned soldiers. Many units were exhausted; it remained to be seen how they would stand up against "cannon and steel," the well-equipped regular armies of Egypt, Syria, Lebanon and Iraq, already poised to attack.

Of the 30,000 men mobilized, only 20,000 had arms. Their artillery consisted of little more than Arazi's five Hispano Suiza 20-mm. guns. Slavin's factories, as they emerged into daylight, were manufacturing as many three-inch mortars as they had the raw materials for. However, the machine gun on which Slavin, Alper and Schalit had expended so much energy in the United States had been shelved. It had been impossible to make it underground; now there was no time for its complicated tooling. The aircraft carrier *Attu*, which if Arazi's scheme had worked, would have been on its way now with heavy equipment, was tied up in Baltimore, doomed to be cut up for scrap. Arazi sent word that artillery and machine guns were on their way from France by sea; the ship was due, but nothing could be seen on the horizon except the vigilant Royal Navy maintaining its blockade.

Other arms had been bought and stockpiled abroad, Ben Gurion told the assembled leaders. "If we are able to bring over not all but a portion of what we have overseas, say another fifteen thousand rifles and four million rounds of ammunition and artillery, bazookas and fighter planes equipped with cannon, machine guns and bombs, then our position at the outset of the campaign will be vastly different. We would be able to deliver a strong blow at the Arabs from the beginning of the invasion and undermine their morale. But the Arab armies are likely to march into the country before the equipment reaches us."

PART
SIX

XLI

THE RED HOUSE

I n later years it would be said that the new Jewish state was fighting a war on three of its four sides—north, south and east—and that only its western boundary, its long Mediterranean coastline, remained open in the grim opening days of its war of independence. But that would be history's long view with time compressed and anxiety anesthetized. In those early days of May 1948, when the leaders of Haganah met in the "Red House," a squat pink building on the beachfront of Tel Aviv which served as their secret headquarters, and looked out their windows to the sea, they saw in the Mediterranean a forbidding obstacle to their survival, in some ways stronger and more implacable than any Arab army. That oval sea which had seen so much of their history, their dispersion, and lately, their return, might yet be their undoing.

It was the Mediterranean, patrolled by British ships, which they had had to overcome to bring in illegal immigrants from the DP camps of Europe. It was the Mediterranean, which the "used industrial machinery" from Alper and Schalit had had to breach to give them the machine tools and raw materials for Slavin's clandestine arms industry. It was the Mediterranean, which the chartered American C-54 had to vault to furtively land guns that helped open the road to Jerusalem. Now, sitting in the Red House, the men contemplated the blue innocence of that fabled sea and looked toward its northern shores, which held the instruments of their salvation.

In Czechoslovakia were the fighter planes—the ten that had been bought in April, the fifteen more that Dr. Felix had under option. In Czechoslovakia and elsewhere in Europe were the arms and ammunition they needed for their armies. Spread out across the world were the Norsemen, the C-46s, the B-17s, the Constellations and the pilots and crews who had been recruited to fly the planes.

But none of the men, planes or arms were of any use until they crossed the Mediterranean.

The Palestinian leaders had hoped, when they began purchasing arms in Czechoslovakia, that Yugoslavia would allow them to pass through its ports on the Adriatic. One shipload had arrived that way, but then something had happened. Marshal Tito's regime had turned cold to cooperation with Czechoslovakia. Only months later would the world learn about his historic break with the Cominform.

There were longer, slower, more complicated routes through the American occupation zone of Germany to Belgian ports, or through Austria to Italy. A few small shipments of arms had been slipped through, but in recent weeks, since Czechoslovakia had moved all the way into the Communist camp, border traffic was carefully watched. The arms were trapped in Czechoslovakia.

Other ships with other arms were on the way or would be coming; coming too were MFP ships with boots, beds, barbed wire for their army. But even these ships would not break the shackles of the sea if Arab navies were blockading Palestine ports, if Arab planes were bombarding their docks, or if Arab armies already stood victorious on the Mediterranean shore. The ships, most of them, would take weeks to arrive. The Arabs were poised to defeat the Jews in days. It was the planes that they needed, planes to fight and planes to fly in guns as the C-54 had done.

None of the planes in Europe could make the flight from Czechoslovakia to Palestine without stops for refueling. The Me-109s, with a range of less than 400 miles, would have to make three. But where? British and American pressure had frightened Italy into closing her bases to Palestine-bound planes. The same pressures had been put on the once cordial Greece; the three Ansons bought in England, which had landed in Rhodes, still were under detention. Only the French island of Corsica still was hospitable, but it wasn't enough. The nine C-46s were sprawled across the world from Panama to Africa. The Constellations, which could have made the long flight non-stop, were tied up thousands of miles away in Panama, New Jersey and California.

The men in the Red House looked at their maps, worked their slide rules and calculated the distances. The answer always came up the same. The Mediterranean, silvery smooth outside their window, might yet defeat them.

Two of the C-46s laid up at Natal still needed work. It was decided to send the other three on ahead to Dakar. They left on May

13 in the evening, planning to fly by night and navigate by the stars. Auerbach, in RX 130, the lead plane, noticed that his propellers were out of synchronization, they did not hold a constant speed. The right engine feathered and there was no fuel pressure. After an hour "sweating it out," he decided the 2,600-mile night flight over water would be too dangerous and turned back. "130 abort," reads the diary of one of his crew, "return Natal, heartbreak and scared."

Auerbach's plane joined the two that had remained behind at a Brazilian Air Force base; they had five days of work still ahead of them.

The other two planes, piloted by Kurtz—his marmoset perched on his shoulder—and Raab, flew on toward Dakar.

Ben Gurion sat in the Red House and watched the sea through binoculars. A ship had appeared off Tel Aviv, undoubtedly Arazi's arms ship, although it had sailed from Marseilles as the *Santa Ciara* and now bore the name, papers and colors of the *Borea*. Aboard it, beneath 450 tons of onions, potatoes, and canned tomato juice, Arazi had shipped five 65-mm. cannon, French mountain guns, meant to be packed on mules, easy to dismantle and move around, an important advantage when an army had only five pieces of heavy artillery. He had also sent 211 French Chatellerault machine guns with 3 million rounds of ammunition.

A note sent ahead by courier told Ben Gurion, "Be sure I am doing everything in my power to hasten shipments, but there are many problems and every day we find new ones. Just now Shaul Avigor tells me he has no more money . . ."

As the *Borea* dropped anchor off Tel Aviv, two British destroyers hailed her, boarded her and examined her papers. New forged documents and a new coat of paint passed their inspection; it was not the ship they had been alerted to intercept. But they did not leave.

In the Red House there was talk of blowing up the *Borea* in the hope she would drift onto the beach, where her cargo could be retrieved. It had been an anxious day and the men in the Red House were ready for desperate measures. Transjordanian Arab Legion armored cars had broken through the defenses of Kfar Etzion, the principal settlement in the Etzion bloc. The road to Jewish Jerusalem was closed again. Jaffa, sister city to Tel Aviv, had surrendered that afternoon, but the Arabs said it was a strategic withdrawal, soon to be regained and who could deny it? Certainly not the representatives of an anonymous "third party" who had asked the Greek government on this day if Greece would prepare itself to give refuge to "thousands" of Palestinian Jews who soon would have to flee the country in the face of an Arab victory.

The men in the Red House decided to wait before doing anything to the *Borea*. They waited and watched all through the night.

Two C-46s reached Dakar in the early morning of May 14, eleven and a half hours after they had left Natal. Second fireman Kurtz sent his wife a picture postcard of a woman with one bare breast. "It was a swell trip. I was the navigator and co-pilot and we made it fine. Our next stop is Casablanca." The other three planes still waited in Natal.

Independence Day dawned sullenly in Palestine. The watchers in the Red House saw the *Borea* move north, under escort of the British destroyers, and they regretted not having scuttled her during the night. The first radio message crackled in from the Etzion bloc: Kfar Etzion had fallen; all but four of its defenders had been massacred, fifteen of them mowed down by a submachine gun after an Arab Legion officer ordered them to line up for a photograph. (One of the four survivors was a girl, rescued by a Legion officer who fought his way into a mob of Arab men to save her.) Now the other three settlements in the Etzion bloc were negotiating to surrender but insisting that representatives of the International Red Cross be present.

It was the first battle the Jews had fought against a modern mechanized army and they had lost.

British headquarters in Jerusalem had closed down and its personnel, under heavy guard, were moving toward the Royal Navy ships awaiting them in Haifa. Egyptian troops had crossed the southern border into the Negev, the desert that, under the UN partition plan, was to comprise two-thirds of the Jewish state. Cairo radio said they would be in Tel Aviv within forty-eight hours.

At 4 P.M. on May 14 the provisional government proclaimed a Jewish state to be named Israel. Homeless no more, at least for the moment, Jews demonstrated in the streets of Tel Aviv. Others, unaware of the new state's fragility, celebrated in cities around the world.

Ray Kurtz and Larry Raab heard the news when they flew into Casablanca. The airport guards, the mechanics, the hotel porter, the shoeshine boys, all mentioned it. Most of them were Arabs and Raab wondered what they were really thinking.

At eleven minutes after midnight, Tel Aviv time—it was 6 P.M. in Washington—President Truman announced that the United States had granted de facto recognition to Israel, the first nation to do so. Truman would write in his memoirs, "I was told that to some of the career men of the State Department this announcement came as a surprise. It should not have been if these men had faithfully supported my policy."

One of the early visitors to the Red House on May 15, Israel's first full day of independence, was Teddy Kollek, on a quick trip from New York to discuss activities in the United States with Ben Gurion. Absent from their meeting was Yaacov Dori—Jacob Dostrovsky when he had been one of Kollek's predecessors in the Hotel Fourteen—who had been taken to the hospital the day before with another attack of ulcers. Now he was chief of staff of the Israel Defense Forces, a pretentious title for a scattered collection of half-armed bands that had been defeated at Kfar Etzion in their first pitched battle against a real army.

Ben Gurion's morning began with good news. The *Borea* had been freed after midnight, suddenly, with no explanation, by the British destroyers that had taken her under guard to Haifa harbor. Arazi's artillery pieces and machine guns could be unloaded and sent into battle. They were needed everywhere. In the north the Syrians were at the gates of the Degania settlements. In the east, the Transjordanian Arab Legion had closed the road to Jerusalem. In the south the Egyptians were lancing northward, the second real army to go into battle against the new state with airplanes, tanks, artillery—and supply lines that went back to well-stocked arsenals.

The Tel Aviv sirens sounded. Two Egyptian Spitfires swooped in from the Mediterranean at 1,000 feet and headed for Tel Aviv airfield. One Spitfire stayed as high cover while the other one bombed and strafed three small Israeli reconnaissance airplanes parked on the ground.

The lesson was clear to the men in the Red House—the Egyptians controlled the skies above Israel. Without fighter aircraft or sufficient antiaircraft guns, there was nothing they could do to protect themselves from Egyptian raids. The bombing of the reconnaissance planes left their army blind.

The lower Spitfire was making another pass over the airfield when a chance shot by a machine-gunner on the roof of a power station hit his engine. The Egyptian made a wheels-up landing on the beach and was taken prisoner. A small victory.

"We cannot," Dori said, "exist on small victories and large defeats."*

Ben Gurion sent for Eliahu Sacharov, the young Haganah agent who had supervised the packing and shipping of the guns from Magenta in Italy. Sacharov had just returned from the United States, where he had been working with Teddy Kollek at the Hotel Fourteen. He had asked to be assigned to duty in Israel during these first crucial days of independence but Ben Gurion informed him that, instead, he was to leave immediately for Czechoslovakia. Some way must be found to get the Czech fighter planes to Israel.

---

* Asked years later by Moshe Pearlman for his thoughts on Independence Day, Ben Gurion replied that while proclaiming independence, he had thought, "Now at last we are responsible for our own destiny. It is ours to shape." He continued: "When, some hours later, I went to inspect the damage done by the Egyptian bombing which marked the opening of the Arab war on the new state, I remember thinking that if we were now responsible for our destiny, the rational question might well be whether in a few days or a few weeks we would have a destiny to shape. For we had no planes to match their planes, no artillery, no tanks."

XLII

ZATEC

Newspapers in Cairo and London were carrying vague and mysterious stories about armadas of ships and fleets of airplanes that were being rushed to Israel to save the state from being stillborn.

In Casablanca, Raab and Kurtz—wearily wondering if their planes would get off the ground once more; worrying about what had happened to the planes they had left behind in Burbank, in Millville, in Panama, in Natal; running out of money and with no place to go but an obscure base in Catania, Sicily—climbed aboard the two battered C-46s of the worldwide Israeli Air Force and took off.

It was May 16.

With all the calm of normally law-abiding citizens trying to sneak two large airplanes through Italian customs in fading daylight, Hyman Sheckman and Danny Agronsky waited in the control tower at Catania, their eyes fixed on the two approaching dots in the sky, their ears expecting an angry expostulation from the airport manager. He had been watching them suspiciously since they had mounted to the control tower. Only a few days before they had been his most welcome guests, bowed in with a sweeping gesture that could only mean his control tower was their control tower. Now he stared at them menacingly while Agronsky picked up the microphone and began talking in the two C-46s. Sheckman watched and wondered "what kind of fish the manager smelled." They had urged him not to communicate with Rome lest their business arrangements be entangled in the Italian bureaucracy. The manager had nodded; he was nodding now—and muttering what were obviously imprecations.

The two C-46s came in and taxied up to the tower. The crews climbed out and looked around. They saw the twisted steel frames of hangars that had been bombed in World War II, some Quonset huts and two men running toward them—Sheckman and Agronsky.

In the hotel that evening Agronsky broke the news—they would have to move on immediately. The Catania airport manager had been in touch with Rome and had learned that American authorities were saying LAPSA was something less—or more—than a Panamanian airline. He was suspicious and might detain the planes.

Raab and Kurtz would fly to Israel in the morning.

Sheckman announced he was going along. He had gone to the United States to navigate operation Yakum Purkan and he was going to bring it home, however fragmented.

At dusk on May 17 Larry Raab turned in his seat, caught Sheckman's eye and pointed at the dark strip on the horizon ahead. Sheckman nodded; it was the coast of Israel. They were flying without position lights, without wireless communication. They were ten hours out of Catania. They saw the blur of light that Sheckman said was Tel Aviv. He slipped into the co-pilot's seat as "we made a perfect hit on the coast. We had instructions to land at Ekron, but I wasn't sure who was holding Ekron. We knew the Jordanians had Lydda. So we came in at Tel Aviv airfield." As the plane came down to 1,000 feet, antiaircraft guns opened fire, the tracers falling just short of the plane as it turned sharply and flew away.

The guns were Arazi's 20-mm. Hispano Suizas which had been hurriedly brought south to guard the airport from the Egyptian Spitfires.

Obviously the C-46s were not expected at Tel Aviv; they now flew over Lydda, where the Jordanians signaled them in a "fantastic code," which Sheckman decided was designed to confuse them into landing. Heading now to Ekron, they made radio contact with the field; the lights went on, but the signals did not conform to the pre-arranged code. Raab circled while Sheckman wondered what had become of SHORTCAKE, TOPPER and MERRY-GO-ROUND. Gingerly landing at the edge of the strip, Raab kept the engines running. "We weren't really sure where we were," he recalls. Sheckman, sitting anxiously next to Raab, said, "Be ready to hit the power if this is the wrong place." They could see the dark figures of trucks and men moving toward them, silhouetted by the landing lights. One of the crewmen handed Sheckman a .45 and said, "You go to the door and talk to them in Hebrew and see what answer you get." Cautiously Sheckman opened the door and peered out. The first man he saw was Aharon Remez, sender and recipient of so many urgent cables, the new commander of the new Israeli Air Force. "Norman" and "Roni" shook hands.

Raab was so tired. "I just sat there in the cockpit for forty-five minutes, exhausted, beat." Men were swarming all over the planes, unloading the BT-13 trainer they had brought. It was, at the moment, the closest thing to a fighter plane in all the country.

Someone tapped him on the shoulder. It was Sheckman, apologetic. "The planes can't stay here. The Gyppos have been bombing; there is nothing to protect the planes when the Gyppos come back in the morning." For the moment, not even Israel offered a home. The C-46 that Arnold Ilowite had flown in two weeks before already had been damaged in an air attack. To protect it—the only big airplane in the country—it had been hidden and temporarily retired from flying supply missions.

The crews got a few hours' sleep and before dawn took off again for Catania, wondering what they would find back there.

"You are either smugglers or thieves or you are up to something else," the angry airport manager greeted them, his worst suspicions confirmed by their sudden unheralded return. The Catania police put them under arrest but, being Italian, they made it a house arrest, the "house" being a hotel, the beach or wherever the boys wanted to go. Agronsky, informed of their predicament by telephone, promised to hurry down from Rome.

In Rome that morning one of the Norsemen had burst into flames and crashed on takeoff, killing two of the most celebrated recruits to the Jewish cause: Buzz Buerling, the Canadian World War II ace who had been so anxious to get into action, and Leonard Cohen, an ex-RAF pilot who had gotten the nickname of the "King of Lampedusa" when he was forced down near the tiny island off Sicily in 1943 and, crawling ashore, soaking wet, persuaded the 132 Germans there to surrender to him—the advance man, he assured them, of a large Allied landing.

Two other Norsemen had gotten off and were en route to Israel.

Both reached the coast, but were unable to spot the lights that marked the landing field. One, flown by Vic Weinberg, a Dutchman, and Al Trop, from Cleveland, went down on the shoreline in Arab territory; both men were taken prisoner by the Egyptians. The other Norseman, hit by an antiaircraft shell over Gaza, came down five miles inland on a farm captured by the Egyptians. The pilot, Bob Fine, who had been selling children's dresses in New York before he joined Service Airways, and his English radio operator, Hugh Curtis, were captured within five hours; the co-pilot, Bill Malpine, an Italian-American from Providence, Rhode Island, hid for two days and nights in an orange grove while Egyptian officers with loudspeakers urged him to surrender and their troops raked the grove with machine-gun fire. Weak from thirst and hunger, Malpine finally was captured by Arab irregulars, who beat him savagely with their rifle butts before turning him over to the Egyptians for imprisonment, with the others, in Cairo for the duration of the war. The four men would be freed in a prisoner exchange in March 1949.

The death of Canadian ace Buzz Buerling got considerable attention in the world press. And on the same day, May 20, the New York *Times* reported that the Israeli Air Force had "gone into action for the first time." Some Piper Cubs with machine guns held at their open doors had strafed enemy troops in Galilee—hardly an action to merit notice in any other air force or one likely to make much of a change in the course of the war.

Yet May 20 was a turning point. Something else of importance was happening, unnoticed and unrecorded by the press—the first of the Me-109 fighters had reached Israel.

Eliahu Sacharov had consulted with Dr. Felix and other members of the Israeli mission in Czechoslovakia as soon as he arrived with Ben Gurion's urgent mandate to—somehow—get the Me-109s to Israel as quickly as possible.

The planes had been reconditioned by the Czechs and were ready to go, but it was impossible, everyone agreed, to fly them there under their own power without refueling stops. The "only alternative," Sacharov would report later, was to airlift them, one by one, inside larger aircraft. An extraordinary undertaking, but Felix and Sacharov were accustomed by then to extraordinary undertakings and desperate enough to try anything. There were technical problems which "appeared insurmountable" even to them. The planes would have to be partially dismantled for the flight and reassembled in Israel, work requiring "the very highest degree of exactitude and responsibility," and for which there were in Israel at the time no qualified technicians.

"We explained the problem to the Czechs," recalls Sacharov, "almost without hope that they would agree to send . . . their experts to Israel during the very darkest days of our struggle. But to our surprise we received, within a few hours, their positive reply to our request."

The Czechs agreed to the airlift, agreed to send technicians and put at their disposal a military field about four hours from Prague, near the town of Zatec. It was, Sacharov would report later, "closed to the public and guarded against enemy agents. The Czech government was interested no less than we were in keeping our activities quiet and guarding the flight of the aircraft from the eyes of strangers."

The chartered American C-54 that had airlifted the load of Czech guns on March 31 in time to open the road to Jerusalem was willing to take on another lucrative assignment. It flew in from Paris to Zatec, and the jigsaw job of fitting an entire Me-109 into its innards began. "There were," recalls Sacharov, "of course, no problems in fitting in the propeller and the dismantled wings."

Next the fuselage was lifted with a block and tackle until it hung parallel to the plane's large doors. Gently the Czech mechanics tried to guide the swaying fuselage into the C-54 without damaging its shell. They tried it nose first, from various angles; nothing worked. There was always a bulge that would not fit.

Stubbornly they shifted the position of the block and tackle, the height of the airframe. For nerve-racking hours they maneuvered, shoved, jiggled the swinging fuselage—like pinball players trying unsuccessfully to sink an enormous marble into the winning hole. Toward dusk, "in a mysterious manner without anyone realizing quite how," Sacharov recalls, the fuselage suddenly slipped into the belly of the C-54 and a shout of triumph went up from Israelis, Czechs and the American crew. To make sure the plane could go into action as quickly as possible, they packed in some bombs, guns and ammunition and the C-54 took off.*

Sacharov hurried to meet with the team of Czech technicians who would follow the plane to put the dismembered fighter back

---

* The successful loading of the Me-109 was less mysterious than Sacharov realized—or reported. Gerald Rowland of the C-54 crew kept estimating the weight and balance of the C-54, vital if the big plane was to be flyable, while Seymour Lerner supervised the rigging. Rowland finally suggested that they insert the Me-109 fuselage backward so that its tail would be "nearly in the crew compartment" of the C-54. Lerner looked at his calculations: "If what you have here balances, you've found the solution." Rowland concluded that "maybe a thousand pounds of hardware in the forward baggage compartment would put it in the green."

together. His high spirits sagged as they explained that there was no point in their going to Israel until at least three Me-109s had reached the country; it took that many to "rationalize" their work.

The C-54 required twenty-four hours for a round trip with time out for refueling and maintenance. Its one crew also had to sleep. That meant it would take days, perhaps a week, to get three planes to Israel and days more to get them ready to fly. Each trip would be more hazardous with Egyptian planes patrolling the sky. Spare parts, bombs, armaments and ammunition also would have to be flown over. And the remaining seven planes. Such a continuous airlift was clearly beyond the capacity of one cargo plane.

Sacharov telephoned Teddy Kollek at the Hotel Fourteen. Would it be possible, he asked, to divert the C-46s to Czechoslovakia to help transport the Me-109s? Kollek, who had just returned to New York from Israel, promised to see what he could do. Sacharov then got in touch with Tel Aviv. There was no point, he argued, in basing the C-46s in Israel until there was "a sufficient number of fighter aircraft in the country to give them protection. On the other hand, there was supreme importance in the establishment of a regular airlift to Israel and the dispatch of the Messerschmitts." Tel Aviv, which had just put one C-46 into hiding and sent two more back to Catania to protect them from Egyptian planes, agreed.

Sacharov hurried out to the field at Zatec to watch the C-54 return from its first flight. "Its crew were dead tired," he recalls, "but when we explained to them how important it was to transport two more Messerschmitts without delay, the American crew agreed to leave on another flight almost without rest."

Back at his hotel in Prague he found a telegram from Teddy Kollek: The C-46s were on their way. "This news was for us," recalls Sacharov, "almost a sign of heavenly intervention."

In Catania Danny Agronsky broke the news to the pilots. Briefly entered in the diary of one crew member for Friday, May 21, it was: "Off again, Italy and Catania not our base. Castigliano and Brindisi NG, no OK, operate from Czecho."

XLIII

BALAK

The C-46 crewmen came into Czechoslovakia groggy, exhausted, like Sunday drivers going home. No one, not even Agronsky, had told them what to expect; no one, not even Dr. Felix, was sure what they would find there. It was a Czech Air Force base, and formerly had been a German fighter strip. There was one long runway, about 5,000 feet long, a control tower and some hangars amid rolling grain fields. The control tower asked them as they touched down to taxi to the far end of the runway, away from the Czech Air Force base, and they rolled a good mile before climbing out at what was obviously the place.

A C-54 was parked just off the runway; a couple of fighter planes on spindly landing gears with the look of long-nosed German schoolmasters had just landed on the grass. The men climbed out, stiff-legged, and met Dr. Felix, who introduced himself in precise English and told them what was going on. They watched the Me-109s being dismantled by Czech workmen and they talked to the Czech Air Force pilots, ex-RAF some of them, who had ferried the planes up from the Avia plant near Prague. The Czechs said, "They're tricky airplanes and we're quite glad to be rid of them," sounding very English and not at all like Communists.

They got into taxicabs with Dr. Felix hovering over them like a bachelor uncle who had never entertained nephews before. They saw the spires of a town not very far away and learned that it was Zatec. Until the war ended, it had been Saaz, a German town, for this was the Sudetenland that had stirred up the Munich crisis and the appeasement that, in another time, in another context, had let another country fall to its enemies.

The Czech sentry at the gate waved them through without a smile, as if he could hear what Dr. Felix in his precise English was saying: They would eat and sleep in a hotel in town where every-thing would be charged to his account. They would, please, operate only from one end of the airfield, the far end, and, please, keep away from the other end. He asked them to stay together, please, and not wander off alone. Even Moonitz had nothing comical to say on the ride through narrow streets into the broad square of the town with shops on three sides and, at one end, the town hall with its dome shaped like an inverted scallion. It reminded them vaguely of the Kremlin and they realized they were behind the Iron Curtain.

The hotel was across the street from the town hall, tucked in a corner of the square. Its name was freshly painted along the façade: Hotel Stalingrad. There was another hotel across the street, the Zlatý Lev, or Golden Lion. It would also house the men who were expected to come—from Panama, from Rome, from Paris, from everywhere. There would be several hundred men here before it was over, includ-ing the LAPSA crews from Panama, some of Schwimmer's mechanics from Burbank and Millville and fresh transport crews recruited all over the world. Fighter pilots would be coming too, for the Czechs had agreed to give them a short course in flying the Me-109 at a Czech Air Force fighter base.

The impossible was about to happen—a complete air base, staffed largely by Americans, was about to operate behind the Iron Curtain just as the United States and Russia were squaring off over Berlin. There would be men of many nationalities taking part—Eng-lishmen, Frenchmen, South Africans, Canadians, Swedes, Norwe-gians, Danes and Israelis—but Americans would predominate and set the tone.

Raab and Kurtz, first in, were first to fly out as soon as they'd had a night's sleep, ferrying one Me-109 between them; a C-46 was not large enough to carry an entire plane. Auerbach and Moonitz arrived May 22 and took off the following morning with another Me-109, its fuselage in one plane, the wings and propeller in another.

There were now four C-46s operating from Zatec of the ten bought from American surplus depots by Schwimmer Aviation of Burbank, insured by Service Airways of New York, registered in the name of LAPSA of Panama and now strung out across the world.

Auerbach had brought along some mail, forwarded to Natal from Panama. Ray Kurtz heard from Ruthie. Brooklyn was a long way off, and Ruthie was riled by his references to the prostitutes in Panama and by the picture of the bare-breasted African girl.

"I finally got your two letters, the ones you wrote me in

Panama," Kurtz replied. ". . . I was overjoyed hearing from you
. . . I wish I could tell you where I am but security disallows it.
Anyway, the last mailing address I gave you in Italy is now canceled
and you can write me care of Rue de Lausanne 153, Geneva, Switzerland. As for my running around, forget it. To begin with, I haven't
seen anyone I'd care to be seen with. And secondly I'm so goddamned
tired I can't even stand up. I never thought I would work this hard
for anyone or anything but here I am doing it. I spent the last thirty
hours out of forty in the air in various parts of Europe." He enclosed
a picture postcard that showed the big central square of Zatec, which
the Czechs called Namesti; the postcard gave its wartime name: Adolf
Hitler Platz.

Auerbach took over as operations chief. Another American, Sam
Pomerantz, an aeronautical engineer, was already at work in Prague
at the Avia factory. He had been recruited by Swifty Schindler early
in the life of Service Airways. A serious older man, he had brought
along his wife, Elsie, when he had been summoned up from Rome
"for a long stay." Next to arrive had been Ernie Stehlik, the ven-
erable former TWA mechanic, in from Paris, where he had been
helping rig the Norsemen. Of Czech descent, he spoke the language, a
great help in working with the Czech mechanics.

At the hotel the LAPSA men met the crew of the chartered C-
54. The two groups, volunteer and mercenary, faced each other with
the wariness of men who are abashed by the others' motives. Only
one of the C-54's crew, Seymour Lerner, was Jewish; on each of its
trips a Shoo-Shoo man, a Canadian, went along as "observer." The
C-54 was a powerful plane, big enough to fly the route to Israel non-
stop while carrying an entire Me-109 in its belly. It wore American
registration and was charging all that the traffic would bear. Yet it had
done the job, a dangerous one, when nothing else was available, and
its owner was prepared to let it continue—the lamplighter in the synagogue on Saturdays.

The C-54 crew, seasoned by two round trips, briefed the newcomers. Whatever your motives, flying was flying.

The Israelis, who treated the Bible like an Esso road map,
already had named the run "Operation Balak" for the son of Zippor,
one of Moses' wives. Zippor in Hebrew means "bird"—the airlift was
to be the "Son of Bird." It was Yakum Purkan in another setting by
another poetically historical name. To the Americans, however, it
became the "Milk Run." Zatec ("Etzion" to the Israelis) became

"Zebra." Israel became "Oklahoma." And Ajaccio, in Corsica, their refueling stop along the way, became "Jockstrap."

On his first trip in, just ahead of Auerbach, Moonitz came over Ekron as a low fog blotted out the airfield. "We made six passes trying to sneak down lower and lower," the first fireman reported later. "Our only alternative was Nicosia, in Cyprus, which meant the plane and its load would be impounded. There was a bright full moon, and I was afraid of being shot down by the Gyppos as soon as dawn came. The Gyppos always came over to strafe at first light." Hyman Sheckman, who had become Hayman Shamir and the second in command of the Israeli Air Force, was on the ground. "We lit smudge pots and we spoke to him. We could see him when he came over the field at about a thousand feet but he couldn't see the field at all. And so we told him to fly out to sea and come down low.

"He flew off and we didn't hear anything. We were maintaining radio silence, of course, so as not to alert the enemy, but after a while it became obvious something had happened." When Auerbach came in half an hour later, the fog had lifted and he "sat down as gently as the dew."

Auerbach was insisting his airplane be refueled so he could go back up and look for Moonitz and his crew, when, he recalls, "we found them—or rather, they found us." Moonitz, on foot, was staggering toward the edge of the runway carrying an injured radio operator, Ed Styrak, on his back and followed by his co-pilot Sheldon Eichel. He had hit a low ridge just west of Ekron; the plane had caught fire in the crash. His navigator, Moe Rosenbaum, who had left engineering school at Cornell to join Service Airways, had gone aft just before the crash. He was killed when the cargo shifted.

Moonitz had bought compasses for everybody in Panama. After the crash he took his out and headed west. It was a two-mile walk, strenuous even for a burly Brooklyn fireman when he is carrying a 200-pound man on his back.

Moonitz went to the hospital for ten days. Auerbach's plane took off again in the morning with a relief crew. Its right engine gave out and it made an emergency landing in Greece, where the Greeks impounded it.

In two days, two of the four C-46s had been lost and half of an Me-109—the half Moonitz had been carrying.

The surviving planes and men carried on.

Ray Kurtz, a captain now, wrote Ruth: "I haven't slept for

nearly three days and I'm thoroughly exhausted. I usually get a few hours' sleep upon arrival there but this time I had to leave as soon as the plane was unloaded . . . We are so short of pilots that I have been using my radioman for co-pilot."

The lobby of the Stalingrad became the ready room. When the crews weren't flying, they slept and when they weren't sleeping, they lounged in the lobby. The first fighter pilots came in, from Rome, including Gideon Lichtman, the boy from Newark in his sky-blue zoot suit. The first South Africans and Englishmen appeared, looking at the Americans the way the Americans had looked at the C-54 crew. The fighter pilots stayed only a few days and went off to a Czech fighter base, Ceské Budejovice, for a short course in flying the Me-109. Their Czech instructors gave them coveralls to wear. The coveralls, left behind by the Germans, still bore swastikas.

Two more C-46s came in. Swifty Schindler, who had been forced to stay on at Natal, arrived, made one trip to Israel, then was summoned back to the United States. Arnie Ilowite brought in the C-46 that had gone to Italy early in March and been the first into Palestine in early May, only to be hidden away to protect it from Arab air raids.

The airlift crews did a little sightseeing. They passed Communist Party headquarters with its bulletin board out front carrying the latest clippings from *Rude Pravo*, the Czech Communist newspaper. They hung around the hotel, complained about the food and studied the girls. Dr. Felix had talked the Czech authorities into giving him ration books for each man. But there was never enough food. Even bread was scarce. When the flight crews coming back late at night would troop into the kitchen of the Stalingrad and ask the girls there for sandwiches, they invariably got them "open faced, a slice of bread and a whisper of meat." They began loading up on meat and vegetables during their stop in Corsica on the way back.

The girls in the Hotel Stalingrad's kitchen, like the hotel's waitresses and chambermaids, were rosy-cheeked country girls who laughed a lot and disappeared when work was done. Soon that changed too. The management added new help: girls who weren't especially rosy-cheeked but wore cosmetics, spoke a surprising amount of English, and asked all kinds of questions, in and out of bed. The Zlaty Lev got a new name: The Sloppy Love.

The men assumed the Czechs, the British and the Americans were spying on their activities. They were especially careful about the Czechs. The country was preparing for an election which the Communist government was determined would legitimize its February coup d'état. Sometimes when a Czech airplane took off from their end of the runway, the Americans couldn't help noting that it was a type of airplane that they all had heard about, but only a few had seen. Auerbach decided the Czechs were developing a twin-jet fighter. "The fact that this was probably a very secret development frightened me," he recalls. "I warned everyone not to get involved because he might very well be hauled in as a spy."*

Most of the time they flew. And when they weren't flying, they dreamed the route in their sleep:

ZEBRA: Up at 5 A.M. Takeoff at 8 A.M. You headed south over Pilsen, where the beer came from, and although you didn't know it, over Ceské Budejovice, where the fighter pilots were being trained. Then into Austria, over Linz. Austria was occupied jointly and nervously by the Allies and the Russians, but it was safer than flying over Germany, where things had become hot over Berlin and fighters patrolled the airlanes.

You flew south until the Adriatic came into sight, like a pane of glass in the morning light. That was Yugoslavia out the pilot's window and Italy on the co-pilot's side. Time to take a heading west and south, even though Israel lay the other way. The C-46 had to refuel and Agronsky, pulling strings again, had arranged with the French in Ajaccio to let the C-46s take on gas there as long as they didn't stay too long and didn't arouse suspicions. So, there you were, crossing the thigh of the Italian boot until you reached the Ligurian Sea; there you could begin letting down for Corsica. You flew around the island's northern tip to Ajaccio.

JOCKSTRAP: Commandant Latour ran the airport at Ajaccio. He was a fat man with a red face and blinking eyes who spoke only French but managed to convey his eager sympathy. He grinned and winked, or seemed to—so hidden were his eyes in the folds of flesh— and wrote all kinds of destinations on the blackboard in his operations room where he posted notices of incoming and outgoing aircraft.

---

* The Americans were being properly cautious as befitted the circumstances. However, the Czech jet fighter was not a secret development, but a German Me-262 fighter, the Stormbird, which had been built in Czechoslovakia (among other places) by the Nazis at the end of the war, too late to have any effect. Of 1,400 produced, only 200 saw action. The Czechs salvaged a few and used them to train pilots, against the day when their new Russian allies would deliver the first Soviet jet fighters.

You took on all the gas the plane would hold, filling the extra tank that had been installed in the fuselage as well as the regular wing tanks. From Jockstrap it was an 1,800-mile hop to Oklahoma. A C-46's normal range, with less of a load, was 1,500 miles; and you took off sure of only one thing—you weren't welcome anyplace else. If you landed in Greece, they would impound the airplane and its cargo. If you landed in any of the Arab countries, they would hang your manhood on a pole and parade it around.

OKLAHOMA: So it was ten hours, minimum, to Ekron, depending upon the winds and the weather and the prevailing temper of Israel's few antiaircraft guns. If the Egyptians had just been over, jumpy Israelis might shoot at any airplane in sight.

But it was when you landed that you realized what it was all about. While you were still taxiing up to the apron, the trucks started pulling up. There were men standing in the trucks, new immigrants who would do the unloading, and the way they stood there, in their gray caps and shabby clothes, with their haggard unshaven faces, reminded you of newsreels and newspaper photos you had seen not very long ago of similar people riding in similar trucks to their deaths in Nazi concentration camps. The look of them came back to you in your hotel room in Tel Aviv that night. And the thought of making the whole trip back again in a couple of hours didn't seem like such a big deal after all.

XLIV

FIGHTER COVER

I t was three in the afternoon when Dr. Felix arrived at the Defense Ministry in Prague in the company of the manager of the Avia factory from whom he had bought the ten Me-109s and optioned another fifteen. The success in airlifting the fighters to Israel had convinced Tel Aviv it should buy the additional fifteen planes. Dr. Felix wanted to exercise his option. The manager of the Avia plant was agreeable, but the chief of staff of the Air Force was raising objections. "We have spent two days with the Air Force and gotten nowhere," the Avia manager warned Dr. Felix as they walked down a long corridor to a conference room where they were asked to wait. Several high officers came in to join them, then the chief of staff, who sat down at one end of a long table. Dr. Felix pointedly took the seat at the other end of the table. He was trying to behave, not like a petitioner, but like the representative of a sovereign state.

The chief of staff explained that the Air Force could not release the additional fifteen Me-109s. Everything suddenly had become very difficult; the Russians had not delivered Czechoslovakia's new jets; there were diplomatic problems.

Felix listened to the catalogue of explanations, then he began talking. He lost his temper, pounded the table and shouted, "You are talking here and my people are dying there."

He had pounded the table so hard that, to his horror, the glasses of water which had been placed in front of each man jumped into the air. Normally mild-mannered, Felix was as astonished as his listeners at the vehemence of his outburst. But he saw that it had caught their attention.

"Could we adjourn for twenty minutes? I want to discuss this with Reicin," he said, speaking quietly now but flourishing the name of the powerful chief of military intelligence with whom he had held so many fruitless dialectical discussions.

The bluff worked. The chief of staff agreed to the sale of the planes.

The Czechs had to be paid immediately. The deal hung on too slender a thread to permit any delay. Yet Tel Aviv's treasury was low, and the bill was a whopping one: on the second batch of Me-109s, the unit price had been doubled. The problem went directly to New York, to the Hotel Fourteen, where Teddy Kollek called upon a few of his friends to ponder it and decide which wealthy sympathizers should be approached.

Joseph Shulman, a textile merchant, knew William Levitt, the builder.

Levitt was a man who thought fast and big; he was making a fortune by applying mass-production methods to the building of houses, erecting out on Long Island the first of his complete communities—Levittown.

Shulman arranged for Kollek to meet Levitt at the latter's office on Northern Boulevard in Manhasset.

Introductions were brief; neither man had any time for formalities.

"We need money," Kollek said. "And I can't tell you what it's for because it's top secret. But if you'll lend us the money, the Provisional Government of the State of Israel will give you a note and pay you back in a year."

Levitt had heard of more promising investments. No collateral; no interest.

"So," Levitt recalls, "I said O.K. and I gave him the million dollars."

More crews arrived in Zatec and the remaining three C-46s came in from Panama, but there were never more than four operating at any one time. They and the chartered C-54 began carrying other cargo as well as the dismantled fighter planes—big wooden crates, five feet long, four feet wide and two feet high. On each crate was stenciled the dainty outline of a wine glass and the English word "glassware," yet they were so heavy it took four men to lift one. They contained steel tubing for Slavin's mortars and a heavy German-designed Beza machine gun, excellent for desert warfare.

If the planes ran into heavy headwinds coming back from Israel, they could, in a pinch, stop at Catania. Danny Agronsky would race down from Rome to bail them out. "Wild-looking guys," he would recall years later, "in tattered clothes with beards this long and their eyes hanging out of their sockets, squinting at you out of a cockpit."

In three weeks the C-46s and the C-54 made twenty-six Balak trips. They carried over a hundred tons of cargo, delivered eleven Me-109s complete with spare parts, and bombs, machine guns and ammunition and brought in the first fighter pilots to fly them.

On the return trips to Zebra they brought back the empty glass crates.

There was a deposit on the crates.

Lou Lenart, the intense Hungarian-born former U.S. Marine, was one of the first fighter pilots into Israel. He had flown in early, bringing one of Mrs. Silverman's Norsemen, gone on to Czechoslovakia for training on the Me-109, then returned as a passenger on the newly established airlift, sitting behind Larry Raab with the fuselage of a dismantled Me-109 jutting into his back.

In Israel he waited impatiently while Czech mechanics assembled the first fighters. The Arab air forces—Egyptian in the south, Syrian and Iraqi in the north—still flew over the country at will, bombing and strafing settlements, airfields and cities. Air raid alerts sounded in Tel Aviv daily. With few antiaircraft guns and no fighters, there was nothing the Israelis could do to stop them. Their own tiny Air Force, consisting of Piper Cubs, Austers and Rapides, was pressed into all kinds of missions for which the planes were never intended: as light bombers (the bombs were rolled out the doors), to parachute supplies (they were dropped overboard), in tactical support of ground forces (with hand-held machine guns aimed out the windows), for reconnaissance (having no radio equipment, pilots would scrawl their observations on a piece of paper, put it in a bottle and drop it to the troops below). Most of the flying had to be done at night to avoid Arab fighters and it was becoming harder and harder to perform the essential job of supplying the isolated settlements and evacuating the wounded.

Lenart watched one day from a slit trench at Ekron air base while Egyptian Spitfires bombed the hangar next to the one housing the Me-109s.

On May 29 the first four planes were ready. "Our plan," Lenart remembers, "was that the very first mission would be a surprise raid on El Arish," a former RAF air base just across the Egyptian border in the south, to which the Egyptians had moved a squadron of Spitfire fighter planes and several bombers; it was their principal base for aerial operations against the new state.

As the four Me-109s were being made ready to take off in the late afternoon, the commander of the Haganah forces in the south, facing the Egyptians on the ground, rushed in to plead for a change of plans.

The Egyptian advance toward Tel Aviv had been stalled by the stubborn defense of the Negev settlements along the way, particularly one called Yad Mordechai. The time gained had been used to evacuate the children of the settlements and to organize their defense. But the Egyptians had regrouped also. That afternoon an Israeli observation post had reported that an Egyptian column consisting of five hundred vehicles, including artillery and tanks—the full rolling stock of an entire brigade—was moving north along the coastal road. It was more than enough to make good the Egyptian boast that they would overrun Tel Aviv, only twenty-five miles away. The column had stopped temporarily at the Ashdod bridge, which had been blown up by Haganah sappers the night before. Egyptian officers had been observed leaving their cars to look over the damage to the bridge; the vehicles were massed along the road, a perfect target and a heaven-sent opportunity to smash the ominous Egyptian advance.

"The decision was made just like that," says Lenart. "Half an hour later we started up the planes inside the hangar, the doors were opened and we made a fast taxi out to the runway going east-west. There was a shout from the guys on the field and we took off. We made one wide low turn. We had to join up very fast so that nobody would see us and we no sooner joined up than we were over Ashdod. We started coming down and right away the whole place erupted."

Heavy antiaircraft fire easily reached the low-flying planes. Lenart could see the plane piloted by Eddy Cohen, a South African volunteer flying his first combat mission, "blow up, just a ball of fire." Two Israeli pilots who had been trained in Czechoslovakia, Modi Alon and Ezer Weizmann, dropped their bombs, then returned to strafe the Egyptians, but their machine guns jammed. Lenart, "holding one hand down for the manual release because I didn't trust the electrical release," dropped his two bombs and tried to strafe, but his machine gun jammed too; his cockpit was peppered with antiaircraft fire and his plane damaged.

Back at Ekron air base they tallied the score of their maiden action: one plane and one pilot lost; another Me-109 damaged in a bumpy landing. Damage to the Egyptians: much less than they had hoped for.

They were bitterly disappointed. But later in the day came a new report. The Egyptians, sobered by the sight of Israeli fighter planes, were digging in at Ashdod, apparently for a prolonged stay. They had not been destroyed. But they would not be in Tel Aviv "in forty-eight hours" either. Some of the 65-mm. mountain guns that Arazi had sent from France were brought up to shell the Egyptian column. That night Haganah began a series of harassing actions on the ground. In the days that followed, the Me-109s returned to make more expert attacks.

The Egyptians had been stopped. They would never get any farther. The danger had passed of a quick victory that would rally the other Arab states with the smell of blood, weaken the will of the Jews to resist, and shake the confidence of Israel's wavering sympathizers in the world.

The Me-109s were being airlifted in at the rate of one or two a day; and as fast as they arrived, they were assembled to fly. Theoretically, they made up a squadron, the first fighter squadron of the Israel Air Force, boldly named the 101st. It was based on a dirt strip bulldozed out of an orange grove near Herzliya, north of Tel Aviv, and was dominated from the beginning by the American volunteers who had fretted through the long wait for airplanes in Rome and now fretted for an opportunity to fly. There were never enough planes. Even under the best of maintenance and flying conditions the Me-109s were fragile and eccentric aircraft. Under the conditions prevailing at Herzliya, they cracked up on takeoffs and landings; their unsynchronized guns shot off their own propellers in the air. Rudy Augarten, a former Harvard student who was the squadron's operations officer, recalls, "We never had more than two in flying condition at any one time."

The men made the most of that one or two.

On June 3, five days after the first raid on the Egyptian Army at Ashdod, Modi Alon, the 101st's young Israeli squadron commander, shot down two Egyptian bombers as they flew in at dusk over Rehovot, about 20 miles south of Tel Aviv. The next day a bombing sortie succeeded in driving off three Egyptian warships which had been approaching the coast.

As in the Navy, the language of the new Israel Air Force would be English, the style American. More than half of all the volunteers would come from the United States—nearly five hundred by the time the war had ended. By July 1949, the official end of the war of independence, sixty-eight airplanes of various types would have arrived in Israel from the United States and seventeen Norsemen from the U.S. occupation zone of Germany. In addition, the largely American-equipped and manned airlift based in Zatec would have ferried in eighty-two airplanes bought in Czechoslovakia, mostly Me-109s and Spitfires; thirteen planes would have arrived from the United Kingdom, eight from South Africa, two from France and two from Egypt—Spitfires which were shot down and salvaged.

A breakdown worked out by Aharon Remez and Hyman Sheckman—"Roni" and "Norman" of Hotel Fourteen days, who had become commander and deputy commander, respectively, of the Air Force—would list one hundred crewmen for the C-46 transport planes, forty-two crewmen for the B-17 bombers, forty fighter pilots, twenty Norseman pilots, thirty AT-6 pilots, seventy crewmen for the various other planes, and a hundred sixty-seven ground crewmen in Czechoslovakia and Israel.

In early June, the fighters had established a presence and that was enough to discourage the Egyptian Air Force, whose zest for combat was slight. Egyptian air raids on Tel Aviv ceased; Arab planes stayed close to the borders. Observes the Israeli military historian Lieutenant Colonel Netanel Lorch: "The material superiority of the Arab air forces continued to exist for a considerable time; however, their morale had obviously been irretrievably lost."

Once the air was theirs, the Me-109s began flying missions in support of the Army, strafing and bombing enemy bases, troops and transport. Under their protective cover the supply aircraft of the IAF could operate freely once more.

The Mediterranean had been spanned; a makeshift air bridge had been flung across the hostile sea, not precisely as anyone had planned, later than they had expected, but in time to make the difference. At the last moment, by an improvisation, the planes and weapons that the new state needed to survive were being delivered by a slender link of cranky, overloaded, undermaintained airplanes salvaged from America's scrap heaps.

As airlifts went, it wasn't much, nothing to compare with the airlift the United States had flown over the Hump during World War II or the airlift the United States with its Western allies would mount later in that summer of 1948 over the Russian zone of Germany to Berlin.

Yet, on its own small scale, short of everything but ingenuity, it did the job. It closed the gap. Without it, for all the indomitable spirit of its fighting men and women, the new state would not have survived. It brought in the first sizable infusion of weapons with which to meet their enemies. And the fighter planes ferried in, a half at a time, threw a threadbare cover over the cities and countryside so that factories could operate, traffic could move, armies could fight, airports could receive more planes and seaports were safe for the supply ships which would arrive.

XLV

TEN PLAGUES

I t was a strange war, interrupted by two United Nations truces, which were intermittently enforced and broken by both sides. A grim version of the children's game of Going to Jerusalem, with the UN attempting to call the starts and stops. Between truces all of the belligerents—the new state of Israel and the Arab armies that had invaded—scrambled for as much territory as they could get. The UN partition plan had delineated boundaries, but no one accepted them as final. Transjordan hoped to annex the portion of Palestine that had been designated as an independent Arab state—or more. Syria maneuvered for a bite of the north and Egypt for a bite of the south, while Israel strove to establish boundaries more secure than the convoluted pattern provided by partition. Even the UN mediator, the Swedish Count Folke Bernadotte, would twice propose drastic revisions of the partition boundaries, both of which would have taken away from the new Jewish state the southern Negev desert that had been allotted it by partition but which Egypt had invaded in the opening days of the war.

It was clear that the final boundaries would be those that were carved out on the battlefield. For the American underground and the airlift crews of Balak, operating out of Zatec, it was, as it had been for months, a desperate race against time. A race to get sufficient weapons to the Israeli armed forces while the game still was on, before a final halt in the fighting was called.

In the United States the men of the Sonneborn Institute charted the course of events at their weekly Thursday luncheons and funneled more than a million dollars' worth of non-contraband equipment a month through Materials for Palestine.

Elie Schalit's "black" operation served as the conduit for an astonishing variety of other goods, culled by individuals and the "special companies" from all parts of North and Central America: aircraft propellers from Buffalo; Colt aircraft machine guns from Montreal; an entire production line for making bazookas, developed by the Eastern Development Company; radar equipment from Danny Fliderblum's Radio Communications Engineering Company; 30,000 pounds of sheet steel sent by Phil Alper's Inland Machinery Company for Slavin's armaments plants; Norden bomb sights from Montreal; aircraft engines from Texas; spare parts for the Connies and C-46s; chemicals for manufacturing explosives; an invaluable bonanza of two shiploads of American Army surplus trucks, jeeps and half-tracks from Panama.

Al Schwimmer made a trip to Mexico to deliver $260,000 in cash to his government friends for the long-postponed purchase of Mexican arms. Despite exposés in the Mexico City newspapers and representations by the country's influential Syrian community, the Mexicans went through with the deal, delivering the arms to the port of Tampico on a railroad train guarded by Mexican Army troops.

Hank Greenspun was on hand to see them loaded aboard the *Kefalos,* a small ship of Panamanian registry that Schalit had bought and had refitted at the Todd shipyards in Brooklyn. It was a smaller haul than Greenspun had expected: 36 75-mm. French howitzers; 17,000 shells; 2,000 aerial bombs; 500 machine guns and submachine guns—including those that Greenspun had obtained in Hawaii and brought to Mexico on the yacht *Idalia*—and 7 million rounds of ammunition.

There was still room in the *Kefalos'* hold. At the last moment the Mexicans put aboard aviation gasoline, in drums rushed down from California by Schalit. Fourteen hundred tons of sugar were loaded on top to hide the other cargo, in case the British Navy should intercept the *Kefalos* off Gibraltar.

On board as first mate when the ship, after numerous delays, steamed out, headed for Israel, was Bob Keller, Phil Alper's former assistant at Inland Machinery, who had been on Pier F in Jersey City on the fateful January day when the TNT fell.

Keller was not the only young American headed for where the action was. Hal Gershenow, the MIT-trained naval architect and former U.S. naval officer, who had startled Rabinovich in the early days of the Hotel Fourteen by suggesting a navy for the future Jewish state, went over to work with several other Americans, improvising a rudimentary fleet from the battered hulks of illegal immigrant ships that had been captured by the British and now had been reclaimed by the Jews.

Land and Labor, which had sent over several hundred men to serve with the Israeli armed forces, was discreetly notified to look out for "specialists," in particular, fighter pilots, navigators, bombardiers, gunners, mechanics and other experienced air force men. Rudy Augarten, a former fighter pilot, left for Zatec as soon as his Harvard classes ended in June. Danny Cravitt, another former fighter pilot, agreed to spend his summer vacation from the University of Miami law school in Israel. Also recruited in Miami was former Navy pilot Ted Gibson, the son of a Baptist minister, who had grown up in an atmosphere of revivals and camp meetings with the Bible and the Holy Land as subjects of daily family conversation. And Wayne Peake, one of five children of "a poor North Carolina dirt farmer," who had joined the Air Force when he was eighteen, got in touch with Land and Labor at the suggestion of a Jewish friend whose service station in Chicago served as Peake's "permanent mailing address" as he moved restlessly from job to job after the war. Former pilot Sam Katz's mother said she hoped he'd "find a nice Jewish girl" when he decided to leave his father's grocery store in Mishawaka, Indiana, to go to Israel. In Canada John McElroy, a former RCAF flying ace who had been recruited by Buzz Buerling, persuaded sixteen fellow pilots to follow him over to Israel.

In all, some five hundred airmen—a mixed bag of idealists and mercenaries, Zionists and adventurers, Jews and non-Jews—would go over from the United States and Canada to help create the new Israel Air Force.

In Israel, Slavin's arms factories, still supplied by Alper, were hitting full production, turning out ammunition, aerial bombs, explosives and a thousand mortar shells a day. Ironically, the light machine gun that had been the inspiration and initial project of the American underground, never went into mass production.

Carl Ekdahl, the Swedish-American gunsmith who designed it, had gone to Israel when "Hai-yum" sent for him. He and Max Brown, the Canadian machinist who had been arrested at Niagara Falls, spent three months working on prototypes. But the ordnance department of the new Israeli Army rejected the gun. Slavin had chosen it to defend settlements; the Army depended upon mobility and wanted something even lighter and simpler. Supplied for the moment with Czech arms, it no longer had to be content with anything that would shoot; it preferred to wait for a superior weapon. Eventually the machines that Slavin and Alper had chosen from their scrapbooks, bought at WAA sales, packed at the Bronx warehouse and shipped in Schalit's crates of "used industrial machinery" would

make the Uzi, an Israeli-designed submachine gun which became the
standard infantry weapon of the Israel Defense Forces, so effective it
was bought by other armies—the Dutch, Iranian and West German—
as well.

In Zatec, Ray Kurtz, Norman Moonitz, Larry Raab, Trygve
Maseng, Hal Auerbach and other Balak pilots continued their exhausting round of flying armaments to Israel, stocking up on fresh
food in Corsica on their return trip, grabbing a few hours of restless
sleep at the Zlatý Lev and taking off again with another load.

On Friday, July 9, Constellation RX 121, the first of Schwimmer's Connies to have been put into service and the only one to get
out of the United States, flew into Zatec from Panama.

The timing was propitious. The first UN truce of four weeks
had ended that morning at 6 A.M. The fight was on again and Israel
had launched a major offensive, to be known as the Ten Days.

Sam Lewis, the veteran Connie pilot whom Schwimmer had
recruited so many months before in Los Angeles, had flown the
Connie from Panama, across the South Atlantic, via Brazil and Africa.
It took off again from Zatec almost immediately, with a load of
machine guns in its belly. Like the chartered C-54, the huge triple-
tailed Connie could carry ten tons of cargo and make the run from
Zebra to Oklahoma non-stop. With its added heft, the airlift was
boosted to a peak capacity. During the following week, while the
Ten Days offensive moved into just about all of the territory allotted
to Israel by partition except the Negev, Balak carried fifty tons of
armaments and supplies into the country, the record in its history.

As the RX 121 returned to Zatec from its seventh trip, the
Connie's hydraulic system gave out. Pilot Sam Lewis, unable to lock
its landing gear in place, circled until his gas ran low, then slid the big
airplane in for a landing on its belly, one wheel locked into place, the
other flapping wildly. The impact thrust a spar up through the wing
as if the aircraft had been stabbed from below. It lay there like a
crippled animal on the grass when Ernie Stehlik came out to see his
pet.

Without spare parts or proper lifting equipment, Stehlik set to
work to repair the RX 121. In the language he had learned from his
parents, Stehlik urged the Czech mechanics to scrounge steel, plywood and aluminum so he could fashion new parts by hand. He dug a
tunnel "from the back end of the airplane to under the wing, deep
enough so that I could set up a couple of jacks and get under the

plane. I just made up my mind I would get the damn thing going, regardless."

Meanwhile, there had been another important arrival at Zatec: three Flying Fortresses, big American B-17 bombers which Schwimmer had bought in the United States. They had flown out of Miami on a "survey" flight, led by Charles Winters, the Florida entrepreneur who had sold Schwimmer two of them (the third was bought in Tulsa).

The planes had American registrations and, although the Miami airport, where they had been checked out by crews recruited by Winters and Schwimmer, buzzed with rumors that the bombers were headed for Palestine, no one had stopped them. They flew to Puerto Rico and, after a twenty-four-hour stop, were cleared for a flight to Santa Maria in the Azores. In Santa Maria, Winters opened a sealed envelope that Schwimmer had given him to learn their final destination. Twelve hours later planes and crews landed at Zatec, as astonished, in Winter's words, to find "an American base behind the Iron Curtain" as the airlift crews were to see them.

Ray Kurtz, the second fireman from Brooklyn, wrote his wife Ruthie, "You'll never guess what showed up here—the same type airplane as the one I flew during the war, the Flatbush Floogie. I'm the one who has the most experience with them and I'm checking them out." Later he wrote, "We have been working like dogs to meet a deadline and met it tonight. The past few days I've practically passed out in my clothes . . . I guess the boys at Brighton Beach know what I'm doing here or don't they?"

On the morning of July 14 Kurtz led a flight of the three B-17s out of Zatec, heading down the Adriatic. Their destination was Israel, but it seemed a shame to waste the flight. Before leaving, Kurtz had sent two of his crew members into Prague to visit the United States Information Service Library; they spent an afternoon studying atlases and looking at a guidebook illustration of Abdin Palace, the 550-room home of King Farouk in Cairo.

Over Crete the planes separated. Two of the B-17s, captained by Bill Katz of Jacksonville, Florida, and Norman Moonitz, the first fireman from Brooklyn, flew east to hit Egyptian bases in Sinai before flying on to Israel. Kurtz took a more circuitous route. At dusk he came over Cairo, flying low, looking for Abdin Palace. It was late and getting dark; the B-17 had no oxygen equipment and a makeshift bombsight. Kurtz was able to drop only a few fifty-kilogram bombs and he missed the palace. It was no more than a token raid, but coming on the sixth day of the Ten Days offensive, it drove a point home to the Egyptians nonetheless.

All three planes arrived safely in Israel. Two of them took off the same night to bomb the Egyptian air base of El Arish. In the few days that remained of the Ten Days offensive, the Flying Fortresses boosted fivefold the weight of bombs dropped by the fledgling Israel Air Force. A military observer would recall later that the "situation changed completely"; the Arab air forces almost ceased activity and "anyone arriving in Israel then would have found it difficult to believe that only one month previously the Arab air forces had been in complete control of the sky."

As Kurtz was preparing his B-17s for their flight to Israel, one more Flying Fortress, piloted by Swifty Schindler, the erstwhile president of Service Airways, flew into Santa Maria in the Azores in an attempt to join them.

Al Schwimmer had decided upon a last desperate effort to get some more planes out of the United States, including the two Constellations still sitting at Millville, and four A-20 attack bombers that he had bought in Florida.

It was an audacious plan, bordering on the foolhardy, but Schwimmer had reasoned it was "now or never" if the planes were to get to Israel in time to help in the decisive fighting just ahead.

Anyway, time was running out for his operation in the United States. From the beginning he had suspected that some of his employees in Burbank were FBI informants. He was pretty sure his planes had been traced to the airlift in Czechoslovakia. The existence of the airlift had been reported by the BBC in London as early as May 29, its first week of regular operation. The American Embassy in Prague had almost certainly identified the registration numbers of the planes; Americans at Zatec had seen men watching them with binoculars from outside the field. Schwimmer had always predicted that "eventually the Federal machinery will catch up with us." The moment seemed near, but perhaps one last time he would manage to be "a step ahead of them."

A mass flight was set for Sunday, July 11, but when pilots appeared to pick up the four A-20 attack bombers in Fort Lauderdale, Florida, they found the planes under such strict surveillance it was impossible to take off. At Millville too authorities had been tipped off that the fuel tanks of the Connies had been filled for a "check flight"; customs agents had seized the airplanes on suspicion. Only the B-17 managed to take off on schedule from Tulsa.

Schwimmer and Leo Gardner flew it to a previously arranged rendezvous at the small suburban Westchester County airport in Purchase, New York. It was a sunny day and the airport thronged with weekend fliers who gawked at the unmarked World War II Flying Fortress which dwarfed the tiny sports planes dotting the field.

Swifty Schindler had been persuaded by Teddy Kollek to take the plane on to Zatec, but he insisted on making a test flight before attempting the long transatlantic hop. He had never flown a B-17 before. By the time he came down, reporters—tipped off to "unusual activity" at the field—had joined the crowd. Finally, against his "better judgment," Schindler took off with a crew of eight, trailed by an airplane owned by the New York *Herald Tribune*.

Mechanical trouble forced Schindler down at Halifax, where Canadian authorities ordered him to return to the United States. Instead, he dodged a U.S. Coast Guard escort plane and flew to the Azores. His odyssey ended there. He and his men were brought back to New York under arrest. The B-17 was seized. The underground found itself, once again, in the headlines.

There was nothing left for Schwimmer to do but flee.

He and his cigar-smoking sidekick, Steve Schwartz, took a commercial plane out to Rome, where they stopped off to see Arazi, who was negotiating with the Italians for surplus Sherman tanks. They went on to Zatec, where Schwimmer urged Stehlik to "get the RX 121 back home if for no other reason than that they can't throw it in my face that I turned it over to the Reds." Then they flew, on the airlift which they had been so instrumental in creating, to Israel. Schwimmer became director of maintenance and engineering of the Air Force; Schwartz was put in charge of personnel for th˜ new Air Transport Command. For neither man was it much of a change. Schwimmer worked with many of the same men he had sent over from the United States. The Air Transport Command, Schwartz quickly realized, was simply Service Airways under another name.

On July 19 the Ten Days of fighting was superseded by another uneasy UN truce. Neither side expected it to last. The Israeli Army continued to mobilize, train and arm more men, including hundreds of raw refugees, transported directly from their arriving ships to training camps. The underground continued its battle against embargoes, its fight for funds, its race with time, to maintain the crescendo of shipments into the new state.

After the Westchester debacle, no more airplanes were flown out of the United States. But in the coming months the underground's young shipping expert Elie Schalit would slip out more than fifty planes by sea. Among them: twenty Piper Cubs for reconnaissance; seventeen North American AT-6 training planes, which once they reached Israel were called upon to perform many other services, from bombing to dropping supplies; and five of the long-coveted P-51 fighters, bought as scrap and shipped, broken down and crated, in the guise of International harvesters.

With Zatec available as a staging area and refueling stop, other airplanes bought in Europe headed for Israel to join the burgeoning Air Force. The remaining Norsemen, Mrs. Silverman's contribution to the war of independence, came in and, when the Yugoslavs in one of their sudden changes of heart granted an additional fueling stop, moved on to Israel. They became a cargo squadron, used also for occasional bombing missions. Three Beaufighters, twin-engined British fighter-bombers, smuggled out of England by a group of mercenary pilots, showed up at Zatec and then went on to Israel. They had been bought from RAF surplus through a friendly Englishman who explained to the Air Ministry that they would be used in making a film.

On August 12 the Czechs ordered Balak to cease operations, as suddenly and as inexplicably as they had let it begin three months previously. The airlift had flown ninety-five trips; it had transferred twenty-five Me-109s as well as spare parts, armament and many of the fighter pilots who would fly them. Some 350 tons of arms, ammunition and steel tubing for Slavin's mortars had been delivered.

Zatec had served the cause well and the Czechs had been served equally well—some twelve million dollars' worth, Dr. Felix estimates—by their decision, whatever its reason, to help the new state.

Even as they irritatedly ordered Hal Auerbach to get his airplanes and men out of the country within twenty-four hours, they were negotiating with Felix for the sale of a squadron of Spitfires the British had given them after the war. Eventually the Spitfires would be stripped down, equipped with extra fuel tanks, and flown to Israel, via Yugoslavia, in a daring series of flights collectively known as Operation Velveta.

The C-46s—by August 12 there were seven of them—took off for a final trip to "Oklahoma," hastily loaded with everything movable, including the diminutive Czech girl friend of one of the pilots.

The only thing that remained in Zatec of the bustling Balak operation was the grounded Constellation and Ernie Stehlik, still laboring to make it airworthy again. Eighteen months later he,

Schwimmer and Sam Lewis would fly the patched-up plane back to California.

The uneasy UN truce dragged on through August and September, broken by sporadic skirmishes and occasional pitched battles. As a result of the Ten Days offensive, the Jews now occupied most of the northern territory allotted to them by the UN partition plan. They had been less successful in the south.

The arid Negev desert, which Ben Gurion called the new state's frontier, its living space for future settlement of the thousands of refugees already streaming through its ports, still was occupied by a well-entrenched Egyptian Army: nine infantry battalions armed with artillery, antiaircraft and field guns and more than a hundred tanks.

The Egyptian positions stretched from the Egyptian border in two roughly parallel lines: one along the Mediterranean coast to Ashdod, the point twenty-five miles south of Tel Aviv where the first Me-109s had halted the Egyptian invasion in May; the second, inland to the Bethlehem area south of Jerusalem. The two were linked by a third row of Egyptian strongpoints which cut off the Jewish settlements in the central Negev from the rest of Israel. They were supplied by air. The Egyptians controlled the roads.

None of the Arab armies had been decisively defeated in the fighting to date. And neither had the Jews. It was a standoff, frozen by a truce that would not last. Both sides girded themselves for the third and final round. The battleground would be the Negev.

Leo Gardner, one of the pilots who had joined Schwimmer Aviation at Burbank, flew into the Negev and picked out a site for an airstrip between two Israeli settlements. It was speedily bulldozed and rudimentary communications and lighting equipment installed.

On August 22, ten days after leaving Zatec, the C-46s began another airlift: Operation Dust—the Americans called it Dustbowl—to reinforce the Negev settlements against the day when fighting would break out again.

The planes took off from Ekron under cover of darkness, circling until they had reached an altitude of 5,000 feet, above the range of Egyptian antiaircraft guns, then leaping across the enemy lines to circle down over the desert airstrip, lit only by rows of kerosene flares, for a bumpy landing in choking dust. Schwimmer remembers a typical night at Ekron, "the rows of trucks waiting all night in the hope of getting their cargo aboard; everyone silent, listening for the sound of a returning airplane."

The object was to build up a force in the Negev that could

hammer from the inside against the enemy ring, in support of the main Israeli thrusts that would come down from the north.

The future military operation already had been given a name—Ten Plagues—by Israeli staff officers who leaned on their Bibles as well as their guns. For the first time they would have the means to mount a coordinated offensive: three brigades of infantry, with enough arms to go around—rifles, machine guns, some artillery, a few tanks—backed up by an Air Force of fighter planes and bombers and even a diminutive Navy to patrol the Egyptian lines along the Mediterranean coast. It was small and rudimentary, but a modern defense force, such as Ben Gurion had envisioned only in hazy configuration when he speculated about the future and asked for American help in Rudolf Sonneborn's living room more than three years before.

No one knew how long the UN truce would last. As the weeks went by and the truce weakened, the pressure to be ready for Ten Plagues mounted. The C-46s made five trips a night, eight trips a night and, on one night of superhuman effort, thirteen trips. Their success almost boomeranged. They were exhausting the supply of high-octane airplane fuel; there might be none left for the air operations of Ten Plagues. But the *Kefalos* was on its way from Mexico with an additional supply; it was decided to continue the airlift and hope for the best.

Operation Dust continued for two months. In that time it made 417 round-trip flights, carried down to the Negev 4,991 tons of material and 10,961 passengers, and brought out as many battle-weary defenders for rest and retraining on the new equipment, which at long last was accumulating from overseas.

When the *Kefalos* arrived, the bombs and high-octane gasoline she had loaded in Mexico at the last moment were rushed to the Air Force. Ten Plagues began on the evening of October 15. The Air Force struck the first blow, pinning the Egyptian Air Force to the ground with a surprise raid on El Arish, the main enemy air base, and battering enemy positions up and down the Negev. In seven days it dropped 150 tons of bombs, immobilizing the enemy inside his strong-points. The Egyptians had had months to dig in, and it took five days of bitter brutal fighting before the three Israeli brigades, supported by more armor and artillery than had ever before been used in one campaign, would open a road to the Negev. On the seventh day Beersheba, the Negev capital, fell, and the Israeli Navy won its greatest victory of the war by sinking the Egyptian flagship *Emir Farouk* off Gaza.

That afternoon the United Nations ordered a cease-fire.

The war was not yet over, but the Egyptians were now the besieged.

Four months of fighting lay ahead before the Egyptians would agree to sign an armistice at Rhodes. The Lebanese and the Transjordanians would follow. In July 1949 the Syrians, the last of the invading armies to acknowledge defeat, would sign an identical armistice agreement.

XLVI

THE PAINTING

———————————

S am Sloan received an order at Materials for Palestine:

Five flutes
Five piccolos
Six oboes
Three bassoons
Five E-flat clarinets
Fifteen B-flat clarinets
Fifteen cornets . . .

The list was headed "Instruments for Israel Defense Forces Military Band."

It was time to quit, decided Phil Alper, the underground's first recruit. He no longer thought of emigrating to Israel. He had married the pretty girl Ricky Hefterman, who had hidden Ekdahl's machine gun under her bed during the TNT crisis, and he wanted to go into business and "start making a living."

His Inland Machinery and Metals Company was absorbed by the new Supply Mission of the State of Israel which had taken offices at 250 West 57th Street, on the same floor but separated by a discreet corridor from Materials for Palestine.

MFP changed its name to Materials for Israel and continued until 1955, but its function changed from supplying the armed forces to supplying the basic needs of immigrants pouring into the country at the rate of one thousand a day. It shipped over medical supplies, foodstuffs, clothing, shoes and trucks.

The military needs of the country were now handled by the official Supply Mission next door.

Teddy Kollek emerged from the chrysalis of secrecy which had surrounded his underground days with a title: Representative of the Ministry of Defense. He had cards and stationery printed and moved out of the Hotel Fourteen.

That small hostelry on East 60th Street, so "convenient to museums and shopping," as Ruby Barnett pointed out in his advertising brochures, reverted to the little old ladies, padding through the lobby to inquire about their pension checks, the buxom beauties of the Copacabana chorus line, and Ruby Barnett, worriedly studying his account books. "While everyone else is celebrating Israel," he muttered to Fannie, "I'm going out of business."

No longer needed, the American underground quietly disappeared—dismantled and dispersed as thoroughly as one of Slavin's machines in the Bronx warehouse.

Eastern Development Company shipped off its assembly line for bazooka production and some of the workmen it had trained, then closed its doors.

Danny Fliderblum liquidated his Radio Communications Engineering Company and emigrated, as he had always dreamed of doing, to Israel.

Schwimmer Aviation and Service Airways continued only on paper, among the records in Nahum Bernstein's law office, where taxes on the salaries of its overseas employees—there were no longer any in the United States—were paid until the last man had come home.

Land and Labor closed down its offices even before most of the hundreds of volunteers it had dispatched to Israel had returned.

The American Israeli Shipping Company, which Elie Schalit had helped to found during the dark days when other shippers balked at making the risky trip to Palestinian shores, continued to carry much of the cargo going overseas from America to the new state, competing with other commercial lines for that lucrative trade.

There were a few legal accounts to be settled before the underground could retreat into total obscurity. The FBI had been painstakingly compiling its dossiers; it was ready to take them to court.

In January 1949 Charlie Winters, who had led the flight of the three B-17s from Miami to Zatec, pleaded guilty in Miami to illegally exporting the planes and was sentenced to eighteen months in prison. Winters, a Protestant, would be the only member of the underground to go to prison. Swifty Schindler, the reluctant pilot of the fourth

B-17 on its abortive flight from Westchester to the Azores, also pleaded guilty, in March, but drew a suspended sentence and one year's probation.

Al Schwimmer returned to the United States in the fall of 1949 to face trial in Los Angeles, with several of the others from the Burbank days, for conspiracy to violate the Neutrality Act by exporting the ten C-46s and the Constellation to Israel. Testifying for the prosecution were FBI agent Ptacek, the persistent airplane dealer Laurence M. Krug, who had tried to sell P-51s to Rey Selk, and some of the mechanics who had worked at Burbank, Millville, Panama and Zatec. Nahum Bernstein testified for the defense, prepared to accept personal responsibility for the decisions to export the airplanes if the government's case dug too deeply. But it did not. The watertight compartmentalization that had been built around each of the underground's projects held. A confused charge that the underground, by setting up an airlift in Czechoslovakia, had somehow given aircraft to the Communists, was refuted by the presence in Los Angeles of the Constellation RX 121 which Schwimmer, Sam Lewis and Ernie Stehlik, who had so laboriously repaired it, had flown back from Zatec. "I didn't want anyone to say I had given it to the Reds," Schwimmer explained.

By the time the long trial ended in February 1950, the war of independence had been won, the first armistices with the Arab states had been signed and the ambivalent American attitude about the Jewish state that the United States had sponsored and then refused to help had changed to open admiration.

Schwimmer, Leo Gardner, Rey Selk, and Service Airways were found guilty, but no prison sentences were imposed; they were fined $10,000 each. In another trial, Hank Greenspun pleaded guilty to smuggling arms aboard the *Idalia* and was fined $10,000.

The Sonneborn Institute continued to meet weekly on Thursdays at the Hotel McAlpin—occupied now, like Materials for Israel, which it sponsored, with the requirements of the newcomers to Israel. In 1955 it decided its job was done and disbanded, with as little fanfare as it had begun with ten years before.

The underground disappeared without a trace, like a murky silhouette on a photographic film floating in a darkroom tub—someone had thrown open the door and the image was gone.

Its records were destroyed, only scattered fragments surviving in the bottom drawers of law-office files, in the basements and attics of some of the participants' homes, in the storage vaults of a Brooklyn warehouse.

The published histories of the Israeli struggle for nationhood would barely mention the American underground. Its members would slip back into the routine of everyday life, their exploits remembered only by themselves and their immediate colleagues of those days, whom—in many cases—they never saw again. A few wrote, or planned to write, memoirs of what had been the most heroic event in their lives, but—until now—no one had pieced together the whole story or even most of it.

While it was happening, nobody knew everything; everybody who got involved—Jew, Gentile, Zionist, non-Zionist—gave something. Thousands participated, responding unquestioningly in many small ways, feeling that they were a part of whatever it was that was going on. Those who did more had more to keep secret, but there were other satisfactions. Al Robison, the gentle New Jersey textile man who was one of the top men, says: "Here was an opportunity that happened maybe once in a lifetime, maybe not even once in a lifetime. That we could be cloak-and-dagger people, that we could live dangerously and feel highly virtuous about it, that we could actually make history. We went around in those couple of years in a state of exaltation. It was a great period in our lives. I don't think we'll ever get over it, and I think it changed our lives; I think it left its mark on us for the rest of our days. And I think it gave us a feeling of accomplishment that nothing else we did before, that nothing we did since, has equaled."

The meeting in Sonneborn's penthouse, where it all began, would become something of a legend, often exaggerated, its details confused. Even Ben Gurion, that usually precise historian, in the few sketchy references he would make to the meeting would be confused about the date—giving it once as June, on another occasion as August.

The only mementos kept by Rudolf Sonneborn would be a letter of thanks from Ben Gurion and a photographic copy of a painting that he, in return, had commissioned as a commemorative gift to the Israeli leader.

The painting shows the living room of Sonneborn's penthouse apartment exactly as it appeared on that sweltering day, July 1, 1945, when Ben Gurion addressed his plea for help to nineteen Americans gathered there. The painting is done in fine detail; it shows the dark walls, the white paneling, the furniture and ornaments of the handsome room in precise detail. The chairs are in a semicircle, just as Sonneborn had arranged them before his guest arrived. Everything is as it was at that fateful meeting with one exception: There are no people.

The room is empty.

EPILOGUE

RUDOLF G. SONNEBORN, industrialist, philanthropist, art patron, and sponsor of a secret American underground, is now semiretired and a director of the conglomerate Witco Chemical Company.

HENRY MONTOR, who organized the meeting in Sonneborn's home on July 1, 1945, now lives in Italy. Amused by the legends that have grown up around the meeting, and particularly by the number of men who claim to have attended it, Montor says: "So many want to be known as travelers on the original Mayflower."

REUVEN SHILOAH (formerly Zaslani), Ben Gurion's "advance man" in the United States, was one of the two Israeli signatories—the other was Colonel Moshe Dayan—to the April 1949 armistice agreement with Jordan. Shiloah (which is Hebrew for "envoy") served as director-general of the Israel foreign ministry and as Minister to Washington. He also was founder and first director of Shin Bet, Israel's central intelligence agency. He died in 1959.

PHIL ALPER settled down in his own machinery business. He visited Israel only as a postwar tourist. While there he toured the arms factories and saw firsthand what had come out of the apartment on West 112th Street. The Israeli arms industry, Ta'as, would grow until by 1967 it produced 70 per cent of the defense forces' requirements for the Six Day War. By then

HAIM SLAVIN had long since resigned as its head. Still the stubborn loner, he couldn't work within the framework of a large and bureaucratic organization. He went into business manufacturing prefabricated housing in Israel. One of his financial backers was

HARRY LEVINE, the Massachusetts plastics manufacturer, now semiretired, who had first put him in touch with Ekdahl and helped on so many of the early underground projects.

323

CARL EKDAHL went back to his home in Vermont, satisfied, his daughter recalls, with his life's last adventure. He died in 1952.

MAX BROWN stayed on in Israel, worked for Ta'as for several years, then returned to Canada, where he opened a chain of household appliance stores.

NORMAN GRANT, who had run the Canadian underground operation, didn't visit Israel until 1959; by that time he was more interested in "seeing the country than machines"; he didn't even visit the Ta'as plants. He is now a manufacturer of industrial and commercial lighting in Toronto.

JERRY SCHWEITZER, the patient secretary of the 112th Street days, became Mrs. William Ungar, a New Jersey housewife and mother.

ROBERT KELLER, who had been on Pier F the day the TNT fell, and who later sailed to Israel aboard the *Kefalos*, works for Atid, Ltd., in New York.

DANNY FLIDERBLUM, the young electronics wizard, emigrated to Israel, changed his name to Avivi, and became one of the leaders in the new country's blossoming electronics industry.

ELIE SCHALIT, Israeli-born shipping expert, chose to remain in the United States. After the years of shuffling "black" and "white" shipments through the port of New York, he knew it as few other young men did. He opened his own shipping firm and settled in suburban Westport, Connecticut, with his American wife, Harriet, a cousin of

ADOLF ROBISON, the New Jersey textile converter, who had been Sonneborn's deputy at the Institute and Arazi's adviser and sidekick. Once the Institute had disbanded, Robison turned to more pacific spare-time philanthropies, principally Fairleigh Dickinson University in New Jersey, where he is a member of the board of trustees.

NAHUM BERNSTEIN, the lawyer and former OSS man who had been the underground's principal legal adviser and strategist, waited until all of the secret projects had been liquidated and then fulfilled a long-standing ambition to visit Israel. He lectured at the new Army intelligence school, where some of the high officers were former students of his school in downtown New York. Back in the United States, he continued his law practice.

LEONARD WEISMAN, who had helped Arazi buy the aircraft carrier *Attu*, found his business in the United States declining and moved on to Brazil, where the opportunities for an "opportunistic trader" seemed better.

ADOLPH SCHWIMMER is managing director of Israel Aircraft

Industries, the largest aircraft manufacturing and maintenance firm in the Middle East and Israel's largest employer. Recently, IAI began manufacturing a jet trainer for the Israel Air Force and a STOL aircraft for commercial use. When he first moved to Israel after trying to start an airline in the United States with several of the men who had worked with him in the underground days, Schwimmer's first associates were

HAYMAN SHAMIR (Hyman Sheckman), the shepherd of Operation Yakum Purkan, who subsequently managed the company that built the Tel Aviv Hilton Hotel, then entered the investment business, and

DANNY AGRON (formerly Agronsky), who ran the Rome "office" of the underground. He now has a crop-dusting service in Israel.

IRVING STRAUSS, Schwimmer's brother-in-law of a brother-in-law who had shuttled between New York and Nicaragua persuading dictator Somoza to front for Arazi's European arms shipments, went back to commuting between his electronics firm in New York and his home in Connecticut.

REYNOLD SELK, who had been Schwimmer's right-hand man at Schwimmer Aviation since that first flight to Burbank to buy the Constellations, did not go with the planes from Panama to Zatec. He returned to Los Angeles, where he is in the electronics business. His cousin,

HANK GREENSPUN, after his Hawaiian and Mexican exploits with the underground, returned to Las Vegas, where he became the crusading editor and publisher of the Las Vegas *Sun*.

WILLIE SOSNOW, the Brooklyn mechanic who helped Greenspun pack the airplane engines and machine guns in Hawaii, worked in an aircraft supply business in Los Angeles until his death in 1967.

IRVIN (Swifty) SCHINDLER, founder and first president of Service Airways and pilot of the ill-fated B-17, is in the real estate business in Florida.

STEVE SCHWARTZ, the indefatigable cigar-smoking recruiter for Service Airways, went into the pipeline business in Canada after trying unsuccessfully to mount a revolution against Fidel Castro.

HAL AUERBACH, Service Airways' operations chief, left aviation to become a stockbroker in New York. Most of the other pilots managed, one way or another, to stay in aviation.

SAM LEWIS, the veteran Connie pilot, became one of the first captains of El Al.

LEO GARDNER, who joined Schwimmer Aviation along with

Lewis, also went to work for El Al and is now its sales manager in Miami.

LARRY RAAB, the baby-faced pilot from Philadelphia who flew with the C-46s from Millville to Panama, to Zatec, to Israel, worked for El Al for a while, then moved on to a career of aerial adventuring in the Congo and Biafra.

NORMAN MOONITZ never went back to the New York Fire Department. He flew for El Al, then for the German airline Lufthansa, and is now with Trans International Airlines, in Oakland, California.

ART YADVEN is a captain with Trans Caribbean Airways.

COLEMAN GOLDSTEIN is a captain with El Al.

PHIL MARMELSTEIN is in the sheet-metal business in Philadephia.

RAY KURTZ, the second New York fireman, died in 1951 while ferrying a plane for Schwimmer's short-lived Intercontinental Airways. His wife, Ruthie, remarried and now lives in Long Island.

TRYGVE MASENG, the would-be writer from Columbia University who flew a C-46, stayed on in Israel with one of the domestic airlines, as did another of the non-Jewish pilots,

TED GIBSON, the son of the Southern Baptist minister, who commanded an AT-6 dive bomber squadron in the Israel Air Force. He was killed in 1951, in the crash of a transport plane at Zurich.

GIDEON LICHTMAN, the impatient zoot-suited fighter pilot from Newark, worked for a while as a test pilot for Schwimmer before settling down as a schoolteacher in Florida.

GILBERTO ARIAS, the Panamanian attorney who served as counsel to LAPSA, was to help the Israeli cause again, wittingly or not, nearly twenty-two years later. On December 25, 1969, five gunboats built in France for the Israeli Navy slipped out of Cherbourg, where they had been trapped by the embargo imposed by France after the Six Day War, and sailed for Haifa. French officials said they had let the ships leave after the Israelis renounced their interest in favor of the Starboat Shipping and Oil Drilling Company of Norway. When Norwegian authorities said they knew nothing about the Starboat company—it had only a post-office box in Oslo—the French disclosed that Starboat's head offices were in Panama. The company had been registered there only a month earlier by the law firm of Arias, Fabrega & Fabrega. The gunboats arrived in Israel on December 31, 1969.

RUBY and FANNIE BARNETT surrendered the Hotel Fourteen to their creditors in 1949. They tried running another hotel in the

Virgin Islands, then retired to Puerto Rico, with Fannie suffering from an incurable bone disease. The Hotel Fourteen reverted to genteel obscurity. None of Israel's leaders stayed there; they preferred the Waldorf-Astoria or the Plaza, where the Israeli flag was now flown to announce their presence. Of the Palestinians who had stayed in the Hotel Fourteen during its underground days,

TEDDY KOLLEK returned to Israel to become director-general of the office of Prime Minister Ben Gurion, then to become the founding director of the Israel Museum in Jerusalem and, in 1965, the mayor of Jerusalem.

YAACOV DORI (Jacob Dostrovsky) served as the first chief of staff of the Israel Defense Forces before becoming president of the Israel Institute of Technology—the Technion—in Haifa.

SHLOMO SHAMIR (Shlomo Rabinovich) commanded a brigade during the war of independence and then moved on to a series of high posts with the Ministry of Defense.

YEHUDA ARAZI, the most daring and colorful of Haganah's "arms procurement experts," made no such easy reconversion. He found himself, when the war ended, with nothing to do; honored but obsolescent. He opened a resort hotel, backed by his Polish Catholic friend of underground days, Count Stefan Czarnecki. He died, unknown to a younger generation of Israelis, in 1959.

DAVID BEN GURION celebrated his eighty-third birthday in October 1969.

ACKNOWLEDGMENTS

First and foremost, my thanks go to my wife, Betty Slater, a writer in her own right, who edited the various drafts, caught my errors, diminished my verbosity, and advised and encouraged me at every step of the way. The errors and misjudgments she and others failed to catch and which were then missed by me are entirely mine. I am deeply grateful also to Michael Chayen of London; Colonel Gershon Rivlin of the Israel Defense Forces Publishing House, Tel Aviv; Moshe Brilliant of the New York *Times;* Alvin Rosenfeld of NBC News; Hugh Orgel, now with the Israel Mission to the United Nations; Julius "Rusty" Jarcho; Bob Luery; Phil Levine; Dan Pattir, press counselor of the Israel Embassy, Washington; Albert A. Hutler of Chicago; James McGunigal of Toronto; a trio of distinguished Los Angeles attorneys, Isaac Pacht, Clore Warne, and William Strong; and, of course, the hundreds of men and women, not all of them mentioned in its text, who cooperated in the research for this book. My sincere thanks also to Paul Gitlin, friend, agent, and attorney, and to Michael Korda and Richard Locke, my editors at Simon and Schuster.

Almost all of the research was first-hand interviews and correspondence—the most time-consuming kind of investigative reporting—although a few records, logbooks, letters, and account ledgers turned up that had survived the passage of time and the insistence on secrecy.

The main sources for each chapter follow, with explanatory details:

PROLOGUE
Based on interviews with Lieutenant Thomas Hynes of the Jersey City Police Department, Captain Sydney Blackledge of American Export–Isbrandtsen Lines, Miss Eileen Ryan, and Robert Keller. Also, the Jersey City Police Department record of the TNT incident and articles in the *Jersey Journal,* the New York *Times,* and the New York *Herald Tribune.*

Chapter I: THE MEETING
Interviews with Rudolf G. Sonneborn, Samuel Cherr, Meyer Weisgal, and Samuel Zacks. Correspondence with Henry Montor, Shepherd Broad, William S. Cohen, Albert Schiff, and Ezra Z. Shapiro. Broad, a Miami Beach attorney, remembers asking BG, "What is the Palestinian Jew like?" BG asked him if he knew what an Iowa farmer was like. Broad said he

did; whereupon BG replied, "Then you know what a Palestinian Jew is like." Ben Gurion's remarks were reconstructed from memoranda by Sonneborn and Montor. His memories of the event, quite colored by hindsight, can be found in these books, among others: *Ben Gurion Looks Back, in Talks with Moshe Pearlman,* Simon and Schuster, New York, 1965, and *Israel: Years of Challenge,* by David Ben Gurion, Holt, Rinehart, and Winston, New York, 1963.

Chapter II: THE JOB
Interviews with Haim Slavin and Phil Alper. The footnoted Ben Gurion quotation "I considered . . ." is from *Ben Gurion Looks Back, in Talks with Moshe Pearlman,* Simon and Schuster, New York, 1965.

Chapter III: THE GUN
Interviews with Haim Slavin, Phil Alper, the late Carl Ekdahl's daughter Mrs. Roland Nordin, Harry Levine, and Rudolf G. Sonneborn. The footnoted information on the Johnson light machine gun comes from *The Rifle in America,* by Philip B. Sharpe, Funk and Wagnalls, New York, 1947.

Chapter IV: THE APARTMENT
Interviews with Haim Slavin, Phil Alper, Harry Levine, Mrs. William Ungar (Jerry Schweitzer), Mrs. Selig Tetove (Diane Schweitzer), and Harry Zysman. Zysman's daughter subsequently emigrated to Israel, and he says proudly, "My grandson is a sabra."

Chapter V: GOLD, PURE GOLD
Interviews with Phil Alper, Haim Slavin, Elie Schalit, Harry Levine, Mrs. Roland Nordin, Norman Botwinik, Charles Frost, and John Kopecky of the Chemists' Club

Library. Correspondence with William Horowitz. Olsen process: invented by Fred Olsen, research director of the Western Cartridge Company, East Alton, Illinois. An article in *Chemical Engineering,* December 1946, was headed "Ball Powder Process Upsets Explosives Industry Traditions" and went on to describe "a totally new form of smokeless powder produced by a process that differs in nearly every respect from conventional methods . . . less hazardous because most steps are carried out under water . . . only about one-fifth the time and so leads to many important operating economies." Some of the details on Abraham Brothman and Miriam Moskowitz are from *Invitation to an Inquest,* by Walter and Miriam Schneir, Doubleday, New York, 1965.

Chapter VI: THE PORT
Interviews with Mrs. William Ungar (Jerry Schweitzer), Elie Schalit, Haim Slavin, Jules Chender. Some facts and figures on the port of New York are from Walter Hamshar, Port of New York Authority.

Chapter VII: CANADA
Interviews with Norman Grant, Max Brown, Samuel Zacks, Ben Ocopnick, General Yaacov Dori, Phil Alper, Haim Slavin, Elie Schalit, and Harry Levine.

Chapter VIII: NIAGARA FALLS
Interviews with Norman Grant, Max Brown, Phil Alper, Haim Slavin, Elie Schalit, Harry Levine, Samuel Zacks, Maurice Boukstein, Robert R. Nathan, Mrs. David Diamond, and General Yaacov Dori. Articles in the Toronto *Star* and the *Globe and Mail,* February 25 and 27 and March 26, 1947.

Chapter IX: HOTEL FOURTEEN
Interviews with Reuben and Fannie
Barnett, Mrs. Charles Shulman, Ben
Edden, Morris Yassky, Mrs. Reuven
Shiloah, General Yaacov Dori, General Shlomo Shamir, Nahum Bernstein, and Ruth Berman. Haganah
history based on David Ben Gurion's
"Last Days of the Mandate," in the
Jewish Observer and Middle East Review, May 13, 1966. Copacabana
background is from *Show Biz*, by
Abel Green and Joe Laurie, Jr.,
Henry Holt and Company, New
York, 1951.

Chapter X: DOSTROVSKY
Interviews with General Yaacov Dori,
Mrs. Charles Shulman, Danny Avivi,
Louis Rocker, Fannie and Reuben
Barnett, Rudolf G. Sonneborn, and
Zimel Resnick. Dori (Dostrovsky)
served with and was trained by
Charles Orde Wingate, the Scot who
became a Zionist while serving as a
British intelligence officer in Palestine
and who inspired and trained the first
elite units of Haganah. Another of
Wingate's pupils was Moshe Dayan.
In World War II, commanding Allied
forces in Burma, Major General
Wingate died in an airplane crash.
Winston Churchill said of him:
"There was a man of genius who
might well have become also a man
of destiny." Haganah history: correspondence with Colonel Gershon
Rivlin.

Chapter XI: THE INSTITUTE
Interviews with Rudolf G. Sonneborn, General Yaacov Dori, Adolf
Robison, Harold Jaffer, Isaac Imber,
Julius Jarcho, Joseph Greenleaf,
Samuel Cherr, Nahum Bernstein,
Theodore Racoosin, Paul O'Dwyer,
Nat Cole, Gottlieb Hammer, and
Moses Speert. A colorful account of

the American League for a Free Palestine and its support of IZL is found
in *A Child of the Century*, by Ben
Hecht, Simon and Schuster, New
York, 1954.

Chapter XII: RABINOVICH
Interviews with General Shlomo
Shamir, Danny Avivi, Hal Gershoni,
Adolph Schwimmer, Major General
Ralph C. Smith, General Yaacov
Dori, Yehiel Elyachar, Harold Jaffer,
and Ben Dunkelman. Ben Gurion "had
even written to Mrs. Blanche Dugdale" is from *Ben Gurion*, by Maurice
Edelman, Hodder and Stoughton,
London, 1964. Some of the material
on the situation in Palestine is derived
from the New York *Times* and from
Both Sides of the Hill, by Jon and
David Kimche, Secker and Warburg,
London, 1960.

Chapter XIII: THE SCHOOL
Interviews with Nahum Bernstein,
Rudolf Sonneborn, Shlomo Shamir,
Mrs. Geoffrey Mott-Smith, Meyer
Birnbaum, and Louis Rocker.

Chapter XIV: W₂OXR
Interviews with Reuben Gross,
Nahum Bernstein, Samuel Sloan, Dan
Avivi. Newspaper reports of hearings
before the FCC in August 1948,
Commissioner George E. Sterling presiding. "The five-letter one-time pad
system . . ." is fully described in *The
Codebreakers*, by David Kahn, Macmillan, New York, 1967.

Chapter XV: F.O.B. ANYWHERE
Interviews with Nahum Bernstein,
Theodore Racoosin, Victor Avrunin,
Harry Weinsaft, Gilbert Seidman,
Hal Gershoni, Sam Sloan, Julius
Jarcho, and Bernard Karmatz. Footnote on Irgun arms collection in New
York: stenographer's minutes, The

People of the State of New York v. Joseph Untermeyer and Isaiah Warshaw, May 1948, Magistrates' Court of the City of New York.

Chapter XVI: PARTITION
Transcripts of Sonneborn Institute meetings at Waldorf-Astoria, October 1947.

Chapter XVII: YEHUDA ARAZI
Interviews with Mrs. Yehuda Arazi, Dan Arazi, Daniel Agron, Ruth Aliav, Elie Schalit, Shaul Avigor, Ruth Berman, Rachel Nachman, Adolf Robison, and Herbert Salzman. Correspondence with Stefan Czarnecki. Undated, unsigned report in Haganah Archives, Tel Aviv. Ben Gurion quotation "You cannot hide a plane . . ." is from *Ben Gurion Looks Back, in Talks with Moshe Pearlman,* Simon and Schuster, New York, 1965.

Chapter XVIII: THE *Attu*
Interviews with Leonard Weisman, Nahum Bernstein, and Al Robison. Information on CVE *Attu* (*Casablanca* class) is from U.S. Navy and *Jane's Fighting Ships,* Jane, London, 1947. Eisenhower's "almost fatal" is from *Crusade in Europe,* by Dwight D. Eisenhower, Doubleday, New York, 1948.

Chapter XIX: SCHWIMMER
Interviews with Adolph W. Schwimmer, Rey Selk, Irving Strauss, Leo Gardner, Sam Lewis, Nahum Bernstein, Willie Sosnow, Ernest R. Stehlik, Dan Agron, Shlomo Shamir, and Ben Doeh. Transcript, U.S. v. Adolph W. Schwimmer *et al.,* No. 20636, U.S. District Court, Los Angeles, October 1949 to February 1950. Transcript, A. W. Schwimmer v. Underwriters at Lloyd's, London; Service Airways, Inc.; Líneas Aéreas de Panama, S.A.,

No. 12574-HWS, U.S. District Court, Los Angeles, October 1951.

Chapter XX: YAKUM PURKAN
Interviews with Irving Strauss, Uriel Doron, Michael Doron, Hayman Shamir, Burya Katz, Boris Senior, Adolph W. Schwimmer, and Louis Brettschneider. Correspondence with Stefan Czarnecki. Haganah report by Eliahu Sacharov, "Arms Shipments from Italy," Haganah Archives, Tel Aviv. Magenta description from *Strictly Illegal,* by Munya M. Mardor, Robert Hale Ltd., London, 1964. The "Yakum Purkan" prayer is recited in the Sabbath service immediately following the reading of "The Prophets."

Chapter XXI: S.S. *Executor*
Interviews with Elie Schalit, Harry Levine, Abe Cramer, Phil Alper, Nahum Bernstein, Jacob Shapiro (Shapik), and Isaac Jaffe (Moosik). When interviewed, Mr. Shapiro was chief of the Israeli Ministry of Defense supply mission in New York; Mr. Jaffe was manager of the London office of El Al–Israel Airlines. Shipping documents furnished the author by Mr. Schalit.

Chapter XXII: PIER F
A report in the Haganah Archives, Tel Aviv, states as fact a belief widely held by the Palestinians in the United States and by some of the more suspicious Americans at the time: "Within each wooden barrel there was a metal container in which the explosives were packed. According to American custom, the longshoremen's wages vary according to the type of cargo handled—and the payment for handling ammunition and explosives is much higher than the general level. One of the longshoremen suspected that the load they were handling con-

tained something other than the chemicals [sic] marked on the cases. To find out what was inside, one of the crane operators dropped a barrel which split open and revealed the contents. Only with great difficulty was it possible to cover up the identity of the consigners and thus prevent their arrest." The author has been unable to find any evidence to document this theory that the cases containing the TNT were dropped on purpose. Furthermore, its reliability is weakened by the known errors the report contains. Interviews with Phil Alper, Elie Schalit, Robert Keller, Max Brown, Jules Chender, Nahum Bernstein, and Mrs. William Ungar. Report, Jersey City Police Department. Transcript, hearings before the surplus property subcommittee of the Committee on Expenditures in the Executive Departments, House of Representatives, Eightieth Congress, U.S. Government Printing Office, Washington, 1948. Articles in the New York *Times*, the New York *Herald Tribune*, the New York *World-Telegram* and the *Jersey Journal*.

Chapter XXIII: Lowy's FARM
Interviews with Charles Lowy, Zimel Resnick, Leonard Weisman, Al Robison, Al Schwimmer, Isaac Pacht, Clore Warne, and William Strong. Articles in the New York *Times* and the Asbury Park *Press*. Transcript, U.S. v. Schwimmer *et al.*, No. 20636, U.S. District Court, Los Angeles, October 1949 to February 1950.

Chapter XXIV: On BALANCE,
  NOT BAD
Interviews with Phil Alper, Elie Schalit, Nahum Bernstein, and Reuben Barnett. Transcript, U.S. v. Martin Adelson *et al.*, No. 127–201, U.S. Dis-

trict Court, New York, February 1948. Report by Eliahu Sacharov, Haganah Archives, Tel Aviv, undated. Articles in the New York *Times*, New York *Herald Tribune*, New York, *Post*, New York *Journal-American*, and Asbury Park *Press*. Quotation from Golda Meir's Chicago speech and figures are from *Golda Meir: Woman with a Cause*, by Marie Syrkin, G. P. Putnam's Sons, New York, 1963. The importance of her appeal is underscored by a confidential memo by Harold Jaffer dated December 17, 1947: "The material has all been purchased and awaits only the accumulation of the necessary funds to pay for it and accept delivery."

Chapter XXV: TEDDY KOLLEK
Interviews with Teddy Kollek, Nahum Bernstein, Ralph Goldman, Norman Companiez, Rey Selk, Nat Cole, Bernard Fineman, Harold Jaffer, Isaac Imber, Julius Jarcho, Danny Avivi, Irvin Schindler, and Phil Alper. Magenta: report by Eliahu Sacharov, Haganah Archives, Tel Aviv. Haganah background: *The Edge of the Sword* by Lieutenant Colonel Netanel Lorch, G. P. Putnam's Sons, New York, 1961; and *Both Sides of the Hill*, by Jon and David Kimche, Secker and Warburg, London, 1960. Companiez and LCIs: interviews with Norman Companiez, Nat Cole, Nat Kohn, and Bernard Fineman. The LCIs were commissioned in the Israeli Navy as *Ramat Rachel* and *Nitzanim*, according to *Naval Operations in the Israel War of Independence*, by Lieutenant Commander Eliezer Tal, I.D.F. Publishing House, Tel Aviv, 1964. M-4 tanks: interviews with Kollek, Fineman, Elie Schalit, Al Schwimmer, Leo Gardner, and Irving Strauss. M-4 background courtesy U.S. Marine Corps.

Chapter XXVI: MFP

Interviews with Isaac Imber, Julius Jarcho, Sam Sloan, Nahum Bernstein, Harris J. Klein, Hal Gershoni, and Al Robison. Robison tells of the time he went down to see the FBI after an employee of one of MFP's warehouses had told them about "parachutes." The special agent who interviewed Robison was a hard-bitten old-timer. "He was not the kind of man you try to flatter or lecture on Zionism," Robison recounted afterward. "He obviously had been around." He listened patiently to Robison's assurances that nothing would be shipped by MFP that was on the embargo list. "You know, Mr. Robison," the FBI man said, "we're in the position of a man who knows his wife is cheating on him. The whole town knows it, but he doesn't know it officially. He can be perfectly complacent about it and go around and not lose face. But if a neighbor pulls him by the arm over to a window and points to his wife in bed with somebody, he can't pretend he doesn't know about it anymore." The FBI man paused and pointed an index finger at Robison. "Now, Mr. Robison, don't put us in the position where somebody grabs us by the arm and makes us look through that window."

Chapter XXVII: Black Goods

Interviews with Harold Jaffer, Isaac Imber, Dan Avivi, Phil Alper, Irving Norry, Harry Levine, Mota Teumin, Nahum Bernstein, Bernard Karmatz, Zvi Brenner, Morris Dolgin, Irving Strauss, and Max Brown. Cyclonite (cyclotrimethyl-enetrinitramine) information from *Encyclopedia of Chemical Technology* edited by Raymond E. Kirk, Donald F. Othmer and others; Interscience Encyclopedias, Inc., New York, 1951.

Chapter XXVIII: Hawaii

Interviews with Julius Jarcho, Al Schwimmer, Rey Selk, Abraham Levin, Hank Greenspun, Willie Sosnow, Bernard Fineman, Leo Gardner, William Strong, and Lee Lewis. Greenspun interview supplemented by material from *Where I Stand*, by Hank Greenspun, McKay, New York, 1966. Transcripts, U.S. v. Herman Greenspun *et al.*, No. 21266, U.S. District Court, Los Angeles, and U.S. v. Herman Greenspun *et al.*, No. 20927, U.S. District Court, Los Angeles.

Chapter XXIX: Schalit's Return

Interviews with Elie Schalit, Julius Jarcho, Morris Feder, Isaac Jaffe, Dan Avivi, David Mersten, Raphael Recanati, Morris Ginsberg, Zvi Brenner, and Moses Heyman. Tel Aviv got some weird versions of U.S. activities in its behalf. One report in the Haganah Archives, Tel Aviv, says that American "gangsters" were demanding the horse-racing concession in the future Jewish state in exchange for any help they might give in expediting shipments out of New York.

Chapter XXX: Land and Labor

Interviews with Ralph Goldman, Harold Jaffer, Samuel Sterling, Steve Schwartz, Gideon Lichtman, Bernard Fineman, Joseph M. Landow, Eli Kalm, Reuben Gross, Maurice R. Commanday, Ruth Commanday, Lee B. Harris, Joseph Greenleaf, Ruth Berman, Sid Rabinovich and Philip G. Levine and other officers and members of American Veterans of Israel; Ben Dunkelman and Walter Reiter and other officers and members of Canadian Veterans of Israel. Research on U.S. neutrality laws and arms embargoes, courtesy of Sylvester and Haimoff, attorneys, New York: Arthur D. Holzman and J. Henry

Glazer, attorneys, Washington. Footnote on Arab volunteers from the New York *Times*.

Chapter XXXI: SERVICE AIRWAYS
Interviews with Nahum Bernstein, Irvin R. Schindler, Steve Schwartz, Martin B. Bellefond, Gilberto Arias, Al Schwimmer, Sam Lewis, Leo Gardner, and Victor Herwitz. Testimony, U.S. v. Schwimmer *et al.*, No. 20636, U.S. District Court, Los Angeles, October 1949 to February 1950.

Chapter XXXII: THE SHEPHERD
Interviews with Hayman Shamir, Steve Schwartz, Willie Sosnow, Charles Winters, Norman Moonitz, Art Yadven, Phil Marmelstein, Lou Lenart, Trygve Maseng, Harold Livingston, Larry Raab, Gideon Lichtman, Al Raisin, Hal Auerbach, Leo Gardner, and Martin Bellefond. Testimony, U.S. v. Schwimmer *et al.*, No. 20636, U.S. District Court, Los Angeles, October 1949 to February 1950.

Chapter XXXIII: WHEN? AND HOW?
Interviews with Aharon Remez, Al Schwimmer, Rey Selk, Steve Schwartz, Leo Gardner, Ernie Stehlik, Daniel Agron, Irvin Schindler, David Michaels, Nahum Bernstein, Leonard Weisman, and Shaul Avigor. Some background on the *Attu*'s legal difficulties from the Norfolk *Virginian-Pilot* and Norfolk *Ledger-Dispatch*.

Chapter XXXIV: CALCULATED RISK
Interviews with Nahum Bernstein, Al Schwimmer, and Rey Selk. Background on Czech arms: *Arms Procurement*, by Pinhas Waser, I.D.F. Publishing House, Tel Aviv, 1966. Beth Darass: *The Edge of the Sword*, by Lieutenant Colonel Netanel Lorch, G. P. Putnam's Sons, New York, 1961; *Strictly Illegal*, by

Munya Mardor, Robert Hale Ltd., London, 1964, and *Israeli Air Force and Mahal History*, by Avigdor Shahan, Am Hassefer, Tel Aviv, 1966. Jerusalem road: Crossroads to Israel, by Christopher Sykes, Collins, London, 1965. Krug and Zadra: Testimony, U.S. v. Schwimmer *et al.*, No. 20636, U.S. District Court, Los Angeles, October 1949 to February 1950.

Chapter XXXV: LATIN DETROIT
Interviews with Hal Auerbach, Nahum Bernstein, Martin Bellefond, Irvin Schindler, Norman Moonitz, and Larry Raab. Testimony, U.S. v. Schwimmer *et al.*, No. 20636, U.S. District Court, Los Angeles, October 1949 to February 1950.

Chapter XXXVI: DR. JOSÉ ARAZI
Interviews with Irving Strauss, Nahum Bernstein, Leonard Weisman, Al Robison, and Moses Speert. Correspondence with David Michaels. Some background on Arazi's arms shipments is from *Arms Procurement*, by Pinhas Waser, I.D.F. Publishing House, Tel Aviv, 1966. "Hasini," in Hebrew, means "The Chinaman."

Chapter XXXVII: CZECHOSLOVAKIA
Interviews with Uriel Doron, Shaul Avigor, Al Schwimmer, and Boris Senior.

Chapter XXXVIII: MRS. SILVERMAN'S AIRPLANES
Interviews with David Miller, Aharon Remez, Phil Marmelstein, André Blumel, Ernie Stehlik, Abe Nathan, Lew Nagley, Coleman Goldstein, Bob Fine, and Bill Malpine. Correspondence with Mrs. Mary Silverman and Arnold Ilowite. Background on Etzion bloc: *The Edge of the Sword*, by Lieutenant Colonel Netanel Lorch,

G. P. Putnam's Sons, New York, 1961. The figure on Red Army deserters is from *Ben Gurion*, by Maurice Edelman, Hodder and Stoughton, London, 1964.

Chapter XXXIX: CATANIA
Interviews with Hal Auerbach, Larry Raab, Willie Sosnow, Irvin Schindler, Al Schwimmer, Rey Selk, Trygve Maseng, Shaul Avigor, Hayman Shamir, Dan Agron, David Baron, and Gideon Lichtman.

Chapter XL: TIMETABLE
Interviews with Trygve Maseng, Hal Auerbach, Sam Lewis, and Harold Livingston. Correspondence with Gilberto Arias; letters of Ray Kurtz. Testimony, U.S. v. Schwimmer *et al.*, No. 20636, U.S. District Court, Los Angeles, October 1949 to February 1950. Background on the meeting of the National Administration and the Mandate's final days: *Three Days*, by Zeev Sharef, W. H. Allen, London, 1962. Haganah's military position: *The Edge of the Sword*, by Lieutenant Colonel Netanel Lorch, G. P. Putnam's Sons, New York, 1961.

Chapter XLI: THE RED HOUSE
Interviews with Larry Raab and General Yaacov Dori. Report by Eliahu Sacharov, Haganah Archives, Tel Aviv. Red House mood: *Three Days*, by Zeev Sharef, W. H. Allen, London, 1962. Borea background: *Arms Procurement*, by Pinhas Waser, I.D.F. Publishing House, Tel Aviv, 1966. Truman quotation is from *Memoirs: Years of Trial and Hope, 1946–52*, by Harry S. Truman, Doubleday, New York, 1956.

Chapter XLII: ZATEC
Interviews with Larry Raab, Hayman Shamir, Danny Agron, Robert Fine, and William Malpine. Report by Eliahu Sacharov, Haganah Archives, Tel Aviv.

Chapter XLIII: BALAK
Interviews with Uriel Doron, Norman Moonitz, Larry Raab, Hal Auerbach, David Baron, Lew Nagley, Les Shagham, Irvin Schindler, Ernie Stehlik, Bob Sprung, George Lichter, and Arnold Ilowite. Author's observations in Czechoslovakia, 1948. Ray Kurtz letters, including this excerpt: "I hope you won't be mad, honey, but Friday night one of the mechanics and myself took out two girls and showed them a wonderful time. They were two Jewish girls who had been in Auschwitz concentration camp for two years. They were 20 years old and looked like 30 or 40. It was pathetic. I saw the numbers that were branded on them and I got sick. It makes me even happier to do what I'm doing after seeing that. Anyway we took them all over and showed them a good time and just took them home."

Chapter XLIV: FIGHTER COVER
Interviews with Uriel Doron, William Levitt, Lou Lenart, Larry Raab, Danny Agron, Michael Doron, Rudy Augarten, and Hayman Shamir. Background on IAF's first days: *The Edge of the Sword*, by Lieutenant Colonel Netanel Lorch, G. P. Putnam's Sons, New York, 1961. Some figures on aircraft procurement: *Israeli Air Force and Mahal History*, by Avigdor Shahan, Am Hassefer, Tel Aviv, 1966.

Chapter XLV: TEN PLAGUES
Interviews with Elie Schalit, Ben Edden, David Mersten, Dan Avivi, Phil Alper, Mrs. Sally Fields, Al Schwimmer, Hank Greenspun, Robert Keller, Rudy Augarten, Dan Cravitt, Reverend and Mrs. Theodore Gibson, Eu-

gene Gibson, Wayne Peake, Sam Katz, Max Brown, Michael Doron, Sam Lewis, Ernie Stehlik, Irvin Schindler, Charles Winters, Stanley Epstein, Norman Moonitz, Willie Sosnow, Hal Paiss, Leo Gardner, Allan Burke, Arnold Sherman, Yithak Shender, and Uriel Doron. Correspondence with Colonel Gershon Rivlin and Michael Chayen. Information on Canadian volunteers: James McGunigal. Background on Ten Plagues: *The Edge of the Sword*, by Lieutenant Colonel Netanel Lorch, G. P. Putnam's Sons, New York, 1961. Background on Dustbowl: *Strictly Illegal*, by Munya M. Mardor, Robert Hale Ltd., London, 1964. Grand Jury charges: U.S. v. Schwimmer *et al.*, No. 7280-M-CR, U.S. District Court, Miami. Westchester airport: New York *Times* and New York *Herald Tribune*.

Chapter XLVI: THE PAINTING
Interviews with Sam Sloan, Phil Alper, Julius Jarcho, Reuben Barnett, Mota Teumim, Dan Avivi, Nahum Bernstein, and Rudolf Sonneborn. The description of the painting comes from a copy in the author's possession. Ben Gurion's confusion about the date is a departure from his usual precision. In his preface to *The Israel Defense Forces 1948-58*, by Lieutenant Colonel Gershon Rivlin, I.D.F. Publishing House, Tel Aviv, Ben Gurion wrote: "In June, 1945, I assembled a group of friends in a certain country with a well-developed munitions industry, and with the loyal aid of these friends, the most modern and up-to-date machinery and equipment were acquired in large quantities for the production of arms and ammunition of all types." In *Israel: Years of Challenge*, Holt, Rinehart, and Winston, New York, 1963, Ben Gurion said: "In June 1945, with Eliezer Kaplan, the Treasurer of the Jewish Agency (later Israel's first Minister of Finance), I gathered together a group of dependable men in the United States, which was about to reduce its arms industry." However, in *The American Zionist* of September 1966, Ben Gurion reminisced: "Most of the machines and tools which are today at the disposal of the Military Industry in Israel are the products of that meeting which took place at Rudolph Sonneborn's on August 1, 1945." The author agrees with Shepherd Broad, a Miami Beach attorney and one of the meeting participants, who says: "Far be it from me to take issue with such a giant as Ben Gurion, but, in this instance, he happens to be dead wrong as to the date." According to Sonneborn, the men at his home on July 1, 1945, were Ben Gurion, Eliezer Kaplan, and Reuven Shiloah (Palestinians); Henry Montor, Abraham Berkowitz, Shepherd Broad, Samuel Cherr, William S. Cohen, Julius Fligelman, Harold Goldenberg, Joel Gross, Charles Gutwirth, Max Livingston, Barney Rappaport, Charles J. Rosenblum, Albert Schiff, Ezra Z. Shapiro, Jacob Shohan, William H. Sylk, Meyer W. Weisgal, Samuel J. Zacks, and Sonneborn (Americans).

INDEX